SCORE

A FILM MUSIC DOCUMENTARY

THE INTERVIEWS

BY MATT SCHRADER

Extended interview selections from
SCORE: A FILM MUSIC DOCUMENTARY
Interviews by Trevor Thompson

ISBN: 978-0-692-82707-9
First edition.

THE INTERVIEWS

INTRODUCTION BY MATT SCHRADER

THE INTERVIEWS

THE INTERVIEWS

INTRODUCTION

BY MATT SCHRADER

DIRECTOR, *SCORE: A FILM MUSIC DOCUMENTARY*

When I was 4 years old, my parents introduced me to the original Batman TV series. The bat emblem lit up the screen as my dad flipped through channels on our new living room television. I was mesmerized.

My parents caught on quickly. They'd record episodes on our VCR that I'd watch over and over.

The bat emblem ended up on all of my doodles. I asked for a Batman costume for my birthday (my grandmother humored me with a homemade bat-sweatshirt). My favorite colors, if anyone asked, were black, gray, and yellow. But there was nothing I cherished more than the theme song. "Na-na-na-na-na-na-na-na Batman," I'd sing as I stumbled down the hallway, ready to fight crime — hearing in my head the orchestral sounds the show famously used for every bat-punch and kick.

In 2008, I waited in line with my parents to watch The Dark Knight, and my love was renewed. As the goosebumps wore off after the film, I realized Hans Zimmer's score was alive; it was its own character in the film. He was pulling the goosebumps right out of us. How could a film score have such a superhuman effect?

I wanted to explore that question, so in 2014 — with a few thousand dollars in savings — I left my job in television news to make a film about these little-known musical geniuses, their experimentation and creativity.

What followed were months of interviews with modern Mozarts that catapulted us into an art form never before explored in-depth — and into a genre of music never before celebrated for its ability to move audiences of people across cultures and languages.

I hope these interviews provoke and inspire you, just as they did us.

SCORE: THE INTERVIEWS

CHAPTER 1

DAVID ARNOLD

COMPOSER

KNOWN FOR		ACHIEVEMENTS
INDEPENDENCE DAY: RESURGENCE (2016)	THE WORLD IS NOT ENOUGH (1999)	GRAMMY AWARD COMPOSITION FOR MOTION PICTURE OR TELEVISION: INDEPENDENCE DAY
SHERLOCK (2010-2016)	GODZILLA (1998)	
QUANTUM OF SOLACE (2008)	TOMORROW NEVER DIES (1997)	BAFTA NOMINATION ANTHONY ASQUITH AWARD CASINO ROYALE
HOT FUZZ (2007)	INDEPENDENCE DAY (1996)	
CASINO ROYALE (2006)		
THE STEPFORD WIVES (2004)	STARGATE (1994)	GRAMMY NOMINATION SONG, MOTION PICTURE/ TV "YOU KNOW MY NAME" CASINO ROYALE
DIE ANOTHER DAY (2002)		
ZOOLANDER (2001)		

As a film composer working on tight deadlines, what's the key to creating music of which you can be proud?

I think the search for perfection is probably fruitless because all you'll do is spend your whole time banging your head against a wall. I can't speak for anyone else but on my own behalf, you know, whenever you set out to write something, your idea of how great it's going to be very rarely ends up being the same as what you end up coming out with.

Because you have to be self-critical. You have to find the faults. And I think most composers, like writers, are probably fairly insecure about what they do, if they're being honest. Again, I can't speak for anyone else, but when you put the work that you've done out there, and you put the in front of people, it's a bit like pleasing your parents, isn't it?

You know, the director becomes the paternal figure. And you don't want to upset him, and you want to make sure he's happy, and you want to make sure he's getting what he wants — and that the film gets what it wants in a way.

The film is this kind of benign creature, which sort of hovers over everyone. And the director is the lion tamer. he's the guy telling it to try — hope that when he cracks that whip it's going to stand up over there and not decide to go and do something else. And I suppose we're all part of this circus to further that metaphor. And I think if you start off thinking that you are going to achieve some kind of nirvana, I think that's deadly.

After the event you can reassess what you've done and whether or not it's any good. Whether or not it could have been better, and I don't know anyone who doesn't think that after the event that they could've done it different or it could've been better. Part of the job, hopefully, is that you move onto another project and every time you try and be better every time you try and get better every time. I think if you start off trying to achieve perfection, I don't know how you can ever say that that ever happens.

How much would you say you know about what the audience wants to hear?

We don't know, do we? we don't know. We make assumptions based on our own love of this genre. And I think to a certain extent, when you are involved in a film series which has been ongoing, you have to be aware of what the audience wants.

To a certain extent, I place myself in the position of the audience, as someone who was a big Bond fan obviously before I had a chance to score them. I always knew what I felt like I wanted to hear at certain times. And so when I watch a film for the first time and we spot it for the first time and we decide where the music's going to go and what it's going to be doing, I always sort of react as I would be if I were in the audience. So that feels like we need something there, we need a bit of Bond theme there or we need some sort of action stuff there or need something sort of tender or tense. And I approach it like I am the audience, because to a certain extent I am the audience. I'm watching the film same as anyone else is. But I don't think there's any way of telling what an audience wants or doesn't want without putting the film in front of them and getting a feel for how they're reacting as it plays through.

Test screenings, whether you like them or not, I think some films definitely benefit from playing to an audience and then just getting an idea about how it's playing. Whether some elements are a little bit flat, whether you need to cut some bits, extend some bits, some bits need to be faster, some bits need to be recut. You can tell that. Like, if you're doing a comedy show, if you think you've written a great joke but no one laughs at it, you might want to rethink the gag.

You've done several James Bond films. How does it feel to be a part of a long-running franchise like that?

I've done five. What's it like being part of it? I feel like I'm still part of it.

You have contact with the producers, especially, Barbara, Michael — two of the most amazing producers I've ever worked with and — I feel like we're friends. And they look after you to such a huge extent whether you're working on a film or not. You're not really far from their considerations. And that's a really rare thing. So I personally think it's a great honor and a privilege to have been asked once, never mind five times, but to still be part of the conversation whenever anything goes on. Live shows or anniversary things, you're still involved, still get asked about bits and pieces.

It's one of those things that will always be a part of your life. You're always going to be the guy who did a Bond movie. But that's true for everyone, you know, that's true for the actors, it's true for the DPs, the directors, it's always going to loom fairly large on your CV.

But I think especially musically, because John Barry initially plowed the field so brilliantly. We're still kind of playing in that sandpit to a certain extent. And it's going to be impossible pretty much for anyone to be able to do a Bond score without being compared to it.

But none of the actors will ever not be compared to Sean Connery, either.

What did the Bond franchise mean to you when you were growing up versus today as someone who's crafted the sound?

I think when you're eight years old, you've got no idea about a franchise or what it is. I just watched a film and the film that I watched sort of took the top of my head off, really. I mean I was eight years old, I lived in Luton. My bedroom looked over an industrial factory and a car park.

And I saw You Only Live Twice, and the film starts with Sean Connery as James Bond post-coitally being machine-gunned to death and then his body dumped in the ocean, and then a giant spaceship eating a smaller spaceship and then going into a hollowed-out volcano.

And then the song, "You Only Live Twice" and the James Bond theme and capsule in space, and within 10 minutes you've basically, you've got everything that is brilliant about Bond kind of reduced into that 10 minutes.

And I thought, "Wow, these places exist." I didn't know. I thought the whole world was a factory car park or school. That's all you can see, you know. They didn't really have travel logs. There was no Internet. There was no way of knowing what a lot of the world looked like. And so Bond, in a way, introduced you to different cultures and different influences and different places.

And that was it. There was something about the feel of the music more than anything, and combined with the fact that this character could do anything he wanted, wherever he wanted with no consequence whatsoever. And if you're an eight-year-old boy that's the kind of life you want to live, isn't it? Do what you like without getting into trouble?

In fact, getting a pat on the back for it.

You've talked in the past about the strategic use of music to tell a story. Tell me about the decision to hold back the famous Bond theme until late in the movie Casino Royale.

Well, the whole idea of holding back the Bond theme in Casino Royale was because the Bond theme is the Bond theme for a good reason. It tells you this is James Bond. If we're to believe that Daniel Craig is James Bond in Casino Royale hasn't become that person yet, then it would seem odd to play that music any other time, because then you sort of disavow yourself of the notion that there is any growth to be had as the film moves on. I think perhaps it was quite an intellectual approach. It wasn't like perhaps an audience-pleasing approach. To a certain extent, when you see a Bond film, one of the things that you expect to hear is the Bond theme.

But this was a reboot, so we're kind of back to square one, and we are to believe that he's having killed Dryden, having had his first "double-0" status given to him. That this is the nascent James Bond and he hasn't become the James Bond that we know or expect or want him to be yet. And I think it wouldn't have done the film any favors, but it was something that I think Sony was a bit worried about it, because they figured that if it's not anywhere, is there going to be some kind of alienation from the character as far as the audience is concerned.

So I went back through it and we thought, well, we should sow the seeds of the Bond theme, the DNA of the Bond theme through the film at moments when he earns it, when he introduces something to us, the audience, that we know is particularly James

Bond-specific.

When he wins the Aston Martin in the game of cards for the first time. When he puts a tuxedo on in the bathroom for the first time. He looks in the mirror and he sees himself and we see him. When he flies into his first location kind of by plane, sea plane. All of these things where you just kind plant the seeds of what the Bond theme is.

And also the song, "You Know My Name," is kind of seated around the same sort of DNA of the theme. That sort of walking bass. And so by the time you get to the end of the film and he says the words for the first time, "The name's Bond, James Bond," you just cut to black and explode into that theme. You felt the whole cinema kind of lift. You're relieved that here he was.

You'd sort of seen these things happen and this thing had grown and grown and grown and grown and grown and then at the end, you know he's just carrying that rifle, and he's got the suit on, and he just looks at this guy, and he says the words and you just cut to black and the whole place erupted. It was amazing.

That was the main reason for it. But it is interesting when you kind of hold back that, because Die Another Day we'd had a hell of a lot of Bond theme. It was like 40th anniversary, there was an awful lot of sort of harkening back to things that happened before the Q Room with then John Cleese, where you had Rosa Klebb's spikey shoe. From Russia With Love, an attaché case with a knife in. All the things you'll kind of like that harken back to that previous film. So we had a lot of Bond theme in there. And then Daniel's were obviously very different. We thought we'll just strip it back as if we were starting again.

17

How would you describe your favorite Bond sounds in terms of instruments?

It's an alto flute, for me, bass flute, and harps. I think going back to Thunderball, really, the underwater scenes in Thunderball. I remember watching that for the first time in the cinema and feeling like it was representative of the exhaled bubbles with his little breather. And the orange wetsuit and that whole underwater fight in Thunderball. And I've always loved the kind of dark rhythm. It feels very human to me. It felt somewhat internal — a bit like a sort of musical pulse, musical heartbeat. A literal heartbeat. Not just a rhythmic device. For me, it was like an echo of John Barry's work. I mean I haven't used it that much, once or twice, but especially like "Night at the Opera" in Quantum of Solace was the most obvious one.

That kind of rolling figure, it just said Bond to me. And it said Bond because John had made it Bond. the same way that he'd made the horns and the trumpet sections scream Bond in certain combinations. So, yeah, it always felt like that sort of lilting, rhythmic, human, pulsing heartbeat. But very musical, which makes it feel like this is a world of Bond that we know we can enter safely.

What did the introduction of jazz to the world of film scoring add to movies?

I think John's style for Bond was obviously very closely related to his love of jazz and Stan Kenton and the sort of big band sound.

Obviously the theme, the arrangement he did of the theme, even though it sounded enormous, it was quite a small setup.

He didn't have like 22 strings, and it was still like a big band sound. And that was kind of cool. The thing about big band was that it was cool, and it swung. And the whole bebop section of the Bond theme felt like this was a guy who could do anything, you know, like so confidant. And that's the voice that John gave to the character. I think it was there in spades in Sean's performance, without any doubt. But you put those two things together and it's unstoppable. So I think the initial thrust of his contribution to it was that very 60s suave — smooth, stylish, swinging, devilish arrangement of the Bond theme. And then I suppose moving on to From Russia With Love, he developed that into perhaps a more symphonic version of the same thing, which I don't think had really been done up until that point. So these combinations of things made something completely unique. And his choice of instrumentation was very particular.

And the fact that it's endlessly parodied. The fact that you will not hear any film which has to do with spying or secret services without a reference to Bond. I mean even in the last year, Spy, the Melissa McCarthy one and Kingsmen. they all touched, they all doff their cap to John's Bond music. It's become the thing to go to in the same way that Morricone was for spaghetti westerns, I suppose. It created a genre of music.

Tell me about meeting John Barry and whether he gave you any ideas for future Bond scores. Did he help you to get a job as the next Bond composer?

I met John in here (editor's note: Air Studios in London). George Martin introduced me to him. And I think he was sort of quite flattered that I was taking quite a lot of time out of my life to record boldly a record which is mostly his material and bring it to a new audience, a different audience.

And so we got on really well right from the start. But I'm pretty sure that he didn't go to Barbara and say, "You've got to use David." I'm pretty sure that didn't happen. I know there's reports around saying that it did.

He was very complimentary about what I was doing. He was very nice to me. And I know that, obviously, his contact with Barbara was constant. And they were sort of deep family friends. So there might have been a little bit of, you know, we'd met and talked and he'd heard stuff and liked it.

But perhaps the best that I could hope for was that he didn't say to not use me.

You've said before that John Williams, despite being an American, strikes you as a more British composer. Why is that?

I think perhaps John Williams had a sort of slightly acerbic British edge to him. And I think there was something about that — he was never anything other than a Yorkshireman. And with that comes a certain amount of baggage. It's like the old cliché: He tells it how he sees it. He didn't really in all the time that I knew him, he didn't really change.

He didn't suffer fools gladly at all. And if he thought something he'd say what he thought. And he did the sort of music that he wanted to do and the sort of films that he wanted to make. And he did it the way that he wanted to do it. And that never really changed.

What are the differences between American and British composers and musicians, in your estimation?

I think it's an attitude. I think it's just a bit of attitude. And that's difficult to pinpoint. It's difficult to actually put your finger on it and say, what is the difference between session musicians over here and session musicians in America. there is a difference.

They're all technically brilliant, but there is a slight character change in the performance style of a British orchestra versus the American orchestra. And that's not saying one is better than the other. But there's a very definite sense of the fact that there's something a little bit different about it. And I'm not quite sure what that is, whether that's a cultural thing, an upbringing thing, or the fact that we are principally, I think, a music culture. I think America perhaps might be principally a film culture, if we're talking about the most influential creative cultural things that each country has brought to the table. I don't think it's that big a leap to say that those things are probably true. It might be the same reason why they made English people bad guys a lot in American films. Why is that? there's a little bit of something. There's a little bit of dirt in the ointment which I think gives it a little bit of edge.

Where do your ideas come from? A lot of composers say they get ideas when taking a walk or while in the shower. Are you the same way?

Honestly, I'll take it from anywhere it comes. I think probably most composers will say the same. If you come up with an idea, you come up with an idea. Sometimes that idea comes after a week of sitting at a piano and sweating it out and actually working through it. Sometimes it comes when you wake up and there's something in your head.

Sometimes it happens when you're having a shower or if you're walking or you're driving. I think most composers, when they're in work mode, are ready to receive most things. Whenever I do that, I know I've become quite useless at practical things. The idea of just doing normal, practical things, it becomes pretty hopeless. You put your clothes in the fridge at the end of the day.

Just like weird stuff because you're really not thinking about what you're doing in your physical senses. Everything's up here. You exist up there completely. And when you're under a lot of pressure to come up with stuff all the time, a lot of the time it starts invading your subconscious. And not only is it when you're not thinking about it that you're thinking about it.

There's a rumor out there that you heard the score for Independence Day in a dream.

I was in Los Angeles. I was renting an apartment and working in a hotel. I rented a hotel room and put all my equipment in a hotel room, and I'd rented this apartment just down the road from the hotel so I could at least get away from everything for a few hours at night.

And I had a dream that I was in the L.A. Guitar Center, I was buying software and synths and this young guy came out and said, "I've got this great new synth and there's a demo on it like it's an alien invasion."

I said, "God that's really handy because I'm trying to think of something for an alien invasion."

So I said, "Press the button." And this theme played.

I go, "That's really good."

And I woke up. I woke up and I sung into a little cassette machine that I had then. We had cassette machines then, and I sang it. And it was about six o'clock in the morning. So I drifted back to sleep, woke up again at half past seven, listened to it, and I thought, "Gee, it's alright."

And so I made sure it wasn't nicked from anyone else, and thought, well, alright we'll try it against the picture. And I tried it and I used it. Shameless.

How much do you take credit for that score, and how much do you admit just came to you in a dream?

Well, I don't know. My name's on it. But do I feel responsible for it? No, I don't.

But then, I don't know if I was really responsible for a lot of stuff that I do, because it comes down to the question of how do you write music and what is music? There are a lot of existential questions about what music is. Written down, music is a set of instructions, right? That's not the music, is it? Because it's just lines on paper. That's not music.

If it's played alright, you've got individual performers who follow the instructions that are on the paper, and they do things to their instruments where sound comes out. Is that the music? The individual line, is that the music? Is the combination of everything the music? Is the music just something that happens when it's played and it's in the air? those are the philosophical questions about what music is.

So it's odd because my job is to come up with the instructions for people to follow to play in order to create this noise that somehow locks to a story that someone else is telling. And it's going to help you, the audience, understand what it is that's going on. It's a weird job, isn't it?

Have you ever had the experience of not being able to come up with anything useful for a score you had to write?

Oh, yeah, I've had that. There was a theme for a film I did with Roger Michell starring Harrison Ford. Morning Glory, it was called. And I needed a sort of gentle theme for this sort of nascent love story that was happening in the film. And you try the usual things. You always try your things because you somehow you hope in your heart that the first thing you're going to do is going to be great and then you don't have to put the real hard work in to get it out.

So I'm already thinking perhaps if I just play something it'll be good. And then it's not, and then you go, "Oh, God. Now I'm going to have to really work hard." so then you sort of try

something else and try something else, and a week later you're
still there and nothing's working. You can't make it work.

So I literally did this, it was like that, like nothing's working.
I just put my fingers on the keyboard, and they fell on the
notes. And just in that little cluster of notes, I just played them
individually, and that felt like the start of the theme. And then
within 10 minutes the whole thing had kind of written itself.

I mean, it's not a complicated piece of music, don't get me
wrong. But sometimes it's about listening and hearing at the right
time. And those accidents are so rare. I mean we highlight them
when we talk about things like this, but honestly, it's so rare. The
majority of the time it's really chipping away a block of marble
until you discover the shape within it.

But yeah, that sort of thing really doesn't happen very often.
But I'm always really grateful when it does. But sometimes
— you know what — sometimes that is the product of having
had a week and a half of actually thinking about it completely.
Even though you might not be sitting at a piano or at a guitar or
wherever. If you're not actually working, like if I'm watching TV
or something, I'm not actually watching TV. I sort of am, but I'm
not. everything's kind of churning over.

So at the point when you actually put your hands on the
keyboard, a lot of stuff has been dealt with a lot of possibilities
have been thought about and thrown out. You're thinking of
approaches. You're thinking of instrumentation. You're thinking of
tone. You're thinking of color.

So when you get to actually sit down to do the hard, heavy
lifting of actually writing the score — the musical concept of

the film — what sort of music it is going to be. Is it thematic? Therefore, we've got to write themes. Or is it tonal? Therefore, we've got to build sound. Working happens from the moment I get asked to do a film to the moment we finish mixing. The hardest stuff is making what you come up with fit to the picture that they give you.

But as soon as someone says, "Would you like to do this?" there is a compartment in my head, which starts processing what it could be. And the writing of it is the ultimate end of that journey, of that huge amount of processing over quite a long period of time. But if you were observing me externally, it would just look like I'm sitting there doing nothing.

But that would happen as well if you were filming someone writing a book, wouldn't it? Or writing poetry or writing a play. Ultimately, you're walking around thinking. And then you might be putting some of it on paper. Ultimately it's about processing the thought, the creative thought, and channeling it and forming it and stopping it from being a nebulous hub and making it a concrete thing.

CHAPTER 2

JAMES CAMERON

DIRECTOR

KNOWN FOR	ACHIEVEMENTS	
AVATAR (2009)	HIGHEST GROSSING ALL-TIME BOX OFFICE, *AVATAR*	GOLDEN GLOBE AWARD BEST PICTURE, DRAMA, *AVATAR*
TITANIC (1997)		
STRANGE DAYS (1995)	2ND HIGHEST GROSSING ALL-TIME BOX OFFICE, *TITANIC*	GOLDEN GLOBE AWARD BEST PICTURE, DRAMA, *TITANIC*
TRUE LIES (1994)		
TERMINATOR 2: JUDGMENT DAY (1991)	ACADEMY AWARD BEST PICTURE, *TITANIC*	GOLDEN GLOBE AWARD BEST DIRECTOR, *AVATAR*
THE ABYSS (1989)		
ALIENS (1986)	ACADEMY AWARD BEST DIRECTOR, *TITANIC*	GOLDEN GLOBE AWARD BEST DIRECTOR, *TITANIC*
RAMBO: FIRST BLOOD PART II (1985)		
THE TERMINATOR (1984)		

How much do you rely on the composer to discover or unlock musical elements to your films?

When I'm making a film, I have to trust the composer enormously. I want to see what their ideas are. I may have my own ideas and from the cutting process. I may have slapped some music in just from generic sources — you know, the temp score. And some composers have kind of a love/hate relationship with the temp score, as I'm sure you're going to hear from all the composers you talk to. Because on the one hand, it's a shorthand, it's a means of communicating a musical idea. On the other hand, it tends to lock people in.

And I think composers like the filmmaker to stay open-minded. Let them bring their best game. So it's a little bit of a touchy area. I think you can be abused by people.

I try to communicate through examples of music but also through a dialogue that starts very early on with the composer.

What are the ideas? What are we trying to say? What are we we're trying to say emotionally? What kind of propulsion do we need? What kind of thematic uniformity do we need? Where can the score do things that I do as a writer, where I'm trying to relate different scenes to each other throughout the film? Where can the score remind me that I'm working with the same ideas of the same emotions?

I think that's where a score beats a temp score every time. A temp score, you can take from every piece of music ever recorded. A composer can never compete with that. But the second you start jamming together music from 10 different movies, you've lost that thematic unity — that sense of a consistent fabric or sound field. And that's where the composer can always win.

So what's it like handing off such an important piece of the film to a composer, who will inevitably be on his own for much of the composing process?

I think it's critical as a filmmaker to always make the time the composer needs to talk, to review, to look at cuts, to talk through musical ideas, to maybe do musical tests in a sense. I like to start working as early as possible with the composer.

James Horner, in particular, would start long before there was a cut of the film doing themes. just doing melodies, just getting the sound, and trying to figure out the musical vocabulary, if you will.

So yeah, look, I mean as a director you're multitasking, and that multitasking gets more multi as you get into post-production and you're doing effects and you're cutting and you are you dealing with all the minutia of finishing the film. But you just have to make the time. It's such an important thing.

I mean the music drives the emotion of the film. It drives propulsion. It creates feelings of tension or beauty or melancholy, if that's what the scene requires — if that's what you need to be feeling at that point.

It's absolutely critical. All your other work on a film can come to nothing if you don't get the music right.

You've mentioned before that a great score is often something you can whistle. What makes melody so important in storytelling?

I think melody is important because it triggers emotions. Once you begin to associate those melodies with something that you've seen earlier in the film, when that melody recurs, it can either reinforce what you're seeing, or it can play in counterpoint to it.

That melody might be associated with a character. You hear that melody after that character's dead, and all of a sudden you're having a response that's emotional. It's visceral. It's happening out of a part of your mind that's not even fully conscious. But it's working on you.

We've heard from a few people that James Horner had a knack for spotting a movie. Can you tell us first and foremost what a spotting session is? What makes it so important to the filmmaking process?

In a typical spotting session, you sit with the composer and you talk through the scene sometimes with the music down, sometimes with a pot handy so you can pop up the temp score a little bit just to see what I have in mind.

Because I might meander along for hundreds of words about some musical idea, or just you know pull a pot up. And it really depends on the composer's appetite and their ability to insulate themselves artistically from other musical ideas and be able to interpret it a different way. their way. So you have to get the ground rules straight with the composer. I feel the spotting session is, is not the first step. I think the first step is to, with James in particular, look at some footage. Not necessarily cut footage, just dailies.

And I think James immersed himself in 35 hours of raw Titanic dailies, just to see what the film looked like — the visual fabric of the film, so he could get a sense of time and place and characters and see who these people were. And then I actually tasked him with writing some melodies, some themes. I said, "Don't even start with scene-specific stuff. Start with themes."

You know, "Where are we going to go thematically with this? You get the sound of the themes right, and we will have a great score before you've scored one note to picture."

And he did that. He went off. He could watch the dailies. He sort of got himself into the framework of the movie. And while I was cutting — we hadn't even cut very much of the film yet — he just sat at the piano, and he wrote some stuff, and he played it for me. Solo piano. And it was the three major themes from the film.

And I cried on all three of them. He played the first one, and I thought, "My God, this is going to be a fantastic story." Played another one, and I said, "You have room for these two themes?" He said, "Ah, there's one more coming."

And I had a deep emotional reaction. And he's sitting solo piano. There's no orchestra, you know. He's just playing. And it really taught me the power of a melody. And I think one of them was in in minor, so it had more of a sense of longing or loss to it.

And they're fantastic. And I knew from that moment that we're going to go through all kinds of gyrations fitting these thematic ideas to the picture, but that we'd already won the battle from that moment onward. So, we haven't even done the spotting session yet.

So that all went on beforehand. Now we get to we've got some semblance of cut picture. And we sit and we go through it, and we see what works. And on Titanic, in particular, I had a lot of Enya laid in, and James ultimately started to refer to her as "the bitch" (laughter), which gives you a good sense of how composers feel about temp scores. But I kept always kind of sticking it in his face saying, "Alright, see, there's no violins here whatsoever. This is piano and voice."

I was I was a terribly afraid of a kind of classic period score with a lot of sweepy kind of lush violins, which seemed to me always a default position when composers felt like they had to go classic. And James freely admitted that that's how he usually solved that kind of period, big drama, big saga-type problems. Or that was his solution to other films he had done

So, I challenged him to try to think without a big string section. Sure, [I allowed] kind of low strings underneath and that sort of thing, but I [didn't want] the main melody be carried by the strings, because I wanted something kind of unconventional.

And so he came back with a Celtic sound, because the ship was built in Ireland, and operated from England and so on. And there was a rich but very bittersweet quality to it. it's very emotional, the Aeolian pipe and so on. So he came back with those sounds, and he found a great vocalist, and he wrote melodies that are sung without words, essentially.

And I think that's what made the score as unique and powerful as it was — his very wise musical interpretation of my kind of blunt force challenge.

What is the overall goal of a spotting session for both you and the composer?

The goal of a spotting session is to have a dialogue with the composer that you have probably been postponing. (Laughter.)

It's really where the rubber meets the road between the director and composer.

In a way it's a handing over the baton. "OK, I've done my work, done my design. I've cast the movie, shot it, we've done our beautiful photography, we've done all our super brilliant editing. Now it's your turn." And typically the composer comes in fairly late in the day after there is picture cut and so on.

And so now it's going through and trying to communicate, as a director, what I've heard in my mind.

The composer, on the other hand, you know, they're not coming in as a blank slate. They've read the script, they've probably seen some dailies, they may have even seen some cut sequences on their own. So it's an opportunity for them to offer up a spectrum of ideas for how to solve dramatic problems, you know. Where to enhance, where to stay out.

You know, sometimes the smartest thing a composer can do is say, "I can kill the scene with music. I'll just stay out," or "Let's stay very, very low threshold, so it's almost not as if music is kind of a deep underscore." Something like that. And this is where the dialogue, the interface, comes in between the director [and composer].

Most directors are pretty visual. They may be very actor-focused, so they understand the emotions of the scene. But I would say most directors don't know how to convert emotions into music. And a lot of them don't know how to even communicate verbally about music.

So the composer has to act almost like a therapist and go through all this mishmash of what the director's saying and get the essence of it, and then go off and try to turn that into something fresh that the world's never heard before — something new, not derivative, and yet something that's going to support and enhance the director's vision of the film.

What made you so sure that James Horner could tackle a project as ambitious as Titanic?

Well James was ambitious right from the get-go. When I first met him, he had just scored a movie for Roger Corman, and I was working in that little Corman stable at the time doing a movie called Battle Beyond the Stars.

The producer of Humanoids From the Deep — I met her on Battle Beyond the Stars — that was Gail Heard, who I went on to do Terminator and Aliens and The Abyss with. And I knew James from that time, and he actually scored Battle Beyond the Stars. And then later, when we did Aliens, [someone] said, "Well, why don't we have James do it?" because he had really established himself by that by that time.

And I thought, "OK, what do I know about James?" I kind of met him in the hallways at Corman, and he was just starting out and his, almost his first score, it was technically his second score out of the gate, was Battle Beyond the Stars. There was this big lush orchestral score on a Roger Corman film. It was unheard of.

Somehow he managed to take a little bit of money, and turn it into this amazing score. So he was he was pretty ambitious musically right from the beginning. And he was classically trained and really knew how to write for orchestra, which a lot of fledgling composers don't.

And so he just went right into it, and it turned out he had a real flair for conducting. He had good rapport with orchestras. He got a lot of bang for the buck.

So I'm laboring in the trenches on this movie Battle Beyond the Stars, and we were being very ambitious on the visual side. We had a little tiny bit of money, and we were blowing things up and doing these very elaborate visual effects. And when we finally saw

34

the film, it all felt like it was much bigger than we knew it actually cost.

In fact, once the score was put to the film, Roger Corman came to me and said, "Jim, what do you think we can say this film cost?" And I said, "Well, I don't know, Roger." we knew that it cost under two million dollars, and I said, "I think you could probably say four or five or six million dollars." And he said, "Really?" (Laughter.) It was all about perception. I don't think he had ever made a film that cost more than a million dollars up to that point.

But the score, the ambitiousness of the score really allowed that, and we got some actually pretty solid reviews on that. I think it's actually kind of a dog, but it was certainly an ambitious dog.

And then James really consolidated that reputation. He went on and did Star Trek II: The Wrath of Khan. I think that was the next one where he really broke onto the scene with a big orchestral score that was very, very memorable. He established himself, and then he just worked very hard doing a whole bunch of different films, showing that he had a lot of range and scope and diversity of ideas, which is important, too.

You knew James Horner for about three and a half decades. Take me back to those moments when you learned it might have been his plane that crashed.

Unfortunately, I've been through this type of thing before, and pretty much the first thing you hear is probably what it is unless there's some miracle. And so when I heard about it, I knew that he'd done a lot of stunt flying and so on and that his plane had gone down. There wasn't a great deal of doubt in my mind. I immediately began processing it as, "Oh, we've lost James."

And then I started thinking, Wow, what was my last interaction with him? That's where my mind goes. how did how did we leave it together between us?

The amazing thing was my last interaction with James — and I'm not the best friend in the world, and I don't always service my friendships and my relationships as well as they should — but an opportunity came up about a month earlier to fly to England to be present at a Titanic live performance, where a major orchestra played the entire score from beginning to end in a screening of the film at the Royal Albert Hall.

And James was going to be there and introduce it. And I thought it was a great opportunity for me to give something back to him, to honor him — not to go there and take any acclaim whatsoever. I was happy to slink in and slink out with without anybody even knowing I was there, other than him. I wanted him to know that I was supporting him and to see him take his bows for such a great score that everybody still loves to this day, you know 18 years later.

And so I went. We had a great time getting back together. We talked a little bit about the Avatar scores coming up, and he was very excited about that. And so it's just that was the last time I saw him.

And it was great because it was it was all about him and his music. He dragged myself and Jon Landau up onto the stage to take a bow with him, which was very generous of him. But there was just as great sense that here a decade and a half or a little bit earlier, we had done something together for the ages. So we really felt this great sort of glow of friendship, and you know, kind of joint artistic accomplishment. And we were really looking forward to the next thing.

What would you say are the fingerprints of a Horner score?

The funny thing is that you can listen to some of his scores like House of Sand and Fog, and they sound so different from other scores like Where the River Runs Black or the big kind of robust science-fiction scores. Apollo 13 with its tension.

I think diversity is an important part of it. I think strong propulsion in high brass, like these crazy high brass figures that just get your heart pounding. Big, strong strings — low, mid and high. he really knew how to get power out of an orchestra.

He always tried to overlay or intersperse his big orchestral stuff with strong percussion, other musical ideas, other musical traditions. I've never really analyzed it, you know.

I think all his scores are so different, but you can always tell that Horner's at the tiller.

It's just a just a big sound, and it's always right on the money emotionally. He's a very emotional composer. He doesn't get too hooked on an intellectual idea. He goes with the feeling, with the emotional thrust of a scene, and I think that's his strength. He knows how to make you cry without overtly manipulating you.

Because I don't think that works. I don't think you tell people cry. I think you offer them the possibility of crying if they feel the film has gotten up to that moment, or they're feeling a sense of jubilation or loss or whatever it is. The music can't tell you to feel anything, but it can certainly enhance what you're feeling.

What is James Horner's lasting impact, not just in the world of film music, but on film itself?

I don't know how you discriminate his role in film music versus his contribution to film in general. I think James has a body of work over a hundred scores that spans 30 years. And they go from very low budget films to the most massive budget out there — in my case (laughter) the highest costing films. Fortunately also has grossing, which is why I'm still in business and not unemployed, and you're not interviewing me at some soup line.

No, I think I think it's just a legacy of being in that cadre of the top two or three composers in the world that really just had such an impact on film music and really made us all collectively realize how important music is — how the hand of the composer is so much an important part of the film experience.

When we were cutting Titanic, James was sending over music as he was, because what he would do is sketch out on synthesizer with his synthesist what he intended to do with the orchestra. And so I was used to getting sort of new ideas coming in. So I was sitting there cutting one day, and a disk came in that said "Sketch." And I thought, OK, this goes for the sketching scene, right? And so I then put them into the Avid, and I put it up to the sketching scene, and it didn't seem to sync up very well. I thought, oh, well maybe, maybe we've trimmed the scene or something and he was working to an old cut.

So I just kind of slid it around until I found a place where it seemed to sync with the scene nicely. And there's a kind of piano downbeat there. I just put it on Leonardo's eyes coming up and looking directly at the camera. A critical moment of eye contact between the two of them while he's drawing her, and then, boy, it just really flowed. It just seemed to hit every movement of his hand, and everything was fantastic. Solo piano. Just a very simple piano melody.

So I was so excited about it. I called him up, and I said, "This is working so well with this scene!" He said, "What are you talking about?" "Well," I said. "You just sent it over this sketch, and I've put it up to the sketching scene, and it's working fantastically." He said, "Oh, no, that's just a sketch. It's just a piano sketch of a melody. We can drop it in anywhere." And I said, "But it works beautifully on the scene!" And he said, "Really?" I said, "Yeah, get your ass over here."

So he didn't live too far away from where I live. And I was cutting at my house, so he came over. He said, "Oh, that works pretty well, OK, alright, well I'll get — " and he was already thinking about what pianist he could get to play it. He said, "Alright, I'll orchestrate it." I said, "No, just the piano, just the piano!" This is fantastic. It's exactly the right thing for the scene."

He said, "Alright, I know the best pianist in the world. He's out of London."

I said, "No, it's you buddy, it's you. We're going with this. You don't understand. You've done it already. You can move on, the scenes done." He said, "But that's just me noodling around!" I

said, "Exactly, you're sketching. It's not a painting. It's a sketch."
He said, "Ugh!"

He hated this. He hated this by the way, because he was very
humble about his playing. And I said, "But it's fantastic!"

So when you when you go see the movie next time, in the
sketching scene, that's James playing. And it might be the only
time he's ever played on a score. I don't know, because he doesn't
like to play. He always thinks he can get the best guy in the world
to do it.

Sorry, I always talked about in the present tense, but he'll
always be in the present tense for us, because his music will
always be there.

What about that famous song from the end of Titanic?

James called me up and said, "Are you OK?" And I'm editing
a film. We think we're doomed. Everybody's mocking us and
ridiculing us for going so far over budget, the schedule and
everything. And I said, "No, no, no, I'm not in a good mood, but
I'll never be in a good mood again for the rest of my life, so what's
your question?" "What's your bullshit question?" And he said,
"No, no, no, you have to be a good mood." He actually came into
the cutting room, and he said, "You have to be in a good mood for
this." I said, "Well, that's never going to happen." So he said, "Oh,
OK, alright."

So he wanted to play something for me, so we actually went
out to my office. It was a DAT tape, and I had a DAT machine
in my office. So we went out there, and was just the two of us

listening, and so I hear the recognizable, kind of Celtic melody start, and then it gets kind of orchestrated in a different way — more of a pop orchestration.

I think, now, here we go. It's a song. And I hear a voice begin to sing, and he's jamming a song on me! OK, alright. And then I'm listening to this song, and I'm listening to the lyrics, and, Wow, this is actually a pretty good song. And, wow, this really supports all the themes in the film. I'm starting to get a real emotional reaction here. By the end of the song, I was convinced that it could be something really important, because previously we had talked about a song, and I kind of crapped all over that idea.

I said, "Come on! You wouldn't want a song at the end of Schindler's List, would you?" This is serious filmmaking." kind of all up in my own ideas. And so he kind of snuck it in, and I listened to it. And I thought about the power of the song in The Bodyguard, the Whitney Houston song, "I Will Always Love You."

I thought, the power of that song in the zeitgeist to always remind you about that movie. I thought, this could be that. This could easily be that. And so I said, "OK, let's stick it in the end credits." And he said, "Well, do you recognize the singer?" And I don't know. I don't know pop singers from Adam. He said, "Well it's Celine Dion," because he had actually done a demo with her, and it was actually her performance of the song. I said, "She's big, right?"

You also worked on Avatar with Horner, and I understand he had to do a lot of research for this film.

41

Avatar was a completely different problem because it took place on another planet, and different culture. We spent a lot of time creating the language for the Na'vi to always remind you that they were not us. This was not some kind of cheesy science fiction film that just sort of glosses over the surface of cultural differences. We were drilling deep on the on the Na'vi culture.

And so I asked James what can we come up with that we can incorporate into the score that sounds alien and sounds indigenous at the same time.

So he went out and did, jeez, I don't know, it was months. He worked with an ethnomusicologist, and the first thing he did was just compile a whole bunch of different sounds. There were Bulgarian throat singers and different vocal styles from all over the world, and different kind of bizarre indigenous instruments — woodwinds, stringed instruments, stuff you've never heard before. And then there were different kinds of rhythms, different kinds of percussion instruments, and he put it all together.

And then we sat and listened to it all, and we agreed that some sounds were really unique and strange sounding. And he could either overlay that, or incorporate it into [the film], but that it probably still needed some kind of orchestral sweep and propulsion to create the grandeur and the emotionality. Some of the sounds were so alien they didn't convey an emotion, other than alienness or strangeness or otherness.

So from that exercise he went out to figure out ways to create a unique sound that felt of another world, but at the same time held onto those ways that music, for a large number of people, encourages them to have an emotional reaction.

And I think the result was an amazing score. One of his best scores, because it has the best of his big kind of orchestral energy and power along with these really strange vocal overlays and some passages that are completely carried by vocals.

How would you convey the importance of the score to someone who has never really thought about the music that accompanies a movie?

If you want to know how important a score is to a film, try watching it with the sound turned down some time. And it just suddenly lacks so much energy and so much emotional power.

I mean, the score is the heartbeat of the film, and that can be literal. It can be the rhythm, it can be the thing that's propelling the film and making you feel like, "Oh, my God, these characters are in danger!" You're racing along at high speed. Or it can be the slow kind of emotional heart of the film.

You'll associate it with characters. Sometimes the score sucks you in right through the character's eyes — inside their minds and what they're feeling in a moment. And you put that together with great acting, and you are having an emotional response.

So, the score is the heart and the soul of the film.

SCORE: THE INTERVIEWS

CHAPTER 3

QUINCY JONES

COMPOSER

KNOWN FOR		ACHIEVEMENTS
THE COLOR PURPLE (1986)	JOHN AND MARY (1969)	28 GRAMMY AWARDS, 79 NOMINATIONS
THE WIZ (1979)	BANNING (1969)	
FOR LOVE OF IVY (1969)	THE ITALIAN JOB (1969)	ARRANGER/CONDUCTOR, FRANK SINATRA
ROOTS (1977)	IN COLD BLOOD (1968)	
THE GETAWAY (1972)	THE DEADLY AFFAIR (1966)	RECORD PRODUCER, "OFF THE WALL" "THRILLER" "BAD" MICHAEL JACKSON
THE ANDERSON TAPES (1971)	THE PAWNBROKER (1964)	
BROTHER JOHN (1971)		SEVEN ACADEMY AWARD NOMINATIONS
$ (1970)		
THE OUT-OF-TOWNERS (1970)		EMMY AWARD FOR MUSIC COMPOSITION, SERIES ROOTS

What initially drew you to the concept of film scoring?

Well, I've been addicted to the idea of film scoring since I was about 12 years old. I used to go to movies — 11-cent movies — and play hooky from school. And after a while I could recognize all the music that came out of 20th Century Fox influenced by Alfred Newman, all the music that came from Paramount with Victor Young.

Alfred Newman was my mentor later on when I came out, and Stanley Wilson at RKO. And they had the style. They influenced the studio. They were huge at the studios. Alfred Newman was bigger than the movie stars out there. I remember when I did John and Mary out there. John Wayne's son was trying to get my cabin, because the composers had all the good places out there. And they

45

would let a movie out.

But it's an amazing thing. When I first started in movies, they only had three-syllable Eastern European composers. Not a brother within site. And at Universal, they didn't have brothers out in the kitchen. It's heavy. The 60s, man? Please.

Same in Vegas with Sinatra. He stopped the racism out there, but it was heavy. And I remember I came in after Pawnbroker, I thought it was going to be easy after that. Not a chance. But I waited a year and Pawnbroker — actually the Swedish one was the first one. Boy in the Tree. And I didn't have a clue what scoring was about. But I came out all dressed in my Italian suit and the producer came out astounded. He was astonished when he saw me. And he went back to his room and told Joe Garcia, he said, "I didn't know Quincy Jones was a negro." (Laughter.) He said given today's world, God dammit, he studied with Nadia Boulanger. You think he's going to write blues solos behind here? And after a while Gregory Peck used to say that it wouldn't have been a bad idea. (Laughter.) But it was so fucked up, man, I can't tell you. When I first conducted the Academy orchestra, man, same stuff, man. You've got 17 brothers in this orchestra. We've never done that before. They said, "Your flute player, who is that?" I said, "Hubert Lawson." "I've never heard of him." I said, "He's never heard of you either. Best flute player in the world. Get out of here."

But we had to go through all that shit, man. It was terrible. I mean terrible.

Several other composers have told us that they enjoy writing for films because there is no limit to the emotions they can convey. Do you believe film music can be that impactful emotionally?

Yes, sir. We used to have these little sessions for the composers to learn some skill with Nathan Scott. He was Tom Scott's father. He did the score to Lassie. And he'd bring in the two-and-a-half-minute clip of Lassie walking through a vacant lot in broad daylight. Just weeds there. And 30 of us would all hit it with comedic or sinister or pastoral or romantic.

We call it emotion lotion, because you can make it feel anything you want it to feel.

You see a girl walking down a dark hall on Elm Street or Friday night, all that crazy shit. We call it the "Oh shit chord," which is dissonance, because all of scoring is about dissonance and resolution, and you have to get the synchronization first. And that's where the science comes in. And that's where you have to really know what you're doing. So it's synchronized. Because if you've got a closeup on someone internal and then you go outside to 300 people, you can't have the same music. It's got to be exterior music.

So unbelievable is the process. It really is. But I love it, man. Scoring is just so much fun.

What are the major differences between producing a record and scoring a film?

Oh, sure. The differences? You've got to please the picture. You've got to be loyal to the picture and deal with the science first, which is about synchronization. Because those brackets don't lie. They keep it the same every time. So you have to make that music feel natural, but cover all of the points. It's a language. It's really like a language, and the audiences are used to it.

There used to be representative scoring where everything you see, you hear. Walk up the steps. Romantic kisses. The eye is doing the same thing the ear is doing. We went another way, way over here, influenced by Fellini.

Fellini would have like a calliope playing at a carnival. And all of that joy is going on over there, and over in the bushes, in the stream, there somebody's getting murdered, with a calliope in the background. And that pulls the viewer right dead into the movie. And that's true. We were not proponents of having representative scoring, so what you see is not what you hear.

How has the technology changed from the time, let's say, you scored In Cold Blood *until now?*

I had two basses play the killers, and really low cellos on that. But Richard Brooks had to go to all the 65 opening theaters, premiere theaters to make sure the sound could go down to 44 cycles, because I had really low shit in there that you wouldn't hear otherwise. They go from magnetic recording to optical and it's over.

And that's why I quit doing movies. And Adobe came in 1971 and, shit, it was a whole different story. Star Wars turned this shit upside down. But it's been an amazing evolution.

What do you wish you had known about the film scoring process before embarking on the score for your first film, The Boy In The Tree?

Well, I wish I had the experience of having to make some mistakes. We need to make mistakes. That's how we learn, man. Just make a lot of mistakes. I made all of them.

You've said before that you have to give yourself some type of boundaries when scoring or else it doesn't work. Why is that?

Well that's what [Nadia Boulanger] said. Nadia told us that. Because if you have total freedom, it doesn't work. You play in any key, any tempo? That doesn't work. There are boundaries. But it's fun to explore, isn't it? Ain't no kind of music scare me, man.

Tell me about your brief stint at Mercury Records.

It was the 60s. I left a job as the vice president, the first black president of Mercury Records. They offered me a lifetime job and I said, "No, I don't want to get up at 8 in the morning with a goddamn tie on. I want to write for movies." And I quit. And my brother was pissed off with me, man. He said, "How do you quit a job like that?" I said, "That's not what I want to do."

You've been quoted before as saying that melody is the voice of

God. What makes a melody so special?

It's important to everything, man. There's rhythm and there's harmony and there's melody. Melody is God's voice. That's for sure. There are only 12 notes, but it's God's voice. And everybody that messes with music has got to find out a way to make those 12 notes theirs with the elements of rhythm, harmony and melody. And melody is clothed with lyrics.

What is it about a great score that gives you goosebumps?

Well, it touches all the emotions in you and it's out of control. You just can't fight the feeling. The series of chords in a rhythmic structure that has this kind of melody. It's hard to explain, man.

But when it gets there, you feel it. It's happening, and you're happy. It's the happiest you've ever been in your life. It's like discovering a whole brand new road to somewhere, and that never stops. And every time you spend a week or so writing arrangements and stuff — because it happens in your mind first, you hear it first and you put it on paper and you get to the studio and you get the guys that know how to interpret it — and then it gets really special.

And it's either as good as you thought it would be or better. Never been worse. And when you drop your hand and hear that sound, man, there's no greater experience in life than that. It's the greatest feeling in the world, man. And all the dreams you had, and you hear it come back to you. And you either interpret it the right way or not. It's just the challenge.

50

Tell me about being a producer on The Color Purple and how that affected your ability to simultaneously score the film.

That's what happened. I forgot all about scoring because it took 11 months to get Steven [Spielberg] to agree to do the picture. He was doing E.T. and I was doing Thriller at that time. And it took about 11 months to get him.

I recommended Whoopi (Goldberg), and she was working the streets of San Francisco. Someone told me about her. And Steven would drive me to work every day and tell me about all the things he had learned from John Ford about color. Where the directors get their first sense of colors, and it was an amazing education for me to be with Steven. Oh, smart cookie, man.

Did you discuss the concept of musical "colors" with Steven Spielberg?

I have synesthesia. I was in art first, and I have synesthesia. And I love it; it's just you get colors with the notes and all that crazy shit. But I'll take it.

You mean like an "A" note is red, for instance?

Yeah, "B-flat" is purple and all that stuff. You change it any time you want to. But it's just a thinking process really. It's just music is crazy, man. It really is. It's not supposed to be logical, right? The science in it is logical, but the interpretation or creativity, forget it.

With that in mind, do you think that great composers are born or made?

Yeah, they can be born. But there's a lot of natural stuff that has to be there too. I don't know how to explain that. But the intuition has to be there — and a certain degree of creativity that goes with that.

And the bottom line, as Nadia said, is music can never be more or less than you are as a human being. That's what it is. That's what it's about: your approach toward life. It never stops to amaze me. (Laughter.) And the things that happen in music — it's just crazy, man.

Who are some of the composers working today who amaze you?

Alexandre Desplat is one of those guys. I love him. And he says he was influenced by a lot of my stuff too. But he's an amazing guy. Amazing.

Alfred Newman, as you've previously mentioned, had big impact on your career.

He had done like 408 movies, and he had a Frank Lloyd Wright home on Sunset, and we used to go over to his house and the sons, Thomas Newman and David Newman, they were bowling with his Oscars. He had them like bowling pins. He had eight Oscars, and they were bowling with them. (Laughter.) They turned out to be good composers, too.

What are some of the things that you learned from Alfred Newman?

He taught me to believe in your "blink" — your intuition. Believe in it when you've got deadlines, and you always have them.

What would you say is your musical "handprint"?

Every composer has sounds. Sonic or romantic. My favorite sound of anything I've ever worked with is one I finally came up with a couple of times. It was four flugel horns, three alto flutes, a bass flute, four trombones, four french horns and a tuba. That's soft with no vibrato. That's the sound that makes my soul smile, man.

But there are all kinds of instrumentations like that that you just fall in love with. And I remember Sinatra — when I first started working with him when I was 29 — he said, "The first eight bars of The Best Is Yet to Come are a little dense. Can you fix it?" I said, "No problem, man."

I changed all the saxophones, the alto flutes, and put the trumpets in harmony and took the stems out. Five minutes. And Frank said, "Damn!"

A lot of composers like to do their own orchestration still to this day. Are you one of those composers?

Orchestration is like a dope habit, man. I love orchestration, man. Oh, God.

And Ravel, please. Ravel was the virtuoso orchestrator. His orchestrations were like virtuosity — all of them. From piccolos down to contrabass clarinets. And living in France, I got a chance to experiment with all that stuff because I could write for horns in the States, but back then they never let us let brothers write for strings. America's got some weird shit going on. And it's finally kind of cleared up now, but it's pitiful. Why can't you use strings?

What are some of the most important non-musical traits that a composer can have?

It changes all the time, and it's just intuitive. It's intuition. But there are so many decisions to make in movies. You sit with the music with the director and the studio and you come to a common direction. But it's beautiful. It's a wonderful journey. It is a really wonderful journey, man. And especially with a director that calls you before he shoots the movie. That's the one. And I only had two guys like that — Richard Brooks and Sydney Lement. They called me first. So on In Cold Blood, I even suggested Scott Wilson, and I suggested him and said he's perfect for that role.

And Capote said, "Richard, I just don't understand why you've got a negro writing music for a film with no people of color in it."

Richard said, "Fuck you. He's doing the score."

Is there any limit to the amount of experimentation you can do in a film score?

No limit. Not one. No. I mean, even with colors and just the sound. I used all kinds of stuff. We used the first synthesizers in a score. It was in Ironside. You had never heard of synthesizers before that.

Alexandre Desplat told us that he believes that composing for a movie is like sculpting or architecture in that it is a three-dimensional process. Do you agree with that statement?

It's like another world. If architecture is frozen music, then music must be liquid architecture, and it is. Brass, woodwinds, strings, percussion. And you're writing it. It feels like emotional architecture, it really does. And I'm sure that — Ravel, Stravinsky, Korsakov — everybody thought of it the same way.

I totally agree, because you're dealing with a total sonic situation. I have engineers that really know how to make the piano make your soul smile when they get the actual sound. And then they find the second layer, which is like surround sound. I don't know how to describe it, really. I just know when you hear it, it really makes you melt.

SCORE: THE INTERVIEWS

CHAPTER 4

RANDY NEWMAN

COMPOSER

KNOWN FOR		ACHIEVEMENTS
MONSTERS UNIVERSITY (2013)	*A BUG'S LIFE* (1998)	TWO ACADEMY AWARDS, BEST ORIGINAL SONG
TOY STORY 3 (2010)	*JAMES AND THE GIANT PEACH* (1996)	20 ACADEMY AWARD NOMINATIONS
THE PRINCESS AND THE FROG (2009)	*TOY STORY* (1995)	SIX GOLDEN GLOBE NOMINATIONS
CARS (2006)	*MAVERICK* (1994)	
SEABISCUIT (2003)	*AVALON* (1990)	THREE EMMY AWARDS
MONSTERS, INC. (2001)	*PARENTHOOD* (1989)	SIX GRAMMY AWARDS
MEET THE PARENTS (2000)	*¡THREE AMIGOS!* (1986)	2013 INDUCTEE, ROCK AND ROLL HALL OF FAME
TOY STORY 2 (1999)	*THE NATURAL* (1984)	MEMBER, SONGSWRITERS HALL OF FAME
PLEASANTVILLE (1998)	*RAGTIME* (1981)	

At its best, what can music accomplish for a film?

I think film music can heighten emotion. That is what it does best. It can occasionally help you tell a story, but it's not usually cerebral things that it helps you do. It's the visceral kind of thing. It can make an exciting scene more exciting, a romantic scene more romantic. Something that's emotional is what it does best, I think.

Of all your classic scores, you've said that Toy Story 2 might be your finest work. Why is that?

Well, I mentioned Toy Story 2 as my best work. I'm not sure it is. There was an opportunity in Toy Story 2 for lots of different kinds of music. It did different genres. I don't like the word "genre" much, but I can't think of a better one. It was a cowboy movie at times; it was a straight action film — people running around. There was, you know, a tiny bit of romance in it. It was animated. It was comedic. There was some danger; you know, a bit espionage, even. So there's everything in those pictures. So it was a real interesting job. I mean, they always say, "I think you'll find this interesting or challenging," and it usually just means it's hard. But Toy Story 2 was an interesting job. I don't know whether it was my best work, because sometimes you can make a good picture seem like a really good picture. You can make it seem like a classier picture than it is. Cases of that happening, I thought that Jerry Goldsmith was very good at that. A picture like Basic Instinct. It's an example I often use. She was a writer. There was nothing much to indicate in her personality that she was a writer, but the theme he wrote for her house, kind of this sinuous kind of snaky thing, I think it was saxophone — I'm not sure. Whatever it was, it lent some kind of class to the operation — some kind of San Francisco cool to it that indicated that she could be a writer.

How much does the rest of the filmmaking team take note of the composer?

You're not there for any of the social stuff much unless you really want to be. The cast parties or the break parties or appearing on the publicity, the talk shows and things like that. So the glamour of the whole thing is not evident. you're not part of that much.

A composer, of course, is often tasked with creating someone else's vision. So you have to constantly remind yourself that you're not working on your own project, correct?

That's right, you do. You just do. It's clearly their name that's on the picture. Music is not as important as the words they're saying. It's not as important as what they choose to show. You're always subordinate. The music is subordinate to what's up there on the screen.

You can get carried away with what you're doing. It used to happen more in the old days when you actually had more of a line going. Now, it's more background music than it was, so it doesn't happen as often. But you see composers getting carried away with what they're doing, paying less attention sometimes to what's on the screen.

I mean, you could write Beethoven's 10th symphony, and if it didn't fit, of course, you couldn't use it.

Some of the greatest composers there have been in the 20th Century couldn't necessarily have written film music. It's different. It requires you to check your ego at the door. Requires you to have some picture sense and extra-musical concerns. Some kind of dramatic sense.

What kind of dramatic sense did you bring to the table for The Natural? I understand Duke Ellington's music was a big part of the sound created for that film.

Duke Ellington was only in that he was in the source music.

Duke Ellington was doing a bit of mystical dance music in the 30s when this was occurring. Clearly it was the 30s when the movie was happening. It wasn't quite Babe Ruth, or was the end of Babe Ruth, which was 1933 or 1934 or right around there.

So we used Duke Ellington as source music pretty often because I think it's some of the best music being written around then. But the mystical stuff was — hell, I mean — I'm trying to think of what the inspiration for it was.

Music post-Wagner is what it was. And movie music, I would assume. Classical music past 1913 is what it was. I don't know how much was Ellington. He was inspired by that music also. again it wasn't "Rite of Spring" or "Firebird," but it was movie music.

You tackled a similar era in the movie Ragtime. What is it about the early part of the 20th Century that draws you in?

It interests me historically. In the era before World War I, there was still some innocence in the world when one could believe that things were good, and it lasted after World War I was over a bit. Things were getting better and better and maybe there wouldn't be another war. And no one knew there would be a war such colossal in size as World War II.

But I was always interested in that era historically, and I think some of my songs have that in it. And it's so rare that they find someone in pop music with that that. I think maybe some of my first jobs were given to me because of that. They heard it in the arrangements that I was interested in that kind of music and could do it.

Then in 1905, the Japanese and the Russian fleet, the fact they had a little war is of interest to me. All that stuff, I like it. And so I did a number pictures, and they do tend to typecast, you know. The fact that I've done in the last twenty years, eight or nine animated pictures and fewer regular pictures. It's typecasting.

If you can do an animated picture you almost can do anything, because they got everything in them. They're more difficult to do. I get some offers for non-animated movies, but I mean I don't get as many. The Pixar things are fine, but I'd like to do one with Meryl Streep. Something with an actress staring up in the air for about half an hour where I could just hit a big, long whole note. And just rest.

Not where Woody's running around or a bug is chasing a grasshopper. That's a lot of notes. And it'd be easier if Woody and Buzz had a love scene or something. But, that's not going to happen, I don't think.

What do you look for in the films you choose to score?

I used to take the jobs on the basis of how important music would be; certainly, in animated pictures, it's important. Maverick I did because it was a Western, and I just didn't think I'd get another chance to do one. But for the most part, Ragtime, I knew music would be important. The Natural, it had to be important. I mean it really had to count when he ran around those bases. Even with Toy Story, the music had to come through at the ending when the kid gives the toys up.

So I would take the jobs based on whether it mattered, because I have another line of work that people will always know me better for. There's nothing I could do in movies that will be more prominent, I think, than what I've done with the records.

You've mentioned before that your obituary will likely mention your songs and not your film scores.

It will, yes. Oh, yeah, it's true. It'd be something like, "I Love L.A.," depending on where I die and how.

Pop music is a major art form to people. They don't take movie music as seriously, and it isn't the main thing about motion picture. It's just as important to me, but it's not as important in the scheme of things as editing or directing certainly, or acting. And it's probably not as important now as it once was.

The importance music is a bit diminished in pictures, I think. I believe it was more important in the 50s, in the 40s, and the 30s, and even in the 60s. And It's been of diminishing importance because now it can be done by non-musicians in that a director, working with his editor, can put up a temp track and just have it sort of replicated, leaving little latitude for some of the guys to do the job. I think the people you're talking to get a little more latitude than some. But very often, technology is allowing people to make their own choices about spotting — where the music's going to be and what it's going to contain.

And it becomes a lot closer to sound effects when you do that. An editor will want music to hit things. And there should be some of that. In fact, more than there is sometimes.

You look at a movie from the 40s, a romantic picture, you watched people getting up out of a chair. Cary Grant or somebody, and he'll happen to be there on the downbeat.

My cousin [Thomas Newman] does stuff like that, and I do when I can. A lot of people do it. It just happens. You'll just be there on the beat of a scene and it gives the actor a grace they don't have.

You look at it without music, and they're just getting out of a chair. And then you look at it with music, and it's got a more gravitas to it or whatever you want the guy to have. He's got it. Henry II gets out of chair, gets up and, you know, some of the English BBC guys, they'll give him something. And it's a subtle thing — just a downbeat — and the music just happens to be there. But it counts for something. And they don't do it much now. It's sort of going away, that kind of thing. Not a big thing, but not a small one, I think.

So the modern movie-making process has rendered scores less important, in your opinion?

Yeah, I think so. Kids learn the right way to do things in school still. I see kids coming out of USC, mostly, and they learn the right way to do things, but there isn't any time to take that kind of time. You know their scores; a lot of the music is done in less amount of time. And they're not making pictures like that where it matters how people get out of a chair.

They do fights differently now. They'll say we don't want someone to get knocked out and go, "Bam!" They'll just sit there and they'll slow the fight down. If you really look at the next fight scene in a big movie, everyone will be excited in the fight. Unless it's those Bourne pictures where they go, "Boom, boom, boom," and it counts for something. But, in general, there's no time. You don't have enough time to hit everything. But, in movies, where they do, it counts for something. And when they don't, it slows everything down a bit. Two superheroes having a fight, and to me, it slows the fight down. And so, instead of making 923 million dollars, they'll make 922 million. So what? They make — who knows what it costs on the dime? I mean it costs them a few dimes, I think. More than that.

A lot of composers who do animated films say it's much harder to score because an animated face cannot convey as many emotions as a real-life actor's face can. Do you agree with that?

You know, I never thought of that. But at Pixar they made the point to me and made it from the very beginning that their characters are adults and they have adult feelings and they want them to be taken seriously. However one does it, they are not to be taken lightly — the emotions they have and the feelings they have. So you treat them as you would an adult character. But I've never thought of that — that their faces don't do anything for you, because they do. When one of them is sad, they look sad. But that could be so. I did James and the Giant Peach. Yeah, sometimes if somebody is like a potato head, I guess he's not going to give you much. But there may be some truth in that. But you don't have to tell the audience much. The audience, they get it. You don't have to telegraph things to them. Audiences are real smart about what's going on. You don't have to play down to them ever, I don't think.

I'm not sure about that, but that's a hell of an interesting thought. What I think is hard about it is that an animated character, for the most part, behaves in an animated manner. But you might as well go somewhere, and sometimes that's hard to get an idea from the themes you have.

Yes, I think it's harder. I think it's harder because there's more notes.

How much easier is it to write a score if you have a song that you've also written for the movie that you can then draw melody or themes from?

When you have a song you come in before you do the score. Sometimes the theme of the song informs the score, and with an animated picture, they'll animate to the song.

In Toy Story 2, "Somebody Loves Me," the song for Jesse, it tells her story. "When somebody loved me, everything was beautiful." Then the little girl — her owner — drifts away from her, loses interest.

That was animated to the song, and so it had to be there. And so it is different, yes.

Any time you have some material, it's a little less intimidating. Unless it's something that doesn't take you anywhere. You always worry about something. Sometimes I'll think that I wish I'd thought about this more, because this song isn't going to do me any good anywhere. Where am I going to use it? I've had it happen: the song in Parenthood. Parenthood was one of the best pictures I thought I did because it was about a subject that somehow they never made movies about: being a parent. It's the biggest job most people have in their lives. No matter what their job is, no matter how important their job is, a surgeon or an astronaut, whatever they are, being a parent is an enormously significant job, and a difficult one, I think. Ron Howard and them did well I thought in portraying the job.

My whole family liked that picture and wish they had parents like that. But I wrote a song for it, and I didn't think the song was right. I wanted it just to be an instrumental, and Ron Howard wanted that song to be in there. And so it was owing to him that the song is in there, and the song has been very successful, both in the picture and outside the picture for me. And I have entirely him to thank for it. I think he was right in retrospect about it. I thought it didn't fit exactly.

What inspired you to write another one of your famous songs, You've Got a Friend?

The cowboy doll and his owner, Andy, are very good friends. They want to emphasize the specialness of their friendship, so "You've got a friend in me." So that's what I wrote. And in this one it was Mary Steenburgen's smile. Her smile is a dramatically great smile, I thought. And I saw it a lot, and it cheered me up. And I think I wrote that with her smile in mind. I don't know why I said that. She's married and everything, so there's no hope. (Laughter.) And I can't remember when I wrote it — whether it was just a cue or whether it was later in the process.

One of the people you look up to is your uncle, Alfred Newman.
Is there anything you took away from his work in film scoring?

Well, I happen to have seen big pieces of Wuthering Heights without music. And he did a lot for that picture. It's remarkable.

I'm not objective. If he were guilty of something and were on trial, I wouldn't be in the jury. He's my uncle. I loved him. But I think he was the best film composer. He had the technique for it. He was a great conductor, which helps. They played his stuff magnificently well, and he could write melodies and his stuff is deeply felt. It really helps the emotional impact of the pictures he did.

The objection that people have to movie music in general is that it tells an audience how to feel. And it would be an objection to his music because it's so strong — the emotional impact of what he does. But what does the camera do? The choice of where you put the camera and the words you choose to have the characters say? It's all a contrivance. I don't understand precisely the difference. Music is, of course, an artificial entity to put into a movie. There's not an orchestra around.

But I thought he was the best. And Nino Rota's very close, and Johnny Williams. Those three guys, I always thought. My two cousins, Tom Newman and David Newman, are plenty good. I'm not saying that the three Newmans are the best — that those three guys are the best guys. Jerry Goldsmith's phenomenal. You ask musicians, they might think he is the best ever. But there's been some remarkable talent that's done this for a living.

But yeah, Alfred was a great composer — All About Eve — and a versatile one too. His Western stuff was great. How the West Was Won and Nevada Smith were great.

One time I remember seeing him in a national magazine, and I can't remember how old I was, but I remember he'd complained about George Stevens when he was doing The Greatest Story Ever Told. He worked on it for a year. It was the longest anyone had ever been on anything, and George Stevens had wanted him to use the Hallelujah Chorus when Christ was crucified. And Al said that wouldn't be the right thing to do, and it's wrong in a number of ways. I don't remember what he said. But it is wrong, I think. Dramatically and historically.

But Stevens insisted on it, and Time Magazine said it was like a big, almost offensive usage of the Hallelujah Chorus by Handel — this Hallelujah Chorus by Alfred Newman. It was the one time I saw his music mentioned in a big magazine.

I had the same thing happen to me with a picture for Gary Ross called Pleasantville. It was in black and white and then it went to color when they went in the TV. It was set back in the 50s and things were turning to color, and he insisted on this picture — finally this artist was seeing a picture of Starry Night — and he wanted this big crescendo.

I wouldn't do it in the orchestra, but then he turned it up in the dub, and it was in Newsweek or something that I had to learn not to get so excited when I saw a Van Gogh.

So you get credit for things you didn't do, and the blame for things you don't either.

Can you give us a brief summary of the different members of the Newman family who have worked or are currently working in Hollywood?

Alfred, Lionel, and Emil were brothers. Lionel was head of music at 20th Century Fox for 45 years. He won a couple of Academy Awards. I think he did Dr. Doolittle, Hello Dolly. He taught Marilyn Monroe to sing. They were friends. And Emil did the Sonja Henie pictures and the Danny Kaye pictures — a very good conductor. Complicated, those Danny Kaye numbers. Alfred won, I don't know, nine Academy Awards. He was a great, as I was talking about, a great film composer. Tom Newman and David Newman were his sons and are both great contemporary film composers. Maria Newman's his daughter, and is a great musician and composer. I am Alfred's nephew, and my son Amos is an agent — a movie music agent at WME. And who knows what else? It's like a bad Bach family in a way. But there we go.

A lot of people consider the Newman family to be Hollywood royalty. Is that a fair description?

No, I don't think so. we have no control or anything. If we ran studios or something, but we don't. You have to have a position of more power.

My son Eric is a producer, and he's more powerful than anyone's ever been, just by the fact that he's been a producer and the job comes with more power than anything. Alfred had power because he ran a music department, and Lionel ran a music department. But I don't think Tom or David or I have held a lot of power over things.

But there must be some genetic talent in the family for music, I think. It would seem. If there is such a thing.

*Besides having a great appreciation for your uncle, Alfred Newman, you're also a big fan of a couple Italian composers —
Nino Rota and Ennio Morricone.*

All the stuff [Nino Rota] did for Fellini and a bunch of Italian stuff. There's American stuff too that I'm not thinking of correctly.

Then there's Morricone, who's close. He did Once Upon a Time in America, those Once Upon a Time pictures for Leoni and The Mission. The Untouchables, he did. Odd score, but a damned good one, I guess. And Morricone had this Italian band in a lot of pictures, and he's just great. It's great. Accurate. He did a lot for those Fellini pictures. It's hard to tell, because I don't understand Italian. Well, a little bit. Sometimes it looks to me like he made a good picture seem great. He was really close to the top there, I think. I never heard him do anything bad. Never.

I wonder what Goldsmith thought of him. You should find out and let me know. And Jerry Goldsmith, John Williams, those guys, I think, are really at the top. Johnny Williams, tremendous composer. Tremendous. He was a pianist. I'd listen to all his music when he was doing Lost in Space and things like that, and I heard all that. I used to work at Fox running a thermofax machine, and I'd copy music, and sometimes I'd copy the music from the engineers. I'd see all those guys down there. It was good.

Do you have a favorite score that you didn't write?

I think it's probably How Green Was My Valley or The Song of Bernadette. The Song of Bernadette is my favorite score that I didn't write. It's by Alfred. But there are a lot of great ones back then. There's Pinky that he wrote. It would be something by [Alfred Newman], no doubt. The first eight on my list would be by him, I think. That's how much I like him. Then there's Goldsmith ones like Magic that I like a great deal.

What's it like knowing a whole generation of kids grew up listening to your scores and songs?

It's a tremendous sense of accomplishment. Very much so. it's a different audience than I would've expected to get. There are young kids too. Very young. I've had 5-year-old hecklers who want to hear, "You Got A Friend, You Got A Friend." One kid was at the side of the stage. I almost had to go smack him.

But it's very gratifying. The Jessie song, "When Somebody Loves Me" — I didn't think that a bunch of 5-year-olds would sit still for that song, but they sat still for the whole thing. Pixar people thought they would. They were right.

It's been an entirely tremendous experience. There are kids but they're kids whose parents pointed them to my music. Those kids survived being brought up with my music.

SCORE: THE INTERVIEWS

CHAPTER 5

RACHEL PORTMAN

COMPOSER

KNOWN FOR		ACHIEVEMENTS
RACE (2016)	*THE CIDER HOUSE RULES* (1999)	ACADEMY AWARD, BEST ORIGINAL SCORE, *EMMA*
BESSIE (2015)	*EMMA* (1996)	
THE DUCHESS (2008)	*SIRENS* (1994)	FIRST FEMALE COMPOSER TO WIN AN ACADEMY AWARD
OLIVER TWIST (2005)	*THE JOY LUCK CLUB* (1993)	
THE MANCHURIAN CANDIDATE (2004)	*THE WOMAN IN BLACK* (1989)	THREE ACADEMY AWARD NOMINATIONS
MONA LISA SMILE (2003)	*A LITTLE PRINCESS* (1986)	EMMY AWARD, MUSIC COMPOSITION, *BESSIE*
THE LEGEND OF BAGGER VANCE (2000)		
CHOCOLAT (2000)		

You've said before that you believe film music is an "intuitive process." What do you mean by that?

Actually, it's really difficult to come into that cold. (Laughter.) I think the art of writing music for film is actually all about intuition, and it's a kind of innate knowing response that a composer has to what a scene should require. And every composer will approach something differently. I think writing music for film is largely about intuition and having a feel for what a specific scene in a story needs, and responding to that. And every composer would do that differently. So much of it is felt as opposed to graphed or analyzed.

To me, it's all about the feel of something and just having an instinct. When I'm writing, I know when I haven't quite nailed what it is that I'm trying to nail. And it's got to make me happy from a compositional point of view as well as from what it's doing to serve the film. And I feel that intuition is the thing that I use the most when I'm working on film. So when I come onboard any film project, anything from like 10 days — depending on how much time there is — to three weeks is really about stepping into the film. And I'll have to really immerse myself to do that for that process to happen. Because, like any project, until it becomes fully part of you, you can't really sort of add to it. The ideas don't really begin to flow.

And there's a thing that always happens for me on every film that I do. At a certain point, I'm sort of knocking at that door, waiting until I understand the film, how the music flows. Music will flow from Day One, but I won't really be in tune with it until I've crossed that threshold — until I'm actually in the film. I'm not actually conscious of particularly what I'm doing anymore. It just sort of becomes really instinctive. And so my process is always just to immerse myself in the film and watch it again and again and go through different parts of the film. I don't start at the beginning and then work my way through to the end. It's much more organic to do that.

You are a big proponent of something known as "the next day test." Can you explain what that is and how your music benefits from it?

One of the things I've learned over the years is that it's very useful to sleep on things. And often I will have an idea at the end of the day, and I will think, "OK, instead of bashing it out, I'll put it down, I'll record it, and then the next day I'll come back to it." And if it still resonates, then I think, "Oh, yeah. That could be good. That could be worth something." It's a hard one — that whole thing of judgment about whether you think something's actually got mileage or not. Again, you're trusting your own instincts to do it. Sometimes it feels that you're not quite there yet. But another thing that's quite interesting is I can be working away on a theme for a long time and go down quite a long avenue just like any artist — whether it's a book or any sculptor working on a sculpture.

And when it's sort of working, you think, "Why? Why isn't it working?" And suddenly you have to come to that horrible conclusion that it's just not right. It's not quite right, and you need to start again and be prepared to throw it all away while the clock is ticking and you've got less and less time. But it's part of the process.

What are some of the things music should never do in a film?

I feel music is there to serve the film. And it's the film that you're putting your music to, so the music should never be too large for a scene. It should never be in the way of the dialogue. It's there to support, and it shouldn't be put on too loud, either, in the mix. I'm often there, in mixes, saying, "You could actually lower the volume of the music. It would be good." Because sometimes, depending on what the music is, you might be writing a piece of music that is meant to be played incredibly subtly, and it's just a little hint of something. So it's almost sort of unconscious.

I think music can be overused and over-labored in films, and certainly it takes me out of films when that happens and there's just too much music. I like it to be a sort of a background thing. Even though by the end, if you're working with something that's the melodic theme, it can have real power if you've tracked that melodic idea from the beginning of the film.

You have feelings about how certain types of instruments should be used in a film with human voices. How do you think an oboe should be used in a film scene with dialogue?

It was actually one of the first things I learned when I was starting. An oboe is in a very similar register, and it's quite a sort of thick, muddy sound. And it's not great to have an oboe sort of playing a melody along at the same time as someone talking. It would probably, actually, be fine if they were really high, so way above the sort of vocal sound — if they were just sort of floating above. But yeah, they do. In a middle register, it's not a great instrument.

You've mentioned in previous interviews that you try to do something different with your music than mirror what's on screen exactly. Why is that so important to you?

For me it's really important not to, what I would call, "over-egg" a scene. So you have something tragic happening in the film, and then you have tragic music going along with it. That is just like same and same. It's more interesting to do something that, if you can, has got a bit of hope in there, or something a little bit bittersweet, or just something that isn't doing the same thing again. And that's the magic for me of writing film music. What makes it the most interesting thing is when you can do something different. A film allows you to just have something other happening. Slightly. Obviously, it needs to match the film.

How does your instrumentation change when you're doing a period piece? How important is it to be historically accurate and only use instruments of the period in which the movie is set?

Yeah, it's interesting. I might put a different hat on if I'm doing a period drama in England — a different one than if I was doing a film set in China, obviously. I think, at one point, I probably had fairly strong ideas about the kind of instruments I would use. I wouldn't use a guitar. I wouldn't have any electronic sort of feel to it or anything like that. Nowadays, I think I probably would be more open to using different instruments than perhaps I have been. I've done a lot of period films. I don't think there are any rules anymore. I think I probably gave myself rules over the years, and now I'm more interested in breaking them.

In a period piece, I'm not really interested in writing a score which is historically accurate unless it's something that the director specifically wants. Obviously, any source music in a Jane Austen story, if one of the characters was playing the piano, then that would need to be accurate. But in terms of the score, there's much more freedom. Often, in the scores I've done, I will give a nod to the period. And so there will be something about it that makes you feel that it's coming from that period. I'd probably use classical instruments, and I'd be happy to put a bassoon in there, like I did in Emma. As a solo, I used it quite a bit because it sort of felt of the period. But if the way the film was made felt quite contemporary, then it would make more sense. And that's one of the things you do as a composer. You look at all the very different sort of facets of how the film's being made and then you try to match them because the music is always put on at the end. So you match them in a way to the director's take and the design and everything in the film.

When you were in your teens you attended an all-boys school. What was that experience like? How did it prepare you for your career in film music?

When I was 15, for my last two years of school, I went to an all-boys school where there were just like about eight or 10 girls. And I went there because they had a fantastic music department there. It was fantastic, and that's where I really started composing loads and loads.

It was really an interesting experience, and I don't know whether it helped me long-term, but I think it might have just in terms of not worrying about my gender at all, and being comfortable to work in what is essentially a field that has traditionally been full of guys, not women. And that still is the case today.

And it's something that I honestly never ever considered. I only considered myself as a composer who writes music for film, not a female composer or someone who has a different sensibility, in a way. And I have a feeling that experience really helped me.

What is your response when a director says they want a female sensibility for a scene? Is there a difference between the music men and women write?

It may be true that I have a different sensibility because I'm a woman. But that doesn't mean that a man can't write music that is a wonderful match for a very female subject. And vice versa, with me being able to write something that has a much more male energy. And it's quite interesting to mix them up, I think.

It's an interesting question. I think if you put a blindfold and played music to anybody, I don't think they'd be able to tell if a man or a woman had written it. I think it's impossible.

What do you think the future holds for female composers?

I know that there are a lot more female composers coming through. There are a lot more film composers coming through, first off. There's a lot more training and many more courses for it. And there seem to be many more composers wanting to work in the field. I think and I hope it's only a matter of time before women are much better represented in film composition, because it's taking its time. And, for that, I would want to encourage women to sort of fight and come through, because we are under-represented. And I'm really not sure why.

Have you ever felt that your career has been held back in any way because you are a woman in a field dominated by men?

Not at all. I've always had the freedom to do whatever I wanted, and if there were an opportunity for me to think that I might have been held back, I really haven't been interested in doing that. I'm just interested in the work. And I think I've been very lucky. So, I'm happy with what I've had and what I have.

When you're starting out on a project, why do you try to avoid listening to music?

I'm very careful actually when I'm writing not to listen to music because I become a sponge. It's terribly easy. We are sort of sponges, so we have to be quite careful. And I don't want to be influenced when I'm deeply working on something.

Who are some of the composers you admired growing up? You didn't necessarily listen to film music as a young composer, right?

For me, personally, my favorite composers are Bach and Ravel, and I mostly listen to classical music. That's what I love. I love Faure. I love Schubert. I love Messiaen. I love 20th Century music, too. So, it's difficult. And in terms of film music, I never studied it. And I never really sort of followed a particular composer. So I think, if anything, I found my own voice through just my own writing, really, and probably classical music more than film.

What are some of today's most exciting changes in the film music landscape?

I think the ability to study film music in school, which is available now and wasn't when I was coming through. There may have been one or two places, but certainly not specifically designed courses. I think it's a fantastic thing. I think it has raised the quality of film music in some senses. Whether the craft of composition is addressed, I don't know. My only worry is there can be a big emphasis on sound and ambience and everything that is available, in terms of soundscapes that are so readily available instead of coming from your head — which I think is a harder place for it to come from. I hope there's enough of that still, but I think it's good that it's so much easier to study now. And it's only going to make what's out there richer. So it's a good thing.

How have you adapted to recent technological advancements in the field?

I think things have changed. Things are changing and have changed so much in the ability of anyone to become a film composer. The technology is there for you to do it without going all through school and university and college like I did to study music and be able to handwrite it and everything. And, honestly, I welcome it all. I think it's all good, and I think that everybody has their different way of doing things, and I have mine. For me, I like the process of sitting with a pencil in hand and actually physically writing my music onto manuscripts. And I work with electronic instruments as well. I work with programming. But for my writing process, I like it to come from my head and from my acoustic instrument, which is my piano. And that's a good tool for me to write with. That's where I do my thinking, but other people work in different ways. I think it's all viable and all really valuable. And anyone who's going to make their own road into an interesting voice to work on film — it doesn't really matter how you get there. It's whether it's got substance.

What advice would you give a young composer on how to break into the industry?

I think everyone has a different story as to how they broke into the industry. And it may be that it was harder when there weren't programs and there wasn't all this information that there is now. And I certainly feel that I was incredibly lucky to have my break that I had when I was 22. From David Putnam via Allen Parker, to write the music for a film for Channel 4, which was a little feature film that had a small release. Now I feel that my journey was very idiosyncratic, and it makes it very hard for me to help and give advice to people. I get a lot of people coming to ask me, "How do you do it? What do you do?" And actually the only advice I can pass onto somebody is it's very tough, and I had to wait a very long time before I got regular work. And I was just determined. And it was the determination that I think saw me through, because I just wasn't going to give up. I knew that's what I needed to be doing.

CHAPTER 6

HOWARD SHORE

COMPOSER

KNOWN FOR

SPOTLIGHT (2015)

THE HOBBIT TRILOGY
(2012-2014)

HUGO (2011)

*THE TWILLIGHT SAGA:
ECLIPSE* (2010)

THE DEPARTED (2006)

THE AVIATOR (2004)

THE LORD OF THE RINGS
TRILOGY (2001-2003)

GANGS OF NEW YORK
(2002)

CRASH (1996)

SEVEN (1995)

ED WOOD (1994)

PHILADELPHIA (1993)

MRS. DOUBTFIRE (1993)

NAKED LUNCH (1991)

*THE SILENCE OF THE
LAMBS* (1991)

BIG (1988)

THE FLY (1986)

ACHIEVEMENTS

TWO ACADEMY AWARDS,
ORIGINAL SCORE,
*THE LORD OF THE RINGS:
THE FELLOWSHIP
OF THE RING,
THE LORD OF THE RINGS:
THE RETURN OF THE KING*

ACADEMY AWARD,
BEST ORIGINAL SONG,
*THE LORD OF THE RINGS:
THE RETURN OF THE KING*

THREE GOLDEN GLOBES

FOUR GRAMMY AWARDS

_____

*When a score is doing all the things it is supposed to do, what
can it accomplish for a movie?*

When film music is at its best it takes the audience into the
world of the film. When the music works together collaboratively
with all of the elements of the film — screenwriting,
cinematography, editing, acting, production design, directing.
That's when it's really working best — when the sum is greater
than the parts.

*Why do you consider film music to be a visual art form in
addition to an auditory art form?*

To a composer, music is as much a visual art (notation) as an auditory one.

How important is it to stay focused on a day-to-day basis and not get behind when you're working on a strict deadline?

Well, I've mentioned before not looking too far ahead in terms of the daily work. I like to focus on what I can accomplish each day, so I keep a very disciplined schedule for writing. And I always try to look at the small pieces and to keep the big picture in mind. Working on Tolkien's *The Lord of the Rings*, you couldn't really capture the whole piece in a short period. It took years and years to write it. So by doing this disciplined work each day, you accumulated the piece and it grew.

I understand you kept the Tolkien books near you when working on **The Lord of the Rings** *in order to remind yourself that you had a monumental task in front of you.*

I did. I kept the books there all the time because, really, you were writing to Tolkien's work as a story. Even though I had imagery — the film and fantastic illustrations of Tolkien's work — all of our jobs as the creators of that film were to put Tolkien's words on screen with a lot of heart and depth of feeling. By having Tolkien's book there and open I could reread those passages that I was working on. It gave me a lot of insight into his world.

You often say that your film music is "painted with a broad brush." What exactly does that mean?

If you look at my concert pieces, the counterpoint is more detailed bar by bar, whereas in the film scores, there's a lot more space in the harmony and the orchestrations. And I think that's just part of the filmmaking process — working with dialogue, action scenes, and sound effects, so it's a more open type of composition. The analogy I was making was to classical concert music, where you're really in complete control. With film, it's a much more collaborative aspect. You're dealing with a lot of different aspects of filmmaking.

Music is also a very linear process to me. I'm not really thinking at the composition stage about a color or orchestration or performance. That comes a little later once I'm satisfied with the composition, which means I'm happy with the use of the theme or the leitmotif that I used in that section, or how the counterpoint relates to the scene in the film. Then I'll start realizing the orchestration. I'll ask myself how to perform this piece? What does it sound like? What parts of the orchestra are required to perform it? And then, again, the orchestration is done in ink and in layers. I then take it to the performers and I conduct the piece. It's another stage of the production, and then I'm interested in performance and recording and acoustics, the physics of the room, microphone placement, etc.

But dealing with symphonic music, orchestral music — that's really the process. Film music is about performance in a recorded art form.

What you're after is really this great recording of the piece, which then goes into the film. So, once you have the recording, then you're into editing, mixing, mastering — the more technical part of the production. So I've now taken you from the pencil and paper, really a 19th Century world to 21st Century technology, and you bridge the gap between all of those periods — a couple of hundred years of music making.

Every composer is different in terms of where they start. Some like to read the script before they get started while others consider it a waste of time and would rather simply watch the movie. Why do you prefer to start with the script or the novel, if there is one?

I always start with the words. I like to read. So if I'm doing an adaptation of a novel, in the case of *The Lord of the Rings* or *The Hobbit* or with David Cronenberg who has made a few adaptions (*Crash, Naked Lunch,* etc.). I always go back to the original source.

And then once I'm satisfied with that I go into research of what led the author to write this piece? What effect did the work have after it? With something like *Naked Lunch*, it had a huge effect, and was very influential in terms of writing and literature and what literature could be. William Burroughs' book was published in the late 50s and it also had an effect on music. I look at the effect this piece of literature had on the culture and I try to bring that into the work.

Once I'm satisfied with the research and the reading, I put it all aside, and then I take the walk. Then I do the nap, where I try to get into the subconscious. What does the subject mean to me? What do I have to say about it? And I try to put myself in a place where I can relate to it on a on a very intuitive or subtextual level. And I love that stage. That's a very dreamy kind of a period, where I'm just kind of absorbing it and thinking about what it means — thinking about certain scenes. And, usually, I'm not looking at the film at that point. I may have looked at the film once at this point. And I just want to feel like the audience.

And then I go about writing, doing the sketches with pencil. And it's not always linear. I'll work in scenes that I most remember from the film and try to capture those scenes in my mind. Usually what I'll do at that stage is not work with the film too much, but I'll work with themes and leitmotifs. I'll try to create a body of work that has to do with the story of the film or what I remember from the film. Sometimes this piece can be 20-30 minutes in length, and to me, I'm trying to incorporate all the aspects of the composition in this suite away from the film. Then once I'm happy with the material that I've collected, I go about placing the pieces into the film. That's also based on the meetings with the director during the spotting sessions — how music will be used in the film. So I have this catalogue of pieces and now I'm placing them in and "scoring" the film.

You've spoken about the whole moviegoing experience as being somewhat of a dream-like state. How do you compare those two?

If you think of films —you go into a room and the lights come down and it's dark. And then images start appearing. Isn't that close to what happens in the dream state? You go into a room. It gets dark. You close your eyes and images start appearing. You're in a dream state.

I like to capture that feeling, and I think I've tried that on certain films. And, yes, of course you get ideas when you're asleep. I've talked about the nap being so important.

And, really what I'm saying is that it's a way to internalize, to get a deeper feeling about the ideas. That's why I'll only watch the film once just to get that imagery. I don't want to look at it over and over. I just want to get an inspired view from it, the way you would with any great film. You go out of the theater remembering certain parts of the film very vividly. Maybe even more vividly in your imagination than what you actually saw on screen. It's deeper.

How does the recording process differ in Los Angeles and London?

There's music recording taking place all over the world. And what I like to do is to try to match the recording to the subject, so I do this with certain orchestras, certain acoustic spaces. In the case of *The Aviator*, I used an orchestra in Belgium in an old movie theater to capture the sound of film music from the early 30s in Hollywood. I've done that on other films like *Ed Wood*. *Naked Lunch* was a good example, where the studio and the orchestra were matched to the recording. So I don't say it's so different in Los Angeles or London. You could look at other places in the world where music is recorded, and I think they're all of great value, in a way. I've recorded in other countries for these reasons.

There are amazing orchestras in Los Angeles, as there are in London. The orchestras in Los Angeles are specialists in recording film music. And in London you have standing orchestras like the London Philharmonic, which I've recorded with many times. You have the benefit of that orchestra as an opera orchestra. They play in the pit for the Glyndebourne Opera season. They have a great maestro, Vladimir Jurowski. You instantly have the benefit of all of the repertoire that they've been performing in opera houses or in concert halls in London and in Europe and around the world.

So I think really it has to do with what the film subject is. One good example of it was the film *Big,* which is a film I did in the mid-80s. And I really wanted the sound of Hollywood. It was the first time I'd recorded in Los Angeles, and I went to Alfred Newman's studio at Fox and they still had his grand piano in the studio, and the screen and the podium were set up as in the past, and we used film projection. And, what I was really looking for was that experience. I wanted that sound. Not perfect for every film, but it was perfect for that one. So that's how I try to match the sound recording to the subject matter. Again, it depends on what you're trying to achieve. Not all scores are orchestral or use acoustics and physics to record, or even use microphones.

After Hours was a score I recorded in the 80s for Martin Scorsese. I didn't use any microphones. It was completely electronic. *The Aviator* — a completely symphonic score. I try to capture the sound of a certain period. So I think with the acoustics of the room, the electronics, the recording studios that I work with, the engineers that I work with — what you're trying to do is capture the sound of the film. And there's a lot that goes into that. There's a lot of planning involved in that. Who are the right players? What's the right orchestra? How are you going to produce the score? What's the right recording studio? Who is the right engineer to work with?

How did your score for The Lord of the Rings help the audience to keep track of the myriad characters and locations?

The Tolkien book *The Lord of the Rings* is very complex. It took Tolkien 14 years to write, and it's considered one of the most complex fantasy worlds ever created. So to write a score to that film, you have to create a mirror image of his work.

The music had to use themes and leitmotifs, courtesy of Wagner's work from the 19th Century, which showed us how you could use music to describe characters and places and cultures and objects. And it helped you follow the story. When Aragorn holds a certain sword in the film, and you hear a certain motif, you may connect it to an Elven culture. You understand the source of that sword. It helps you to understand the relationships in the story.

That's how the music was used in in those films. Not always a technique used in other stories. Not a technique I used working with David Cronenberg. We're working around the edges more with the Cronenberg films. It's just to bring the audience into it, and you can decide how you want to feel about these characters and places and things. But the Wagner technique can be very good for clarity of storytelling. And it was one that was used extensively in the Tolkien scores, and I believe that it helped to make them accessible to a wide audience. People who have not read the book, don't understand the story — "Who are all these people on screen?" They can watch the movie and enjoy it on a level that was just pure fantasy and myth and entertainment, but it has an inner logic.

Why do you believe that the Tolkien movies came at just the right point in your career for you to be able to tackle them?

Well, I think I was in my mid-50s at that point, I had been working on films for maybe 20-25 years. I'd probably worked on 60 to 70 films, so I really had a point of view, and I had the experience of working, I might add, with some very good filmmakers.

I think that when that project arrived, I was just ready for it. I was ready to compose, orchestrate, conduct and to produce it. I would create it for the London Philharmonic, an orchestra I had worked with for many years going back to *The Fly*. So I had already had at least 15 to 16 years of recording with that orchestra, and the score was written and orchestrated for them. It came at a point that was very much the right period for me to create such a large symphonic work.

Some composers say they get tired of doing a series of movies. What is it about Tolkien's work that keeps you wanting to come back to do the next picture?

I like his writing, and I'm very much interested in nature as he was. A lot of what Tolkien wrote about was based on his love for nature. I live in a very beautiful forest that I love, and I think that connection to nature and to everything that was green and good resonated with me. I believe that was really my strong connection to Tolkien's work.

Whenever I went back to Middle-earth, it was always of interest to me. I never really tired of it. It was hard work and difficult work, but I didn't tire of it on a mental level. I just always felt that I had more to say. And at the end of *Return of the King*, after having written, I don't know, 10 or 11 hours of music and recording it over four years, I still felt I had more. I think they had to pull me away from it. They had to drag me away — (laughter) — from writing those scores. And I had so much discipline writing every day that it was difficult to actually put the pencil down and stop.

How much music did you write and record that didn't make it into the final cut of the Tolkien films?

There wasn't much that I put aside. What I may have been doing was rewriting and adjusting to a new edit. It's not a new piece, but it's taking an earlier piece and conforming it for a new edit of a scene.

Do you go back and look at your movies years or even decades later and wish you had a chance to rewrite some of the music?

I don't go back and look at the work and try to second-guess. I accept it for what it is. There were things that I wrote, and I remember when I wrote them at the time, thinking, "This is it," late at night. Or "I'm sure I'm going to revise this." And I didn't.

And at a certain point, I just accepted it. That's what it was, and I think as an artist you just know at a certain point you have to learn to accept your ideas and your work and just say that was created on that day or that evening, and this was the performance that day in the studio. And that's really what it is. Then go on to write another piece. Accept and carry-on.

SCORE: THE INTERVIEWS

CHAPTER 7

HANS ZIMMER

COMPOSER

KNOWN FOR		ACHIEVEMENTS
INTERSTELLAR (2014)	*BATMAN BEGINS* (2005)	ACADEMY AWARD, ORIGINAL SCORE, *THE LION KING*
12 YEARS A SLAVE (2013)	*THE LAST SAMURAI* (2003)	
MAN OF STEEL (2013)	*PEARL HARBOR* (2001)	TWO GOLDEN GLOBES
THE DARK KNIGHT RISES (2012)	*GLADIATOR* (2000)	FOUR GRAMMY AWARDS
PIRATES OF THE CARIBBEAN SERIES (2003-2011)	*THE THIN RED LINE* (1998)	FOUNDER, REMOTE CONTROL PRODUCTIONS
	THE ROCK (1996)	
INCEPTION (2010)	*CRIMSON TIDE* (1995)	
SHERLOCK HOLMES (2009)	*THE LION KING* (1994)	
	DRIVING MISS DAISY (1989)	
THE DARK KNIGHT (2008)	*RAIN MAN* (1988)	

What can a score accomplish for a film?

For years, until very recently, I actually thought really that the job was to serve the film. Serve the film, support the film, support the story, support the characters. But thinking about it, and I'm not thinking about my own work, but I'm thinking about just being a fan of film music, great film music can elevate the movie. And I think that's really what you should aim for. You should try to elevate, you know, everything that is there — the story, the acting, the camerawork, and the director's vision. And I think part of what we do is we get to tell the story — that part of the story you can't elegantly tell in pictures or words.

And so part of it is this — our job is we can invite the audience into an emotional experience. Not to tell them what to feel, but to tell them that the possibility exists to feel something.

You've said before that in film music you don't have to be stuck in one style. You can move around. Why is that appealing to a composer?

Years ago, I read this Keith Jarrett quote when he was starting out as a musician. Everyone was telling him that he needs to find his voice, and he was saying that's rubbish. I was born with a voice. I was born with the voice, and now I need to find out how many different stories I can apply it to. And I'm paraphrasing here, and I hope he forgives me. But I just thought that was absolutely correct. I'm interested in many things, and I like working with filmmakers who are equally interested in many things. If you think about the movies I did with Ridley Scott, Gladiator sounds very different from Thelma and Louise, which sounds very different from Matchstick Men, which sounds very different from Black Rain, which sounds very different from — I can't remember what else I did with him — Hannibal, let's say. So he himself is picking all these different subjects and these different styles.

And that's what you want to do. Or that's what I want to do. And at the same time, I think there are other composers who do absolutely make it their life's mission to hone their voice, to get better at their style, whereas I'm sort of this kid in this big candy store going, "Yeah, give me a bit of Driving Miss Daisy and give me a bit of Dark Knight," and somehow that all makes sense in my head.

We interviewed one of your protégés, Henry Jackman. And he told us he remembers you saying film music has "nothing to do with music." What do you mean by that?

Yeah, of course. That's one of those flippant Zimmer things to say. Of course it has everything to do with music. But I'll tell you what it really has everything to do with — storytelling.

When I first started working in this town, I became friends with Penny Marshall, and Penny keeps the same hours as me. She's really good at 3 a.m., and she used to phone me at 3 a.m., and we used to have these endless chats. And I would use these chats to basically go, "Penny, explain to me how filmmaking works." And she would say, "It's really simple. Just stay on story. Stick with your main character. Protect your main character." In other words, protect your story. Don't let him say anything stupid. Don't let him have a funny, stupid haircut. Just protect them and then you protect the story.

In other words, why does Driving Miss Daisy not sound like Dark Knight? It's obvious, I'm on story. But at the same time, yes, I do have a musical ambition and I have a musical aesthetic, and the game really is, "How can I go and get as many of my cool notes that I want to go and play and still try to elevate the movie?"

For instance, I know that Henry Jackman has an amazing tune — a brilliant tune — hidden away in a drawer. He's played it to me. And the movie hasn't been made for this tune. So there is this amazing piece of music that Henry has.

Just like John Powell was telling me at one point that he had written this really, really great theme. And it just didn't work with the movie. It was a great piece of music, so he put into a drawer. And then when he was talking to me, he said he had gone to the movies and there was the movie and it was a different composer and there was his theme. I said, "Did he rip you off?" And he said, "No. If it's a good piece of music, sooner or later somebody is going to write it."

You've mentioned a lot before that your formal education in music lasted about two weeks or so. How can that be possible?

I think it lasted actually less than two weeks. But, you know, I'm trying to make it appear to the world that I had some education.

How can that actually be seen as beneficial?

The actual education part was beneficial because it really is just a child getting it all wrong. We had a piano back home, and I was just making a racket on it. I loved making noise on it, and my mother asked me one day when I was five or six if I would like a piano teacher. And I thought what a piano teacher does was he teaches you how to get that stuff you hear in your head into your fingers. And that's not what a piano teacher does. A piano teacher makes you go and practice scales and practice other people's music.

And, of course, I instantly rebelled against that. But in those two weeks I learned enough to learn chords. I learned how to go and figure things out for myself. And there's another part that's maybe not formal education, but I grew up in a very musically rich household. So I was listening to music from, I suppose, the day I was born. My mum took me to my first opera when I was two and a half. I would go and probably hear a classical concert once a week, and it's just like we learn language. I have this funny accent that's somewhere between German and English, with a bit of American stuck in, and really I think you learn music the same way. At a very young age, you get an ear for it, and you learn how to listen and you learn those accents.

My accent in my music is, without a doubt, German, and maybe you can't quite put that into formal education, but that doesn't mean I don't know how an orchestra sounds. I do know how it works. Plus, I'm not proud to sit in front. I've done it before with violinists or trumpet players, and I'm saying, "Can we just sit down, and can you really explain to me what your instrument can do?" There's something great about having access to a musician and just being able to have that conversation and learning from them. And the great luck I have is I'm in a position where I can phone up just about anybody.

Sunday, I was working with Lang Lang and just seeing his fingers fly across those keys, and I'm going, "Oh, this is interesting. There are things, there are possibilities there." So rather than saying I've had no education, I think what's happening is I have an education every day. It's just not in a formalized, structured way. It's just what I need to have at any one point to solve a problem.

What would you say an audience needs to get out of a film

score for it to really resonate with them?

I don't know if this is hubris but I do think that a score needs to be able to stand on its own two feet. For instance, last night Bob Bademi and I — Bob Bademi is a legendary music editor — we were trying to look up something on YouTube and we got stuck on this Ennio Morricone concert that he had given in the amphitheater in Verona. We never looked up what we actually wanted to look up because we just watched Ennio. And one tune after another could stand on its own two feet. John Williams. The music we love are things that can stand on their own two feet. And at the same time — I never asked him this — but if you guys get the opportunity I would love you to ask him this. There's always the bravura part of the John Williams theme — the first eight, 16, 32 bars. The great Raiders of the Lost Ark theme. But then comes the "B" part, and it's less well known, but it's so beautifully crafted. And I always think that's the part he writes for himself. But I do think film music needs to be able to stand on its own two feet. It needs to transcend.

I'll give you a very simple example of something like that. Sort of being at the periphery of what Pharrell Williams was doing in Despicable Me 2. And I remember him writing "Happy." On the surface, the simplest song in the world. It took him a while. It took him a while and there's some real craftsmanship that goes into it. But what the song managed to do is it managed to sort of transcend the sort of form that it was written for. And, for me, that's the perfect definition of what great film music can do. Chariots of Fire transcended and became iconic beyond the movie.

So those are far and few between but you should certainly try to have a go of it.

I can give you the bad example of this as well: the really simple brass "brahms" of Inception. Now, when Chris (Nolan) and I did those, they were a story point, an absolute story point. They were in the script. And then they sort of became ubiquitous, in a funny way, in trailer music. People were just sort of using them as transitional pieces. So the idea that they actually tell a story got lost. They're just a sound effect. So their meaning got distorted, and so there's a sort of misuse of that.

Or Jaws — if you think of that. Everybody goes, "Oh, Jaws, it's just those two notes." It's not. It's this amazing orchestral, symphonic piece that takes place and is just being triggered by those two notes. Now, all of John's music could stand on its own two feet.

Can you talk briefly about the importance of subliminal suggestion in film music?

Look. It's maybe because I'm German, or maybe because I don't have a formal education, but I'm always interested in the psychology of it, and I love the games you get to play with music. An example being, for instance, Gladiator. The script was titled Gladiator: Into the Battle. I remember thinking, "We can do more than that." Look, part of it came from — I'll tell you the whole story. I'll go backwards.

Ridley [Scott] phones me up at nine o'clock in the morning. And I'm useless at nine o'clock in the morning. He knows that.

This is not my time, so I'm weak and vulnerable. And he goes, "Hey, do you want to do a Gladiator movie?" And I just started laughing going, "men in skirts." And the way he said, "It's not that sort of a Gladiator movie," made me sit up, and that became an hour-long conversation. Finish the conversation, and my wife says, "What did you two talk about?" I said, "Oh, we are going to do a gladiator movie." And she goes. "Oh, you boys."

And I realized that was exactly the trap we were going to fall into. We were going to go make the "Oh, you boys" gladiator movie, and I sort of made it my ambition — because I know what an artist Ridley is and what a poet he is — to figure out something which would give him license to be poetic, because I knew he had shot all this poetic stuff. And the first thing that gets yanked is the poetic stuff, because the movie's inevitably too long and it's the poetic stuff you can point at and say, "It doesn't advance the story."

So Pietro Scalia, Ridley, and I — actually this was the cutting room. You're sitting in the cutting room of Gladiator. So we had this idea: It had to be a woman's voice. It had to be poetic. So the next day we came in, and there was the hand on the wheat field. And that shot holds for a minute. And if you had written that in the script, that wouldn't have even made it to being shot. Why would you hold a hand on the wheat field? The only way that shot can work was because of the music, because of [Lisa Gerrard's] voice. But it sort of gave license for the rest of the movie to be a little bit more poetic and to be a little more expansive.

And is this a subliminal message? I think sort of in its best sense. and at the same time, maybe that's me, but I can know

John (Williams) is the same way. And I can imagine that Danny (Elfman) is the same way. There's a lot of banter and a lot of laughing and a lot of jokes going on while we work with the team and the director, etc. So, yeah, sometimes the subliminal message is we're just having a joke.

You've talked before about making the beginning of a movie not what you'd expect, but still something that is interesting. Why is that important to an audience?

This whole idea of taking the audience on a journey that they might not expect — you learn more from failure than you learn from success, let's face it. Years ago, I was working with Jim Brooks and we tried to do a musical, and Prince wrote the songs. I mean, we had everything. We previewed the thing and, God, the audience hated it when we broke into song. And it's only afterwards that I realized what we hadn't done; we hadn't invited them into this and [said] "This is going to be strange and different" and whatever. And an audience comes to a thing with a certain expectation. And, of course, the worst thing you could possibly do as a filmmaker is to ask an audience what is it they would like to see. It is not their job to answer. It is our job to go and create something that they can't imagine, but there is this sort of — you have to invite them in. And after Jim's musical and the failure of that and figuring this out, the next thing I was working on was The Lion King.

And here the expectation was, up until then, Beauty and the Beast. These movies had been very much these Broadway, princess fairytales. And here we were doing this weird thing in Africa and what have you. So I thought, if right at the beginning, I put my friend Lebo M.'s voice — I mean that chant. It just sort of says, "We're not in Kansas anymore. This is going to be different, but it's going to be interesting. So come along on this journey."

So I always try to grab those first few moments. I try to get into the logos. Give me that little bit of real estate for the music to just do that. In Sherlock Holmes — you hear the timbales and the violins and you know it's not going to be a normal Sherlock Holmes movie.

For Batman, you hear the bat flap. So just tiny little iconic things that will tell the audience to sort of expect the unexpected.

Tell me about the beginning of the whole process. How much exploration and experimentation do you do before you know the path the music will take?

Everything comes from conversation. Everything comes from conversation with the director, which can involve meeting with the DPs, meeting with the actors, going on the set, whatever you have. Whatever makes you figure out what the tone of the thing is. And I come at music from a slightly different history I think than other composers. I started out as a synth programmer. So my thing is I'm very interested in sort of the sonic world of things. And in a way, sometimes I think that all I do is like I'm a cook. And it's really just going around the shop and going, "Oh, look, the carrots are fresh, and, look, there are some great potatoes, etc." And then I'm standing in the kitchen and I'm peeling potatoes forever and cutting carrots and onions, and I know the guests are coming at eight o'clock. And I tend to just throw it all in a pot. And whatever was fresh is going to hopefully go and create a delicious meal for our guests. And I don't see it any more or any less than that.

It's great to have a little bit of company in the kitchen, and that could be other musicians or it could be the director. You're on this sort of weird thin ice, because you're not trying to do the director's vision. You're trying to go beyond the director's vision and trying to do the thing he couldn't even imagine, because otherwise he'd be doing it himself. And that takes time. It takes time to get to know each other. It takes time be comfortable with each other so that we can push and pull each other.

And I'm very fragile when I have to play a piece of music to anyone. Listen, right now we could chat for hours and, in a funny way, I'm very secure about this because I hide behind the words. You'll never really figure me out. But I think when I play you a piece of music, I completely expose myself. And that's a really scary moment.

So, part of the getting ready, part of the experimentation is just being in the room and being — I love it when the director is here. When I'm really comfortable, I can write in front of the director. Ron Howard being a prime example, or Chris Nolan. It's just I know instinctively that they are there to cheer me on, because if I succeed, their work will be done.

And they invite anarchy and craziness, and every sentence starts with "This is probably the worst idea you've ever heard." But it opens up the possibility of this adventure. It opens up the possibility of this experimentation.

It was actually Ron (Howard) — I remember him sort of walking out of this room and pausing in the door and going, "Hans, just remember, don't close the laboratory doors too soon. Just keep the spirit of experimentation alive." And if I really had my way, which I did, for instance, on Interstellar — I spent two years on and off just experimenting, making sounds, trying things out.

And then came that 10 minutes before we had to go and finish, but I now know the language. I now know the vocabulary I want to use, and I have an intellectual construct of the whole score. I might not know the notes, but at any one point I will be able to answer your question of why I'm doing something. You might not like what I'm doing, but I will have an intellectual foundation why I'm doing it. This is a John Powell phrase: "I haven't gotten it under my fingers yet." He once said to me, "The thing about movies is you just got to get them under your fingers." And he's right. When I'm working on Interstellar, I can only play Interstellar. If you ask me to go play Gladiator, I won't know what that cue is. It's just gone once I'm in that in that zone and that style. But it takes a while to get there.

Christopher Nolan said at one point you gave him up to 9,000 bars of music to work with. How does he sort through all that and what's the purpose of that much music?

Well hang on, that was The Joker suite. That was just, first of all, embracing that character and the idea of anarchy and the idea of fearlessness. I think that character — not only Heath and his performance, but that character — is first of all the most honest character in the movie. He always tells you what he thinks. And the idea of anarchy I just thought was really interesting. So I just set on this endless path of experimentation, because I sort of heard something in my head but I didn't quite know how to do it. And Chris kept dropping by, and we kept talking about it, and he had to go to Hong Kong to finish shooting the movie. And I said, "Look, I've got all these experiments." It was actually over 10,000 bars of sheer mayhem. I'm actually quite surprised he survived it and he stayed sane. So I said we'll just go out and buy an iPod, and we'll put all that stuff on there, and literally L.A. to Hong Kong and Hong Kong to London, that's what he did — listen to all this stuff. And I don't know how he survived it. But then he knew that, somewhere in there, the character was there. I knew somewhere in there the character was there. And that's where the collaborative process really starts. And literally Chris has such a great memory that he would go, "Oh, at bar 870, there's something really interesting there." And I would go, "Oh, what's bar 870? So I go there, and I go, "Yeah!" Because I just instinctively work forward. I just make things.

The way I work is very much like keeping a diary. I come in every day and just move forward. I don't actually listen to what I did yesterday. Very rarely. And I don't change it. So I write these suites, which are my way of getting into the movie and my way of describing the movie, and really all the material is usually drawn from that.

But sometimes, at the beginning, the theme isn't quite the theme. And the theme doesn't find me until bar 10,000 or whatever, or two weeks or three weeks or whatever into the process. But just steadily working forward trying to get inside the beast — that's my process.

Since we're on that Batman train of thought, I might as well ask you about the famous bat flap sound. What were you trying to convey subliminally with that sound of batman flapping his cape in Batman Begins?

Well, this is again where we come to this idea of I have to have this sort of intellectual framework. One of the things, plus part of my job is to support the filmmaker. And there's an inherent structural problem with an original story, because the audience thinks they are going to go see a Batman movie, but Batman doesn't appear until reel four.

So I thought if we have something really iconic at the beginning that sort of promises them that. And then literally the way it worked is as we get closer to really meeting Batman, you hear that sound, and it's like, "Oh yes, I kept my promise." Chris (Nolan) kept his promise. "This really is a Batman movie, guys."

So, you try to function on many, many different levels. Look, subliminally, there's him witnessing his parents being shot and the guilt. I was playing very much with the idea, and I was very obvious about it — arrested development. I'm so obvious about it. The tune there is a little choirboy, and he gets a certain note, and I just electronically freeze that note. The note in the movie lasts for four minutes. It's just subliminally that note. That voice is there.

And I finished that note in The Dark Knight Rises. So, yes, that note in one way or another managed to — and look, I didn't know we were going to go do three Batman movies, but it came. The idea that the intellectual construct was there from the first movie helped complete the arc.

I've heard that at one point in time the creation of that bat flap sound was a big secret. Can you tell us about it now?

Well, it's really my friend Mel Wesson. Mel and I have known each other since I think I was 18 and he was 16 or something. We've known each other for a long, long time, and Mel is a great synthesist. And he was in London, and James Newton Howard and I were over here.

There isn't a big secret about it. It's just really good bits of synthesis. And I described exactly what I sort of wanted from him. And the danger is when the composer intrudes into the world of sound design. You usually get a raised eyebrow from the sound design people, and you're usually not doing it as well as they are. And I just remember Richard King going, "Yeah, that works." And so it wasn't so important if Chris liked it. I needed the sound effect guys to go, "Oh, yeah."

Maybe that sound wasn't that big of a secret, but I'm sure you've worked on plenty of movies in which the score was kept secret.

Let me just define this idea of secrecy as opposed to the way I look at it. It's not secret. It's private. And there are many reasons.

One is — the most obvious one — if we tell you everything beforehand, if we show you everything in the trailer, the thrill is gone. You go and see the movie, and all you're doing is you're waiting for the shots from the trailer to happen, and we've told you the story. So I don't think that is the way to make movies. I think there has to be a level of expectation. But the best example for me is The Dark Knight. Everybody knew we were making a Batman movie, but nobody really expected us to make that sort of a Batman movie. I think the Joker sort of surprised everybody.

I remember reading on the Internet and the papers and whatever — you could read it everywhere — what a terrible mistake Chris (Nolan) was making casting Heath Ledger. There was no way that Heath was going to be the right thing — because they're the audience, they lack the imagination. And this is not a criticism. It's just that it's our job to have a vision, and it's our job to keep that very close to our chest.

The other part of it is the only way anything really new can happen is if we are allowed to fail in privacy. What if you fail in front of the whole world? You've got to play it cautiously. And imagine if I had taken some of those 10,000-bar screeching, horrible noise experiments for the Joker — and remember, they're actually really quiet — and if I had gone to some of the executives at Warner Bros. and gone, "OK, big summer movie. OK, this is your main theme for your main antagonist," without context, without having finished it. I would have gotten fired on Day One.

And that's where the play between the director and the composer comes in. This is where we just circle the wagons and we just make the movie. And when we finish making the movie, we will let you see it, and we will let you hear what we're doing. And nobody questions it because it all makes sense, but it only makes sense when we finish it.

The idea of Lisa Gerrard was really questioned a lot — not by Ridley (Scott), but by the studio, basically. Why do you want a woman's voice in a gladiator movie? And the agreement was basically to let me finish it, and let me put it in front of an audience. And I'll be the first one to go — because of a focus group or somebody being asked a pointed question that they then answer. But you just sit among the audience, and you know what works and what doesn't work. You can feel it. Like, "Oh, I've just overstepped the mark," or "They're not getting this. They're not getting this crazy idea."

I had it on Sherlock Holmes: the solo violin theme. There's a big action scene in the first one, and I'm playing a solo violin, and we're going to the preview in Phoenix. And I'm not mentioning names, but somebody pretty high up sitting opposite from me on the plane going, "You're ruining the movie. Just take that out. You're ruining the movie." And it might seem like a short trip to Phoenix, but that was a really long trip.

So we're sitting there in the preview, and I'm sitting next to — I have no idea who she is — just a member of the audience, a woman. And we get to that bit, and she just turns to me and she goes, "That's brilliant." And my reaction was, "Tell him, tell him!" But, it's different. Once you put it in front of an audience, it's different.

Part of the idea of Inception — this idea of shared dreaming that we can do — we're all alone in this together sort of thing in the cinema. That's why I love that. I still love cinema for that.

You've said before that you reinvent the method of work for each movie. What do you mean by that?

I don't reinvent. I don't reinvent the method for each movie. That's typical Zimmer hubris, you know. Something that I probably said somewhere, but didn't mean quite as grandly. But I do try to figure out a method of working that's appropriate for the film. 12 Years a Slave, low budget, but somehow appropriate to have four musicians with Steve McQueen in the room, and we're just sort of — we're hand-crafting it. Interstellar — I locked myself away for quite a few months in my — I have a flat in London. I just wouldn't leave. It was like I was in this lonely spaceship universe, and it's just me. It was just me. Nobody else was allowed anywhere near it. Rush — you have the band, and it's rock and roll and it's that. Blackhawk Down is a prime example: We had very little time because they moved the release date forward, and I thought, "Let's just all pile into a room like the rangers, like the guys," and just — oh, God, I was so grumpy! I was the general, and I was such a dictator. I was horrible. And to this day I should still beg everybody for forgiveness. But every time I felt they were losing focus, I would get one of the real rangers to come down and just sit amongst the musicians and just tell them what they real Battle of Mogadishu was like. So it's sort of method composing. My wife always likes me to do romantic comedies, because I'm a much nicer person. We finish Gladiator, and Ridley is screening it for us, and she's sitting next to me and

I'm sort of thinking, "This is pretty cool, it worked out. It's a pretty good movie." And suddenly — bam! She punches me, and I go, "What did you do that for?" And she goes, "Now I know why you were such a bastard for the last six months." And she was absolutely right, because I was sort of strutting around being arrogant, and probably speaking in weird sentences, and being all butch and all that stuff. And truly I'm not that.

So yeah, you live in that world of the movie. You can't help but take on some of the characteristics. My arguments with Tony Scott during Crimson Tide were just like the characters in the movie.

Let's talk about the instrument you play. A lot of people have asked you before what instruments you play, and you usually have a response that most people wouldn't consider to be an instrument.

I play the computer. I'm very good at playing the computer because I realized early on that all instruments are technology. They're just technology of a different era. When I was a teenager, I sort of started playing around with computers and figured out that this is a legitimate musical instrument. This is a legitimate writing tool. Do they think of journalists or authors, that they're not creative because they work on a word processor? There's this weird sort of anachronistic way of thinking in music that if it's not a violin, it can't be any good. Or if it's not a piano — if you're not a virtuoso piano player. Trust me, we started this conversation off about my formal education. But part of it is there was no way to have a formal education in what I ended up doing. Because computers, music with computers, didn't really exist other than in academia and avant-garde music.

But, trust me, I practiced how to get good at manipulating the computer, and that just became my musical instrument. That just became my tool. And there are quite a few people here who are incredible instrumentalists and practice their scales for eight hours a day. And to this day, I still try to explain to them that "No, no, you've got that under your fingers now. Now go and really figure out how the computer works." Because it can be a legitimate voice in the orchestra. And it is a great writing tool.

You've also said that you enjoy the recording process with the orchestra. What does the human interaction between musicians in a recording session add to your music?

God, hang on. There are so many things that go through my head when we're talking about orchestras and musicians in general. One of the things — and I keep saying it over and over again, so it's redundant, but I'll say it again. I think one of the responsibilities we have as film composers in Hollywood, or anywhere, is we're the last people on earth who on a daily basis commission orchestral music. And the responsibility basically is, without us, and orchestra is a very expensive hobby, and without us orchestras might just disappear. And I think that might create a rift in human culture that's much larger than a bunch of musicians out of work. I think it will be such a loss to humanity.

And part of why that is because there's a thing that happens when you get musicians into a room and they really start playing.

You get to that point when they're really starting to dig in, when they know what they're playing and they're telling you a story with great passion through their instruments. That's why these film directors keep calling us — because we can do that thing they can't do with the camera, that they can't do with the dialogue.

And really I was thinking about it very much during Interstellar, because we had really just finished the score with me completely playing everything myself, synthesizing the whole thing. And everybody was going, "So you guys are done." And Chris and I sort of struggled a little bit trying to explain to people that no, no, it's this other thing that we hear in our head, which we can't prove to you, and we have to go do, even though we're going to be jet-lagged, and we're going to be tired, and it's going to be really a lot of work and cost a lot of money. But we have to go and use and work and play with these real musicians. They are going to be the last actors who are going to join this movie. And they are as important as any actor in the movie. It's just this one more thing that happens — one more great performance — that hopefully is going to go and just take that thing and push it into what we really want it to be.

Regarding the idea that creating music can leave you feeling open and exposed. Can you elaborate on that feeling?

I had an interesting chat at this Oscar nominee lunch. The Oscar nominee luncheon is this thing that's sort of setup that we're all supposed to go to and meet each other, and everybody is a winner in the room, and all that stuff, right? Which of course is completely fake. So I just started asking the people I knew at that lunch, and I knew a lot of them, "How do you feel about your nomination?" And every single one of them said, "I'm a fraud. I feel like a fraud. I shouldn't be here. I'm just lucky." We all feel that. We all have this fragility, which drives us. The thing of trying to create something new — you don't know until you've done it, and until it's out there with an audience, and it's been either accepted or rejected. Because really, truly, it is a completely personal statement. It is truly being able to communicate on a level that I can't do in words. Yes, a great writer can do in words. But it is not what I do. And it is really just standing at the edge of a cliff and going, "OK, I'm shutting my eyes, and I'm just going to let myself fall. And hopefully you'll catch me."

And at the same time, a while back, Claudio Abbado, the great conductor, died. And I was up at night, the way I am. And I remembered, "Oh, Claudio Abbado died today." And so I went onto YouTube, and I picked any performance at random. And it was him doing a Tchaikovsky symphony. Not one of my favorites pieces, but you know. And just watching him and watching him struggling with the orchestra and giving to the orchestra and feeling the emotion of the players and the communication with the audience, and him going through a rollercoaster of emotions while he is creating this piece, basically — while they are creating this piece. And I get to the end of it, and it is a transcendent performance. I picked a good one. But the thing is, I get to the end of it, and the audience — it takes them like 10 seconds to recover, because they realized they were a part of something that was intensely personal and at the same time spoke to all of them. And 10 seconds, then they start applauding, and they're going crazy. And all I could think about was that was a life well lived. I realized that, as a musician on a daily basis, you have that opportunity to go on that emotional rollercoaster with other musicians, with the audience — the struggle, fighting with the notes. So, to get back to the fear — because that's what it is — the fear of playing something, of exposing yourself, of playing something. Are they going to be kind to my baby, that little piece of music I sent out into the world? Or are they just going to kill it?

The reason that you do it is because you get to live this life. And sometimes, yeah, you crash into a wall, and sometimes people are mean and horrible, and they forget. The weird thing is — when you read reviews, or you read about yourself — I'm reading about this person that I don't know, because they don't know me. The assumptions they make about why, how, whatever, I write a piece of music, why I do things. As opposed to that, everything I do is intensely personal. It comes from a completely personal point of view. So, yes, I should have thicker skin. I shouldn't get hurt by the snide comment on a Facebook page or the review that whatever they call you. And I'm not saying don't criticize me. Do criticize me, because I learn something from it. But I'm not saying it doesn't hurt intensely on a personal level.

Speaking of that roller coaster of emotions, what words would you use to describe how you're feeling at the beginning of a project before you know the direction the score is going to take?

(Laughter.) Here's the trap. Every project starts roughly the same way when somebody comes into the room and says, "I have this idea for a project. It'll be fun to do." And they tell you this idea, and you get drawn in, and you get excited, and you're flattered that they're even considering you. "Woo, me," you know, "I get to go along on this ride." And this is the lesson I never learn. You go, "Yes, please. Yes." Right? And then they leave the room, and you have a moment of reflection where you go, "I have no idea how to do this. Oh, my God." And then the first few weeks, you just sit there, and you have nothing. You just have a blank page. And after a while you think, should you be phoning them and saying, "Hey, I think you better phone John Williams. I have no idea how to do this"? And the panic sets in, and I get grumpy, and people don't even go near this room, because they know I'll bite their ankles or whatever. And it's sheer panic, because the weird thing about music is it's not like you can really learn how to do it. The mechanics aren't as important. The blank page is always the blank page, and just because you learned how to fill it the last time doesn't mean you know how to fill it now. Plus, I have no idea where music comes from. So there's always the fear that somebody's going to switch off the tap. This and other paranoid thoughts then go through my head on a daily and nightly basis.

And then, so far, I just think I've been lucky. I've just been lucky that so far a solution presents itself somehow at a certain point. But I've done enough movies to sort of watch myself, observe myself. I just have to go through the torture, and there's no shortcut. It just is. You're struggling, and you have self doubts, and it's quite a lot of weight to carry on your shoulder as well, the more expensive the movies get. And they do let you know this.

The occasional hint gets dropped by the studio that everything is riding on this, and you better — you know — whatever. And this isn't necessarily inspirational; it's just terrifying. So that's my process. I get seduced by the idea. I get seduced by what it could be, and sort of in that first conversation with the director, I have glimpses of what it could be. And then I sit there, and I have no idea how to do it. And really I just have to learn how to do it each time all over again. I'm not saying I've revolutionized anything, or I've found completely new ways of speaking the language. It's just, for me, it's new at that moment. And it's new and very distant and far-removed, and you have to sort of just sneak up on it, because you have to get to this weird state. You have to be in the zone, and to get into the zone you have to learn what the zone's going to be. The zone you were in for that last one is definitely the wrong one, and you can't rationalize it. I'm trying to rationalize it now, and it's not going to happen. It's a mystery, and it's terrifying.

Why do you think the average movie fan should be excited about the future of film music? What does that future hold?

I have no idea. If I knew what the future of film music was, I'd be doing it. I think that's an impossible question. I'll tell you what. Why they should be excited is because it's opening up. It's letting new talent in. It's letting people have voices that maybe 20 years ago those types of composers wouldn't have been able to have had access to a big movie or a small movie or a movie that communicated. I think there's far more experimentation.

There's far more freedom, and inviting artists who would never have thought of doing a film score and who no one would have ever thought of doing a film score before. And to me that's really exciting.

This next question will be much easier to answer. How much do you enjoy what you do?

Well, I have this saying. I've done it all my life — all my film life. Every day, when I wake up, I check with myself. "Do I want to go to the studio today and write music?" And I tell my directors — they all know this — the day I go, "Well, this is it," they better go and look for somebody else.

I love, I love, I love what I do. I love what I do even when I sit there driven by paranoia, fear, and neurosis, and pulling my hair out. I still wouldn't trade it for anything else.

I don't have weekends. I once tried an experiment; I said to everyone here, "OK, it's Christmas. Everybody, we're going to shut down from, I don't know, the 20th of December through the 6th of January. We're going to shut the whole place down." And then, Christmas Day, I was at home unwrapping presents. But just for fun, I hit the speed dial button, and lo and behold there were a ton of people here doing music, and I'm going, "Why aren't you at home, and why aren't you celebrating Christmas? What happened?" And you realize they're passionate. They love what they do. They'd rather be here. So I'd rather be here.

You've talked before about the "spirit of experimentation" and the importance of keeping it alive. How do you keep that spirit going year after year?

The spirit of experimentation — it's just that I get bored. I get bored easily. So — the poor people that work with me — just when we've figured out how to make it sound really good, etc., I've got to go tear it all apart, and tear all the patch cables, and I have to go and reinvent how the orchestra is. Everything has to change, because I can't sit still. I have to at least try something new. So it's that boredom would kill me. The question is the interesting part, not the answer. The answer is tedious. I love the process. I love the process. I observe myself. I love doing the work, and then we get to the end of it, and we have a premiere, and it's sort of like an Irish Wake. It's really sort of over, and you're going to miss working with those people. You're going to miss the work. And then there's that one more moment you get to have when you go and sneak into the theater and watch it with a real audience, and that's who I work for. I work for the people who've worked hard to earn the money to go and buy the theater ticket. And I want to have done good work for them, because I know the world is a tough place, and I have a responsibility to have done my best.

And the only way to do my best is we have to go and shake it up. We have to go and shake it up. We have to go and reinvent. We have to go and try to do that. Sometimes I succeed and sometimes I don't, but I try my hardest. And that's what keeps me going. The possibility of something new. I don't always hit the mark, but I really do try.

When you hear a score that you made five years or 10 years ago, what goes through your head? Do you ever think, "What was I thinking back then?"

I think everybody does that — the idea that you hear something from 20 years ago, and you go, "What was I thinking? Or what wasn't I thinking?" But at the same time, it's like your kids. You can't be really angry at them. You learn, you try to get better. And the problem is you don't actually know what better is, and the only thing that hopefully you get better at is communicating or experimenting and the experiments landing.

But, yes, of course, I listen to the sins of my youth and you go, "Yeah." Some of them, of course — they're embarrassing. But that's part of it. You have to live with it. We did our best then. I'm trying to do my best now. It's not so bad. It didn't kill anybody.

You're often up against a very tight deadline, which some composers see as a good thing. Would you be able to work without a deadline or would you constantly be tweaking your work until the end of time?

I've done — what, 120, 130 movies or something like that? And I'm always left with the "Oh, could it only be a little bit — if only I'd had a bit more time, it could be better." Whatever.

The first time I didn't have that was on Interstellar. It's just we worked in a very different way. Without getting all into how and why, one of the things we would do is every Friday we would screen the whole movie with the whole score, and we'd just adjust and write a couple things or whatever. And there came a moment, like one week before we had to finish, and Chris is going, "Hey, do you have any more ideas or anything you want to change?" And for the first time in my life I was going, "No, I think I crossed every 'T' and dotted every 'I.'" And for the first time I actually felt like I'd finished something. Then straight away went into something else, which, actually no, I actually didn't go straight away into something else. I actually gave myself a bit of time. But it was interesting to feel that, "Nope, this is all I have to say on this subject." But I don't think I'm going to be doing a space movie in a hurry, again. I try to pick my subjects to be as diverse and as far from each other as they possibly can.

I mean Driving Miss Daisy and Black Rain were written in the same month. But other than the fact they were written at the same time, I don't think they have anything in common.

We talked about Thomas Newman briefly before we started this interview, but I wanted to ask you formally what you think his lasting impact on the film music industry is.

What's his lasting impact on the film industry? Elegance. That's just the first word that comes into my head. I think his music is so incredibly elegant and so beautifully original and original isn't necessarily good. Original can get really in the way. It can be very inappropriate to the storytelling, but he manages to do both brilliantly. Don't misunderstand me, but the year I won an Oscar for The Lion King, Shawshank Redemption was up. That's the lasting piece of art. Shawshank. so I don't feel bad. I don't feel guilty. But I do in my heart know he deserved it.

You've also talked about John Williams briefly, but what is his lasting legacy in the world of film music?

I don't want to talk about his lasting legacy. I can only talk about what he means to me. I suppose that other than Ennio Morricone, it was John Williams who made me, first of all, realize that film music can be of a quality and distinction that is as great as any of the classical composers I grew up with. And really for me it's not Star Wars or Raiders, it's Close Encounters. And it's not really those notes that we all know. That whole score is I think one of the great symphonic poems of the 20th Century. And his constant transcending. We take his craftsmanship for granted — which is so incredible and so beyond anything. But it's really just this sort of amazing storytelling that at the same time never lets go of the quality of the music. He manages to do the impossible. He serves and elevates the movie and at the same time never ever betrays his own aesthetic and his own style.

Composer David Newman told us that he would call this era of film music "The Hans Zimmer era." What terms would you use to describe this era of film music?

I have no idea. I think it's wrong calling it the Hans Zimmer era. I think music is constantly evolving. Film music is constantly evolving. It's the constant. Films are constantly evolving. Why can't it be the John Powell era? Why can't it be the Alexandre

Desplat era? I don't know what that means, because does he mean Hans Zimmer of Driving Miss Daisy and As Good As It Gets? Does he mean Hans Zimmer of Pirates? Does he mean Hans Zimmer of Blackhawk Down? I'm all over the place.

I think, if anything, there is more invention. Johnny Greenwood, for me, it's amazing what he's doing. I'll tell you what it is. I think partly it's the era where film composers are being seen not just as the guy who comes on at the end. We're not just plumbers anymore. And this is very much down to the John Williams and the Jerry Goldsmith and the Elmer Bernstein side more than anything else. That we have become the popular music of our day, in a peculiar way. There's so many concerts these days devoted to film music. I've got Pirates out there, I've got Gladiator out there. Our music has transcended the confines of the medium it was written for. And at the same time, we're making people come back to the concert hall. And that's a great thing.

It used to be film music was described just as background music. I think people like Giorgio Moroder stopped it being background music pretty early on. We're now a noisy bunch, and I know Jerry Goldsmith said that if he wrote it, he wants it to be heard. Yeah, it's like, "Play it loud. Play it proud. Play it appropriately." But the idea of, "Oh, what do you do?" "Oh, I write background music." I think we all managed to transcend that. And it's not actually — thinking about it — it's not us the composers who did that. It's the new generation of filmmakers who have done that. It's the directors.

Hey, I didn't turn up once on that dub stage on Interstellar. The huge division of "Oh, my God, the music is too loud, it's drowning out the dialogue," or "I was truly moved by this movie." I loved the extremes we ended up with.

But don't for a moment forget who did that. The writer-director, the man who wrote the words, decided this is how he wanted to present the music and his words. That was the balance he sought from it. And yeah, we're rock and roll.

CHAPTER 8

GARRY MARSHALL

DIRECTOR

KNOWN FOR		ACHIEVEMENTS
MOTHER'S DAY (2016)	*PRETTY WOMAN* (1990)	FOUR EMMY NOMINATIONS
NEW YEAR'S EVE (2011)	*BEACHES* (1988)	ONE BAFTA NOMINATION
VALENTINE'S DAY (2010)	*OVERBOARD* (1987)	LAUREL AWARD FOR TV
RAISING HELEN (2004)	*HAPPY DAYS* (1974-84)	WRITING ACHIEVEMENT, WRITER'S GUILD OF
THE PRINCESS DIARIES (2001)	*LAVERNE AND SHIRLEY* (1976-83)	AMERICA
PRETTY WOMAN (1999)	*MORK & MINDY* (1978-82)	STAR ON HOLLYWOOD WALK OF FAME
RUNAWAY BRIDE (1999)	*THE ODD COUPLE* (1970-75)	INDUCTEE, TELEVISION HALL OF FAME
THE OTHER SISTER (1999)	*HEY, LANDLORD* (1966)	
FRANKIE AND JOHNNY (1991)	*THE DICK VAN DYKE SHOW* (1961)	

What does music add to film?

Well, I only hum public domain. That's what I learned to hum. I used to hum everything; now you hum public domain because you try to use public domain. Because music for film costs money! We go through different budgets and everything so, what does music do for a film? Well I think it's very important, because it covers all the mistakes you make and a lot of times you use it to make it better. I use U2 a lot. Music group. They cost a dollar, but when U2 has songs, when you hear them you think something important is going to happen. And a lot of times if your picture is dull, you're going to make sure they think something important is going to happen. I have pictures where something important did happen! But I like U2 for that. I opened my film Overboard with U2 and Runaway Bride. So it really is a big part of making a movie, is the music. You try to find people you can work with. And most of the adversarial relationships are with the studio rather than the composers.

Talk about the raw creativity needed to come up with an hour and a half or more of music.

I work with various composers. My two favorite are James Newton Howard, which I did Pretty Woman with, and Runaway Bride, and John Debney, who of course I've done a lot of films with. Five of them, I think. He's done my last five films. Now, is it because he's a creative artist? Yes. It's because he's a nice guy? Yes. But mostly it's because he's near me. He's like three blocks from where my office is, so it's always nice when they're in the neighborhood.

But I was very lucky that I found a great artist in my neighborhood. That's where I work with John Debney. He has to come up with a lot of hours of music and he has to make me happy with what I think and sometimes make the studio happy too. But I like John because he's quick, he can rewrite. Lot of composers say, that is what I do and that's it. But he can rewrite, and he's not a guy who just sits at the piano or hums it, he brings it out.

I say, "I want a sound like…" so he goes, "Wait, wait." He goes to the end of the room, finds some guitar or some old India piece of music Ravi Shankar used in India and he uses it and, "you like this sound? Fine." So he's quite flexible and quite artistic, and he's always there for you.

And we're also big Lakers fans — I know that has nothing to do with this, but Lakers fans is when we meet each other at the game. We can talk music during halftime. There it is! The key to music composition and the director — meet at a ballgame.

How do you convey what you want to a composer?

I learned early that I talk a lot of the time. I'm from the Bronx, New York. You guessed? I'm not from Alabama. So, I used to talk, and I remember I did a movie with Patrick Doyle, a wonderful composer, and I was saying, "Well, here, I need some of that harp shit that goes underneath." And he said, "Wait a minute, I want to write that down, 'harp shit.' I never got that as a note." So I learned to talk a little more elegantly with the composers. I don't say that anymore. Mostly when I listen for music, I truly listen: One, I use something that makes the scene become important, or what's ahead. Two, I make it look pretty, and melodic. And three, I always pick music that makes me cry. Because I don't cry that much, so when I get to the music I like to see something that will I remember.

I remember with Bette Midler, I did a movie called Beaches, and she called me 8 o'clock and said, "Come on over, I'm here with Marc Shaiman, and we're playing some music." I don't want to come, it's 8 o'clock, and I have three kids. But I went, aggravated a little, and they played. She said, "Maybe this," and Marc Shaiman said, "Maybe this," and then he played "Wind Beneath My Wings." And I sat there, angry at 8 o'clock at night, not wanting to be there, just the three of us, and I cried. I said, this could work and I must say, "Wind Beneath My Wings" was quite big in Beaches, and helped make that film.

I did a film called Frankie and Johnny. Al Pacino, Michelle Pfeiffer. And so I got Marvin Hamlisch, may he rest in peace, to do the music. So, the studio says, "Let's not have too much of that Marvin Hamlisch, with the violins." "It's a love story. It's a short order cook and a waitress, we don't need beautiful violins." I said, "What do you mean? When rich people fall in love they hear violins, and poor people hear accordions? What are you talking about? When anybody falls in love they hear violins." So we had violins in Frankie and Johnny. And if you ever run a clip, there's a moment in Frankie and Johnny where they kiss for the first time. You got to use everything you got, it's a competitive business. So we not only have all the Marvin violins, but as they kissed a guy opened the back of the truck, and all you saw was beautiful flowers. So we had flowers going, we had music going. Al and Michelle are not bad to look at, and they kiss so that's putting everything together, and music was a tremendous help in that film.

Tell me about a spotting session and what you're looking for, watching the film for the first time with the composer.

When we spot, we usually do it just us, together. I don't want to shock you, but many composers don't work by themselves. They always have a guy named Murray, or a girl named Denise or Martha, or some other person who gets involved with it. John

Debney has a wonderful guy, Jeff Carson is his name, and he also makes suggestions. So the three of us usually do the session together, and the producers come. But it's funny, you just discuss how something here, how about there. He has ideas, I have ideas, and we go.

I think to be different is what you want to try, and what's the trickiest — I'm giving an inside look here — if you use odd things, like in Frankie and Johnny actually we used some Greek music. We used some Greek folk music, they were at a party and they played that. But what happens, the trick they do, is when you have music like that, they say, "We can't find the rights, we can't get the clearance," and so sometimes alright we'll do it anyway, but as soon as you put it in the picture, suddenly the clearance shows up that you couldn't find before, and charges you a lot of money. So I have more than once had to cut a song out of the picture because clearance showed up and wanted too much money. So you battle through these things, but I think you look for stuff that the composer himself writes.

Why John Debney is good — I have Taylor Swift in my picture, not doing bad, Taylor Swift, has a career and so we want her to have a song, so some composers, well, "I don't like when you have popular songs." I like popular songs. So in Valentine's Day, Taylor Swift sang a couple of songs, so you always should be welcomed by the composer to stuff that might have worked in the temps, or that maybe you could use in the real score.

The composers often come later on the filmmaking process. What are the advantages and disadvantages?

The composers come late in the process because they're the last stop to fix it. If you're messed up where your problems are, sometimes the only thing you got left as a tool is music. It's very overwhelming because, I was a drummer, right? Not a great drummer, and I didn't read music very well, so when you come to a scoring session and there's many — I do studio films so my scoring session is 100 musicians, it's a big orchestra, hundred people. And it really is very moving and the only time — I have a wife — and the only time my wife ever comes is the scoring sessions. That's the only thing she comes to. She comes in one day on set once in a while, acts, but the only thing she insists upon coming, every one of my movies, she's been at the scoring session because it's emotional — the most emotional part of the film, and so it is a very emotional and exciting thing to come to scoring sessions. A hundred people playing music is quite a thing; it's not like a quartet we're scoring with. It starts with 100 and they get down to four because they let the other ones go as soon as they're done. And then they do the little stuff but it is it's really hard to describe. What they have never done yet — look I'm making money — they should let tours hear a scoring session because it's something much more special than just saying "oh, here's a set." It's a very emotional time.

What's the value of having a tight relationship with your composer?

Well, I'm not so much for long-lasting partnerships. I like to try this when I was very upset that there are not that many women composers. So I said that I did this picture The Other Sister and I said, I've got to have a woman composer. Well, there's not so many. So you'll find one, there must be somebody, and I got Rachel Portman who is very good, by the way. And she did it and it was a pleasure to work with her, so I like to work with different people. On Dear God I worked with a guy named Jimmy Dunn, he never did one before. He was from one of my TV shows. So he did it and I like to try, Maurice Jarre did the first picture who was a very famous composer, did Young Doctors in Love, and it was great working with he and I didn't know quite what I was doing.

He would have to explain to me, and he had a French accent so I didn't know what he was saying half the time, but we got along and musically, with rhythms we got along.

I always want more drums because I was a drummer. So it's part of my thing, but it is good to develop business then you don't worry or have to explain but who you are, what you're like, but that's why I think the last pictures I've done I had to do in a hurry. Post gets shorter and shorter — five, six months, now some three months, boom.

So it's better you got a guy who you can talk shorthand with. And John Debney talks shorthand about the Lakers basketball team and about the music in the movie.

Why are there so few female composers doing Hollywood movies?

I don't know why, because if you see the orchestras at the scoring sessions, a lot of women are there and I don't know why they don't let them do it, but my family comes from — I'm digressing a minute — my family comes from drawing. My sister Penny was one of the first film directors who broke the $100 million mark. Before Penny, no woman had ever directed a picture that made a $100 million. And they said to her, "We don't think women directors are good, because they have a mind that does not come up with ideas that appeals to a mass audience." That's all my sister had to hear and (she said) "I will show you." And not only did she do one, she did two. She did a movie called Big with Tom Hanks, made over $100 million, and a movie called A League of Their Own that's still making money. So she was the first one, so I don't know who's going to be the first music composer to win a lot, but we're making progress.

How do you create art with so many cooks in the kitchen, making a studio picture?

You got to understand, the biggest problem is the 'they.' Me and John get along fine, then 'they' comes in, it's the music, 'they' always — I like to make a movie, right? And I like to have music in the movie. The studio likes to make a record album. Two different businesses. So the combination of the two often mix up, so you need a composer and you need to be on the same page, and then you can fight the third page. I'll do one story. So we're doing Runaway Bride. James Newton Howard, who I worked with Pretty Woman, he does my Julia Roberts pictures. So I had this opening song in Runaway Bride, U2, she's riding a horse, running around and, oh, something important is going to happen,

U2. They, the studio, the music people who pay for the music that's part of it, don't want to do that. They want another — I'm not going to mention, because I love them — this other group to do it. So they send me this and say try this. I try it, I said no, no. I like U2. And they send it again and, "No, no thank you." Now they send it again, and they do something rarely done, they got the film and they edit the opening scene to fit the music they send me. So now we're going crazy, and I say — sometimes, you have to be from the Bronx again. So they send this nice CD with the music, and I took it and — this is all true.

So we took the CD, and we put it in the microwave, and we burned it, and it got all wrapped up. It's all distorted, and I put it in the nice envelope and bag and sent it back to them, and said, "You keep sending this song to me, and I have the right song. I know it's expensive, so if you don't want to pay for this, get me a song that sounds like that, not because you're pushing this group." And I said, "I'm sorry, I got a little crazy," but what can I tell you? They never sent any more, and from the way the story goes, I hear the executive took that rotten thing I did in the microwave, he hung it, he had it framed. And he has it on his wall, saying you shouldn't drive composers and directors crazy because they get too crazy.

Francis Coppola told me a long time ago, and he's smart, he says, "There are no copouts in a movie." If anything's wrong, there's no copouts. So he said, if you got to do it, pay for it yourself, so I offered truly to pay for the U2 song in Runaway Bride, I felt so sure that that was the right thing to do.

So the fights then are not just the composer and the director, it's a part of the 'they' factor. Now other guys will talk to you just about working with the composer, and my sister uses Hans Zimmer, who is great, and they work very well because you think it's all sane — it's not a sane business. Penny often hired composers that like to eat what she likes to eat. Because when you make movies, you eat a lot together at film edits, so first thing she says to a composer, "What do you like to eat for supper?" It's a different way of approaching films, but you want to get along with the composer, and sometimes you don't personally. And sometimes I work with composers and — I wouldn't take lunch, let's put it that way. But they did well and they compose very well. Very important for composers breaking in. Find out what the boss eats, what kind of food, because then you'll hang out together, it'll be easier. I'm a little finicky with food, so you can't do that with me, but John and I often go to lunch. And he has snacks. I love John Debney, he always has snacks around when you're working.

How does music impact the climax of a film?

It all depends. I am from the school, you must have a beginning and an ending in the film. Sometimes in the middle you can tap dance, but you got to have an opening and you got to have a closing. And I love theatrics, and we do plays, I have a theater here. I like big finishes, and so I always look for the big ending that involves music, and sometimes you need such a big ending that you just can't come up with. The biggest ending I ever needed was in Pretty Woman, and I said we're not going to get a song that does this, so when in doubt go to opera. Opera is bigger than life, and this picture is bigger than life so Pretty Woman ended with the Opera. But that was the biggest I ever could come up with. Other times John Debney has ended, and we have had songs that are memorable, and that's why I think guys like John Debney, they understand sometimes it's a song. And he writes wonderful songs. He wrote a wonderful song, "When You Smile," and we had it in Valentine's Day. But I remember in New Year's Eve, the love song at the end was written by a kid who never wrote anything. A kid out of Cincinnati sent me stuff. And he sent me this one song I used it in the temp, and it seemed to work very well, and studio loves nobody ever heard of them? Good, we get them cheap. That's the way they think. But it was a very nice song, and it did, "Whattya Say" is the song he wrote, and first time he had a song in a movie. Jacob Saylor was his name, nice kid. So you never know, it's not an exact science. But I think if you get a guy like Debney, who knows how to use popular songs, public domain songs, folk songs from other countries — every country has their own song — he's very versatile in that he knows you can get music from anyplace other than him just composing himself.

The business is very competitive, it's good to have a guy like that on your side and we get along very well.

How do you decide between a pop song, original song or something orchestral?

Well, a lot of thought process in the modern day is usually John and I are talking, and we think "Well, maybe this'll be a song," or not, and we discussed it and then we play something and then what we do — which a lot of people don't do because I don't want to shock you, but women go to movies. So very often we bring, I work with women producers. So a lot of my sessions are John and me and Jeff, and we have a woman even if it's my own producer Heather Hall, who's been with me for many years, and she comes in, "What do you think?" Because we like to get a female opinion and a male opinion and that's a part of the decision.

Sometimes we'd say we need a song here, or we don't. And what is wonderful about flexible people like John Debney is if you put it in and it's no good, you take it out. Sometimes you're allowed to make a mistake in the movie, and the song goes in and the song goes out. I tell you, these battles I won — I did get a short order cook and a waitress to have violins, but I lost one of the battles in a film called Nothing in Common with Tom Hanks and Jackie Gleason. There was a wonderful song, sometimes it's not a new song, it's an old song that fits, and it was a wonderful song Air Supply did, "The Power of Love." And I used it as a temp, and it was just beautiful in this scene where one of the best scenes in Nothing in Common where Tom Hanks with his new girlfriend runs into his old girlfriend, who has her boyfriend and because I did it, I wrote it, I did this and it just didn't work. And I finally figured out we shouldn't hear what they were saying, just play music. And that is always what you talk to a composer about. It's a lot of dialogue, but you don't hear a word of it, you just hear the music. And Air Supply "Power of Love" was great. But then they couldn't get the money for it, and we wrote another song or some other song was there, it was not as good. It's still a wonderful scene, but with Air Supply's "Power of Love," one of the most powerful scene I ever shot as a director in a movie, and I lost that battle. But after that, I won a lot. I learned.

What's the value of being a team player, and how does that shape your work with John Debney?

He is a team player. He likes the Lakers. A man who likes sports knows that a team is more important than an individual. Yes, you have that Kobe Bryant, but you have to have a star sometime in a movie, that makes it all. Julia Roberts did it a few times. She's OK. But I think a team player is a good expression to use for a composer because he comes in late so he can't say, "Well, you should have done this." It's over, the picture's coming out. I did a lot of TV and the composing there is even faster. I always tried to use new people. The first TV show I ever did was called Hey, Landlord. The composer of the song in Hey, Landlord was a guy who never composed before. He was a nice guy. His name was Quincy Jones. He told me he wanted to compose. He was Frank Sinatra's conductor of his band in Las Vegas, and we became friends and then he wrote the song in Hey, Landlord which was quite good. He did very well with himself. I didn't make his career, but I'm very proud his first TV composing job was for me. And he went on, and he's a genius, and so you don't always have to say who's the genius, you can say let's find one. And they're out there. I get excited about this story. We were going to act together. We both like acting. So we're saying relax. I wanted to use him as an actor. His star got too big. But he's certainly a good composer. I think Michael Jackson did help Quincy Jones more than I, but helped him get going.

Composers don't often seem to frazzled, even though they have a lot of pressure on them.

Everybody's a different personality. Some composers get crazy, and some are very calm. I like John because he's calm, and before the scoring session I go out, say hello to the band. I am talking about music. I am a lifetime member of Local 802 and a lifetime member of 47, so I'm in the union forever, and not the best drummer you ever heard, but I did play, and it kept me going in my field. When you're struggling music can help me, as it did as a drummer. But I don't think John is very frazzled. I've seen him frazzled at a basketball game, he's pulling his hair out, but I never saw him pull his hair out at a scoring session. And he is kind of a perfectionist, and once you're in this business for a while it's — I have an expression, delegate or die. You can't do everything yourself, but you got to do most of it yourself, so John has people who are listening as technicians and people working with him that are experts at the sound, and more violins and more trumpets, more drums. They always hide the drummer in the thing so you can't hear the drummer. Doesn't dominate. But I would say the less frazzled the composer is, the better he is, because everything's on a time clock. When you compose, when you have 100 musicians, it costs a dollar, so you want to move them along so now you're down to 80, 70, and the fifth day there's a quartet.

But I think that he's very organized and not hassled. I think he's been around awhile and seen everything and he's not thrown by crazy "they said this" or sometimes an actor is acting a certain way and too over-the-top, you want music calm them down, or not energy enough and you want the music driving underneath, so he is adaptable to what he end up with when he comes in late.

Do you think music from movies can outlive the films for which it was made?

I think sometimes, yes. I think whatever Robin Lopez, who's a genius; I'm dying to work with him. That Frozen song is going to last longer than the Antarctic, the way it's going now. So I think many songs do that, and they keep doing them again. I think those purists who say, "Well, these songs in the picture should be brand new" ... no, sometimes for the story you're telling, an old song is really right.

And you do it, and it's annoying sometimes, it's a real hassle just to play "Happy Birthday" in a movie. A big fight, so you got to play "For He's A Jolly Good Fellow." It's not as good as "Happy Birthday," so sometimes you got to play "Happy Birthday." I wish John Debney would write a new song for birthdays so we wouldn't have to play "Happy Birthday" and pay all that money. Two ladies in Jersey own "Happy Birthday."

Talk about music needed for comedies versus music for more dramatic films.

There is a difference in the — it's hard to pin it down — there is a big difference of scoring for comedies and scoring for dramas. The best stuff for comedies is Vivaldi. "Four Seasons." It was voted in 1984 the most boring song, because it doesn't get in the way. That "Four Seasons" just plays under a comedy scene, and there are no flutes and high instruments are enemies of comedy because they get the same octave of what the actor's speaking, and it hurts the joke. I like cellos and violas and because in comedy you have to stay out of the way of the humor, but still accent it. As a drummer, I was very big with rim shots. I could do it. But I think that's why you try — when you ask a composer or try to hear a composer, I always say what comedies they ever did, to hear exactly how he might have done a comedy. It depends on the comedy, you need some relief. Comedy is a lot of transitions, so the composer in a comedy has to not only do the scene, but a lot of times it's just required to take it out and move it into the next scene, what we call transitional music. It's more often in comedy than in drama.

Sometimes it's music that stops. You're playing it and suddenly it stops and the silence is so powerful. But if you don't have music before, it doesn't — the suddenness of stopping the music is very big with drama.

What would movies be without any music?

What is that song with the track it opens with the runners — Chariots of Fire. They do it on TV, they made the Chariots of Fire opening scene without music, and everybody fell asleep. It was terrible! Really boring. Suddenly, they put that Chariots of Fire music underneath, and there it was. So that was a prime example of what — if you don't have music, you're in trouble.

But now you can do any kind of music. Used to be the orchestra but now you do reggae, hip hop, this and that, all different sounds, different instruments, different things to kind of take different moods. Music is not so much the "Hey, I'll go listen to music." Music in movies is to create a mood that brings you into the movie and hits your emotions. You try to hit it with dialogue and pictorially, but sometimes the best way to hit the emotion through music.

How important is music compared to acting and script and everything else in a film?

I think all forms of art are important. There's no question that if it ain't on the page, it ain't on this stage, so you got to have it to get started. But the big things that enhance it after you get started. I think music has saved a lot of pictures, and saved a lot of my moments that music have saved, and I didn't quite get what I wanted out of the scene or I shot it wrong or the actors didn't — and the music will make it work. When I'm writing, I hear music. I write screenplays, I wrote TV. TV music is a little different. Charlie Fox did most of my, Norman Gimbel did most of my TV thing and in TV the music is the theme song, it's not the music in the show so much as the theme song. You get the theme song. Happy Days, you can remember how to hum that. So they do that but in movies, it's the scene within the scene what it's conveying. And what it means and sometimes it's not conducive. More and more now with superheroes and special effects and all of this, there's no dialogue so you got to have music.

Interstellar — without music, Interstellar would be Anne Hathaway making all different faces in a spaceship. And she's my idol, I love her, but it also is with Princess Diaries I did with Anne Hathaway, the music in those things had to appeal to young people, not just "Well, we'll do music."

What would young kids like to hear? What kind of feel? Because music does have age groups, so if your composer understands — and usually a good composer will say what age, who you're going for with this audience. Who you're trying to get. And they do it according to that. Not to too far, but you keep that under consideration.

I really think there's infinite ways the types of music you use; you don't have to use a type of music. It's instruments, every instrument is different. I remember playing — I was not the best jazz drummer, but I was very good at backing acts, because when you back an act it's like composing for a scene. You want to enhance the act, so if I played this kind of music under the act it was better than this kind of music, and sometimes I played them on the cowbell because it made it funnier, that sound.

So what is fascinating about music is there's so many ways — there's no rules that you got to do this, or you got to do that, and I think more and more directors saying what kind of music can I use to never do that — Zorba the Greek, and stuff like that, they use music that mostly America had never heard and it was very exciting.

But I think more and more young people are open to different sounds and every kid you see has something in their ears and everything. So more and more young people are into music and the sounds you put in a movie should appeal.

I have a granddaughter likes a band called Garbage. Never heard of this band, but it's good. I've heard their music, and it's good. So maybe my next music, just cause she likes it I may put a song of Garbage.

But who knows? If you want to hear what music is going on, you ask a teenager. They'll help you as much as a great composer, I think.

You mentioned hearing music in your head when you write. What do you actually hear?

We did a movie called The Grasshopper. I did it in the sixties. Jacqueline Bisset was in it. But we were trying to write an opening and we got stuck with it, and so we just said, "What music do we hear?" and I heard kind of soft traveling music going in the end there.

That's what we wrote; a girl leaving home that gave us the idea that she's saying goodbye and nobody talks to her. She leaves when they're all asleep, and music gave us the idea how to write that, and this guy Jim Webb, one of my idols scored on that, wrote the songs, Jim Webb is a genius.

He can write a song that says more than 18 pages of dialogue I can write, and part of this process of making Pretty Woman into a Broadway musical is to take the dialogue. We had J.F. Lawton write the screenplay of Pretty Woman, and he and I are writing the book, and so much of dialogue that we had in the book and that came from the movie we're trying to now turn into lyrics and make into music. So, whenever you can, turn dialogue into music. It gets to the audience more clearly if you do it with music, we've discovered that. So a lot of times you can't do that in the movie particularly, but in a musical, you sing it is as good as a dialogue, and what they say in musicals is how you do — this is what we were taught they tell you — is that when it comes to the part where the actor just can't say the line, sing it. And that's why they reached that other dimension. And I think it's interesting. I think it's more gut feeling, and then there is a fact that has to do with movie-making that helps if you're not deaf. When you show it to an audience. Most comedies you test a little bit, not all of it, but some. You work a year at a movie; there can be a few jokes. My partner Jerry Bells used to say, "Four people are going to get this joke," — I would say, "Four people are going to get this joke," and he'd say, "More than enough." So sometimes you do that, but I think that you hear if the audience is restless. You can hear if the audience really dislikes something.

I think it's really a gut feeling in what moves you, and if you're the filmmaker, what's moving you and moving the composer is what should move the audience. I think you should use music in all art, whether it's plays, television, movies, whatever. You should use music.

J.F. Lawton wrote the movie Pretty Woman and J.F. Lawton and I now are doing the Broadway musical of Pretty Woman. We're writing the book, I'm not going to direct, we're going to get a big Broadway director. But I think that in taking the dialogue we had in the movie, and transferring it to musical, we're trying to do more of that. Take out dialogue; make it musical because it gets through to the audience better if it's sung.

A lot of people think of the Golden Age of film scoring as the 50s and 60s. Do you have a favorite era?

Well, because I'm in comedy, I think film scoring in the 30s and 40s. They took all the European composers who had to leave because of the war, and they brought them to Hollywood, and they wrote for Lassie. They composed for all the pictures, for the comics, Buster Keaton, Schoenberg is writing. So I think that was the era where these guys had to adapt. That wasn't their job, scoring movies. But they adapted, and they adapted so well, so you got some great scores of those days. I don't remember all the guys' names, but I remember hearing all the great music they used in comedy and drama. Frank Capra wouldn't be so sweet without the music. I would say that I thought honestly that the score of Pretty Woman was not all scoring, it was a combination of songs, and that and I would say Chris Montana a big factor of that, the musical supervisor. I thought that was one of the best scores. It is appropriate, it helped and I know we reached for opera because we were desperate, but it worked. It worked, and they think I know opera, and I was on panels, like "I know nothing!" But they said, "You used it," and, "Well, yes I used it." But I must say I have directed opera, and it is a whole other fascinating thing to use for music. When you come there and do it right, that really moves an audience. I do a lot of love stories. Elixir of Love is one of the great opera love stories. Donizetti wrote it and that score, when they sing those songs, it's beautiful, it really is something. So the power of music is in so many different things that it'll never run out.

Did I leave out any anecdotes? Oh, I've got to say one more thing about what's his name. John Debney — we talked a lot about him. John Debney has a lot of ability. He's one of the few composers who ever did a movie called Passion of the Christ all about Jesus Christ, and he also did for my son a picture about Jewish bar mitzvahs, which was called, Keeping Up With the Steins. We're not Jewish, we're Italian. But John is also not Jewish, but to go from a bar mitzvah movie to Passion or Passion to a bar mitzvah movie, I would say that's called versatility. And that's what I think of John Debney. The creative arts are not like laying bricks, you lay a brick, you could yell at the guy, hurry up you can do it faster maybe. I worked on the railroad for three days. I almost died with the pickaxe. They yelled at you, "Faster!" We were building tracks in the Bronx when I was in high school. But the creative arts, a man has to come up with something. There's no, "Well, you'll come up with it in a few months." So this art of composing on deadline, I think is one of the hardest to do. I know I write on deadline. It's very difficult because writing is the closest, because you're alone. Even if you have a partner, you're still alone. Directing, you got all these people. So for a guy to just sit down at the piano and pick out stuff is very hard. Now I have an opinion, because Hemingway was one of my idols, and he always said that the best creativity comes in the cracks. It doesn't come when you sit down and say, "I think I'll create now."

It comes when you sit down, you grade, you get nothing. You go, "I'll take the kids to school." You take the kids to school. On the way home, that's where you get the idea. So I'd found that myself as a creator, that it comes and goes. You never know where, so I greatly admire music composers who have to sit down and come up with something. A lot of the time I'll say to a composer, "Did you ever have something in your trunk that you once did in high school even?" And sometimes they do. They have a thing that was about the songs hardest to do about the music cues for breaking up, the love affair is over, or I love her — the love affair is starting.

Those are always the hardest cues, and for them to come up with it time after time. Very few successful composers only did one movie. Many directors only did one movie, but composers, if they're any good, they do more and more and now we have a new world which is called the Internet, which is a new challenge to music composers because now, in my instance, they're asking me who created TV shows. They like TV shows that are six minutes or 11 minutes. So you're going to have to have music in that short of time. So composers are now composing for six minutes, and 11 minutes, a new field. And I hope they're doing well because on the Internet we see it, but I think the emotional side of music is most seen clearly with the Internet because suddenly you see these stars. You never heard of these people. Suddenly they're all over the place, they get a thousand million hits, and they sang a song or they did something musical.

That's just a million people say, "Oh, that's good," so I think now it's a much more vast of field than it ever was music. It's in everything now.

Who are some composers you admire and hope you have a chance to work with someday?

I like Hans Zimmer, he does great stuff. And I wish I could've worked with Maurice Jarre more, but he got busy in France and passed away. But Rachel Portman, I'll probably work with again, I like her stuff and I come from the school of helping new young people.

I'm not that young, but I'm not — (my hair) is gray, when it started it wasn't gray. So now I like to help new composers, and John is very good with that too. He will bring in new people.

I think, as I said, songs that do make me cry — that "Wind Beneath My Wings," and Celine what's-her-name Dion, what's her name.

Everything becomes a Broadway musical, is now in the process of becoming a Broadway musical. And James Newton Howard's song that he just wrote without lyrics just under the love scene we're now putting lyrics to and it's going to be in the film, so music has a way of lasting forever. And that's why I think it's so important to a film to have the right music.

CHAPTER 9
BEAR MCCREARY
COMPOSER

KNOWN FOR		ACHIEVEMENTS
THE WALKING DEAD (2010-16)	*CONSTANTINE* (2014-15)	EMMY AWARD, ORIGINAL MAIN TITLE, *DA VINCI'S DEMONS*
10 CLOVERFIELD LANE (2016)	*DEFIANCE* (2013-15)	
	EUREKA (2007-12)	FOUR EMMY NOMINATIONS
THE BOY (2016)	*HUMAN TARGET* (2010)	TV COMPOSER OF THE YEAR, 2016, ASCAP
OUTLANDER (2014-16)	*CAPRICA* (2009-10)	
AGENTS OF S.H.I.E.L.D. (2013-16)	*TERMINATOR: THE SARAH CONNOR CHRONICLES* (2008-09)	TELEVISION COMPOSER OF THE YEAR, 2016, WORLD SOUNDRACK AWARDS
BLACK SAILS (2014-16)	*BATTLESTAR GALACTICA* (2004-09)	
DA VINCI'S DEMONS (2013-15)		

How much of your line of work is creative, and how much is purely business?

The film scoring business, I think, is a misnomer, because it is primarily art. You're telling stories. You're collaborating with people. And ultimately there is a business component to it. But I've found that I've just always done what I wanted to do and found projects that I like. And at a certain threshold I started getting paid to do it. And that was great.

But it's a foolish business to get into for business. There are much easier ways to make money. So while that is a factor, and you have to be smart about business, and at a certain point to be able to sustain yourself and build a career that makes sense and pays your bills, I've never made any decisions for financial reasons. And so far that's worked out for me.

What kind of business skills do you need to be a successful composer?

The kind of business skills that you need really are social skills. ultimately, you get to a certain point where you have a team that helps you with the business stuff. So l don't get into details about contracts or royalties. My eyes glaze over. But I had to be smart enough to get to the point where I could get people to help me with that. So doing budgets and things like that was a part of the earlier part of my career. But otherwise, you know, the smartest business move you can make is just being smart socially, politically. Understanding how to walk into a room and make everybody feel validated, make everybody feel like they're they made a good decision in hiring you, or they should make a good decision in hiring you. These are things that are political skills and social skills, but they're sort of necessary in any business. If you walk around with an ego, if you walk around making people feel like you deserve the job, then ultimately that's a bad business decision because you just will quit getting hired whether or not your art is good.

So I did reach a point in my career where I started thinking about that actively. I think I lucky because I started off being just purely the idealistic artist. And I was mentored by Elmer Bernstein, so I was fortunate to be in the shadow of someone that great. And I picked up a lot about how he interacts with people and how he treated people. But there was a point after

I'd been very established that I realized that in order for my career to progress I would have to start thinking about my social interactions both professionally and personally in the same way that I thought about thematic development. It's just a thing I needed to be a little better at in order for my career to move forward.

What's the value of conducting your own score on the scoring stage?

Being in the room conducting an orchestra and hearing music that I've worked on for a long time become realized is — it's sort of the adrenaline blast that keeps me going through the whole process. It's the part of the process I think I enjoy the most. Because it gets me out of my studio, it gets me out of my element. I get to interact with people. I get to see the reaction from hopefully happy producers and filmmakers. I get to tweak all those little details that I imagined when I was writing it. I spend most of my time in here, so being able to get out of that environment and into a recording studio is really, it's such a high that I've structured my entire life to be able to do that as often as possible.

I always conduct my own work. Look, I grew up worshipping Jerry Goldsmith, Elmer Bernstein, John Williams, and I worked very closely with Elmer. I met him when I was in high school. And he sort of told me the skills you need are the following: You need to be this tall to get on the ride. Conducting, orchestration, theory, counterpoint. All these things I hadn't studied in high school when I met him. So I got in the habit of always conducting my own scores. It's become a vital part of my own self-expression that I can work swiftly. I can interact with musicians. And there is an experience to being in the booth with the filmmakers, but I've found that everybody I've worked with, all the filmmakers I've worked with feel better with me out there. With me in the room with the musicians and I engage with them through the talkback mic. I'll say, "What do you guys think?" I keep them engaged.

But I think they see a level of interaction with the musicians. I think it helps my process with them, because they understand that first they were talking to me. They had me for this whole process, but now I'm out here with all these other people. And I think that it helps them relate to the bigness of the process, that we're not just at a zoo watching an exhibit on the other side of the glass. This is this is an essential part of the process, that I interact with these musicians to be able to get their vision for their film or their show to bring it to life.

But I also have an excellent team. And I've worked very closely with my engineers, my orchestrators, my assistants. Everybody out in the booth with those filmmakers understands socially the things that they need to do to make the filmmakers feel comfortable, to make them feel involved.

What's your job during a scoring session?

Any little thing you could do to help a filmmaker feel comfortable. I make sure that that happens because that is a part of the process I'm not part of when I'm out on the other side of the glass. Conducting for me is the primary way that I can express myself to musicians outside of what's actually on the page. What's on the page is the notes, the dynamics, maybe a little bit of the expression. But all of the emotion comes from the context, the greater context of what is this scene about. What is this music about? What is the style of the music?

I could have a long conversation. I could show them the scene. We could talk about it. Or I use my body and my face the way an actor does to communicate very quickly what the m¬¬ood is. I use the way I use my back, my face, my breath, my hands. And it tells them what the music should sound like, so as they start playing right away, they understand what I'm going for.

It's an incredible shorthand. And the reason I like to be out there is that it eliminates a lot of dialogue. It cuts a lot of dialogue out of the process because as I'm hearing it I'm usually conducting and making myself some quick notes. But I can make adjustments in real time with my hands and my face. But then even afterward I can immediately launch into a bunch of quick fixes before the producers or my orchestrators or my engineers — before anybody else says anything, I just quickly make a bunch of corrections, let's run it again, and then I open it up to the room. It allows me to work very swiftly.

Studio time is something that I like to use very effectively. I don't ever go in unprepared. I know exactly which cues I'm going to record every hour. Every hour is planned out down to the minute. My musicians often joke they can see the secondhand ticking on the clock and when it gets time to take a break I am somehow able to end a cue. But I like to be prepared and in that way when I'm conducting, I'm more in control of that environment. It just saves time. And I think the musicians respond to it, because at that point, the first time we start a cue, I'm the only person who knows what it's going to be. So it in a way — I can use my body language to communicate a lot very quickly. And I just got good at that. And I would never — I don't think I could go back. I don't think I could be on the other side of the glass.

Tell me about the talent of the orchestra musicians used in a scoring session.

I often hear from producers or filmmakers that visit one of my sessions that have never been to one before. They say, "Well, how many days do they have to rehearse this?" And I say, "None, that was it. They never saw it before." And they go, "What? What?" I go, "Well, yeah I just wrote this two days ago. You only heard this two days ago." Like, "How could they have been rehearsing it? You know I just wrote it." Sight-reading musicians, the studio musicians, really are an incredible breed. It takes a certain level of experience in studio to be able to do that. Not all good classical concert musicians are immediately good studio musicians. There's a technique to being able to sight-read, to being able to congeal as a section, as a studio sight-reading orchestra. I also try to work with the same orchestra as often as possible. I'm very fortunate to have worked with largely the same number of musicians hundreds of times in the last 10 years. Actually, I shudder to think how many. 300? 400 times? There's a shorthand between me and all the musicians. Between the musicians and themselves, when they come into a session of mine, they've got the experience of all the previous sessions. So while there is a huge amount of skill in sight reading, there's a lot of — it's easy to forget the importance of familiarity, and that feeling of being a band or a group that's played together before. And it's my music and even if it's on a new project, most of the people in that orchestra know what my tastes are. They know the style that I tend to write in. And I really value that. That again gives me the ability to move very quickly. Because I'm not reinventing the wheel with a new group every time.

How much of the artistry comes from you, and how much comes from the musicians in the scoring session?

The orchestral musicians and specialty soloists bring a degree of artistry to my music that can't be underestimated. Sometimes it's in the research phase, I will bring in someone. Like on Outlander I'll bring in someone who plays bagpipes. Actually I did all my bagpipe research long before Outlander, that's a bad example because I knew all about bagpipes. But for example, if I'm doing something that needs some ancient Hebrew singing. This is a new thing for me, so I bring in a singer and say, "Teach me all about this." And before I start writing, I meet with musicians; sometimes I even do recording sessions just to give myself a crash course.

So on the on the early side, musicians have a huge influence on me. When I'm working with a specialty player on an ethnic instrument I'm not familiar with, I'll call that person and say, "Can you play this note? What about that note? What's the good note? I want to do this. Is this going to work? What's the better key?" I like to make sure everything I'm writing is idiomatic.

On the other side you get surprises with the orchestra. You get things that as you're up there conducting and hearing it for the first time, suddenly new ways of expressing a melody or new ways of articulating an ostinato, things will sort of start happening in the room. It inspires me. And sometimes I'll say something like we started doing this and it's not what was notated. But as a group we all started leaning this way and I like that. Let's do that. Let's push it further. That's a really fun part of the process. It's why I love working with live orchestras and working with live players, because it allows you to add a layer that that's beyond what you can bring to it.

Do you enjoy the writing process?

I don't like spending my time doing this (on a piano). Tweaking stuff. This is sketch. This is like idea barf. And it's fine tuned as much as it can. I get it as good as I can possibly imagine it. And then when we work with live players we make it better. And that makes me better as a musician. And I get new ideas and then I'll come back the next week and say alright now I've tried this. Let's see what that sounds like.

That process has made me a much better orchestral composer and orchestral musician than I would be if I had just read a book about it and learned the theory about it.

A sketch of an orchestral cue or a cue for a film or television is a highly personal thing. It means something different to everybody else. I always think of that fantastic scene in Amadeus when Salieri is looking at the manuscript and he goes, "No, no, no, I don't want to see this. I want to see his sketches." And Mozart's wife says, "No, that is his sketch." And he says it came out of his mind like this? This is the first draft? And she said yeah. I'm not like that. But I always think of that. I love that scene.

For me, sketches are highly detailed. I probably would be faster if I could sketch quickly or do like a piano sketch. But I usually will watch a scene and I bring up a piano sound or some kind of string sound or something. And I write something very quick. Whatever I'll do some drums or something, I don't want to think about it. I move very quickly so that I can stay in this childlike emotional place. I'm very careful not to get bogged down in details because as soon as I start going, "Should it be that, or wait, is it that?" then I'll kind of lose the emotion in the scene. So I work very quickly.

Once that's done then I'll spend hours sometimes days going over the sketch and getting all the details. I'm very specific orchestrally. I think that comes from working with working with Elmer (Bernstein). I orchestrated a lot of sketches that he had done.

The way that he used to work — he had four staves and he would write them all down. And you'd just look at it and go it's kind of a piano part. Cool. But then you look carefully and realize everything is there. Everything.

And I've found that that's the way that works for me. And my synth programming is very detailed. I do all of it myself. And it also means that the mockups sound pretty good. They sound pretty close to what the final will be. They never sound that good. I've never had someone go, "Oh, wow, this — why did we record? Your mockup sounds great." But sketching is a balancing act between staying in a zen-like state of creative inspiration, and then getting into the details of how you're going to realize that idea. And for me that's a two-step process.

In Amadeus, it showed that Mozart was a one-step process. For everybody else, they have their own way. You know I think everybody probably has their unique way of approaching it.

I tend to sequence sketches that I that I record out. I tend not to notate things just because of speed. Again, it sort of slows me down to write things down. So that's just the process that works for me.

What parts of the process do you delegate and which ones do you do yourself?

When I started, I did almost everything. My career started as a two-man operation. It was me and my co-producer engineer Steve Kaplan. Steve mixed, recorded, did all the engineering. I wrote, I orchestrated, I copied, I printed up the parts on my little inkjet printer. I stayed up all night before the session, taping them together. I went to the Warner Brothers scoring stage with a full orchestra and I put them out myself. That was it.

I felt like I was really realizing my vision at this time. This was Battlestar Galactica, was my first job. And there came a point where I realized I have about a week to do an episode of

Battlestar. And I'm spending two days of that week — that's a lot — orchestrating and copying and taping parts. I'm doing 20 episodes a year. That's like a month, more than a month of my life.

So I thought, "Alright, I'll get some help." I was very nervous that I wouldn't be able to express myself. I found that bringing in orchestrators that I trust, and I only work with a handful of orchestrators on everything, so that they understand my shorthand. I've found that that process was incredibly liberating. I had to rethink the way I write. I had to put into markers; I had to put into words, things that I could ignore before, that I would just catch when I was orchestrating it. But that process would add an extra two seconds as I'm writing to put a little marker. Oh, you know, "change the bowing to this," just so that the strings sound the way I want. Well, I can do that in two seconds, or I can take two days to orchestrate that myself. And I have found since then that just the process of delegating the things that are not essential has been such a core to my success. Anything that does not involve the most intimate creative process shouldn't be done by me. I feel like it's almost irresponsible for me to indulge in two days of orchestrating, as much as I enjoyed it, because that's two days I could spend writing, coming up with better ideas, more worthy ideas. Or being able to take on a movie while I'm still doing a TV show.

These are things that — these are decisions that I made early on, and I'm very glad that I did, because it's absolutely liberated me creatively to be able to take on more projects.

And I find that a good orchestrator also cannot only pull the ideas out of my brain. Everything gets on the page. They obviously have their own ideas, and they'll make suggestions. And there will be times where I'll just say, "I want a bunch of absolute crazy woodwind stuff. I want the woodwinds going crazy." I'll be doing this kind of stuff playing it. And the orchestrator would be like, "Oh, my God. Oh, my God! It's so much work." But now I can just say, "woodwinds go crazy. you know. You know what I like." And that's fantastic. Things like that that are very labor intensive, but they're ultimately sparkly little details that are not what I consider like the core of the music. It's fantastic to give that to a team that you trust. And it allows me to work quicker. It allows me to write better music. That efficiency allows me to serve my clients. Because ultimately my clients don't care if the woodwinds are like doing this, or this, or doing this. What they need is my attention and energy and creative enthusiasm. If I ever said to a client, "No, I can't get together with you, man, because I'm writing out all the woodwind rips" ... like, I can't. And I used to do stuff like that. I really, early on, I would just say to clients "we're going to spot the show, and then you're never going to see me again. Because in order to do this amount of work, for you to understand what I'm going to bring to this, I'm going to do so much work I'm not going to sleep for a week. And then at the end it's going to sound great." Which is a stupid way to do it. It doesn't matter if it sounds great, if they don't feel engaged.

So ultimately, it's a long-winded way of saying orchestration, copying, proofreading, taping, all this stuff, sample programming, sample recording. These are things that for me I have found I can influence and I need to trust that my team knows my taste. I guide them, but I can't spend my time doing that or else there won't be work for all of us to do.

What are the first things you do when you start on a new project?

Typically, when I'm working on a project the first thing I do is I interface with my clients as much as I possibly can. It means on a social level, I want to get to know them. I want to understand where they're coming from, why they're making the project they're making. Is this a passion project for them? How long have they been working on it? I want to ask things that help me understand what it means to them.

Then I'll spot the project with them, which means we sit down and actually go over musical details. And again, that's not the first time I've met them. I want by the time we spot everybody to feel really comfortable with me. I want it to feel like I'm connected with them as a filmmaker.

That's actually the first thing I do. I connect with them as a filmmaker. I want them to feel like a filmmaker, like them, has come into the process and I'm the one that specializes in this one thing that they're uncomfortable with. Because they don't really speak the language. But I'm not here representing music. I'm not here to say, "I'm here to do music for your thing, and just let me do my thing." I'm here as a part of their team and I just happen to specialize in that.

What do you look for when you're spotting with a director?

When we spot I try to get a sense of what their insecurities are. What are the things that they're nervous about? What are the things that are not working? What are the things that are working? Very often they're more eager to talk about the things that are working, which is great.

But you're sort of very carefully asking them questions and trying to understand the things they don't want to tell you. You're trying to get to the subtext of what's of what's really going on. Some filmmakers are very open about that. Others are a little more guarded, which is fine. The more time you spend with them the more you get those answers. After having done all that, and I've watched the movie a dozen times, I've spotted with them — then I come here to my studio, and this is where I kind of take the phone off the hook and I just try to keep myself as creative as possible, as undisturbed as possible, and just try to find that childlike place where I'm imagining things.

In a way, that's my favorite part of the process, because it's the most pure and simple. And if I've done my homework, by the time I'm done spotting, I already know what I'm going to do. If the filmmaker has given me enough information by the time I'm done doing my specialty research, the gears are turning so fast.

Sometimes I get in the studio and it just happens very quickly. After that, that's when it's all hands on deck.

That's usually when I stop sleeping as much. Everyone on my team stops sleeping as much because we go into what I call production. Production, like production on a film. You go from script. Script is tough, but it's like a handful of people getting their creative ideas together. And when you go to production it's all hands on deck.

So production for me means I am demo-ing for filmmakers. Either they're coming over here or I'm sending them QuickTimes. I'm talking to them. I'm getting feedback. I'm rewriting. We're booking sessions. There's a huge process that happens where we know basically when we're recording, and now that I've written a bunch of music, we have a sense of how many minutes is it going to be. How big is the orchestra? Do we need specialty players? Do we need them for the demo? Do we need them to come in early so that the filmmakers are hearing live instruments when they're hearing my sketches?

If I feel like that will help the approval process, If I'm working with a filmmaker who will freak out if they hear a crappy synth guitar, then we bring in a real guitar. It's not worth putting them in a place of unease when a guitar session would fix it.

Once cues get approved, they move into another track of production where it's orchestration and copying. Music prep. My orchestrators take my MIDI mockups with very detailed markers. It looks like the great American novel in there, all the markers that are for them. They translate my computer notation and my notes for them, my verbal notes, into scores. Into the music that is put out on the stands. I don't know how much detail to get into, but what the hell.

They make the score that I look at. They make the score that I read from. The copyist then extrapolates all of those individual parts so the violins just have the violin part, the flutes just have the flute part, and the whole orchestra has the notation of my ideas. And it is as accurate a representation of my ideas as we could possible get, as much musical detail is on the page as possible.

Then we go into recording, where those sessions that have been booked, we all know when they are. We go and invite the filmmakers, the producers if they want to come. They usually do. Usually, for me, we're usually doing not only multiple days of recording but multiple days of simultaneous recording.

So I will be out conducting orchestra while my producers will go to smaller studio studios, my producers will go to smaller studios and do percussion, ethnic woodwinds, guitars, vocals. There are too many sessions for me to be at. I can't possibly be at them all or it would take three weeks to record the project.

Then I'll listen on MP3s on my phone on a 10-minute break from the orchestra date, if I even need to. I mean the great thing about having the team that I've built up is that when they go record percussion or ethnic woodwinds, the players know what I want, the producers know what I want, it's going to be great.

So that's a very efficient way of recording a whole bunch of different sessions in a short time span. Then it's mixed. My mixing engineer takes all those tracks. The orchestra, my synth stems here, which are numerous, ludicrously numerous. And he takes all of these as individual WAVE files in ProTools and he mixes them. Then he sends me back mixes and I get to the point where I feel like my musical vision is there. And the musical vision that I believe my clients are expecting is there.

Once I sign off on the music, it's printed into mixed stems, meaning the strings are separate from the brass. Percussion, soloists, guitars. Well, high percussion, pitched percussion, small percussion, big percussion, synth percussion. There's more. But basically anything — the reason that I do this is on the dub stage is I fully expect to get notes. I expect my clients are going to want to be able to change things. And they should, because when they hear it all for the first time with the sound effects, the dialogue has been properly mixed and edited, ADR has been recorded, most of the visual effects are in, sometimes, they're going to have comments on the music. And they're very often hearing the fully mixed music for the first time. So if they say that little drum thing, I don't like that.

Actually, you know, here's what happens. They don't say that. Here's what they say: "That cue's too fast. It's too fast. The cue is too fast." Which, of course, to the inexperienced composer, if you were taking them at their face value, you're thinking, "I have to rewrite that. I have to turn the tempo down and re-record the orchestra. Oh, my God! How is that possible?" It just means that there's a hi-hat that's too loud. You know?

And you just go, "OK. I agree and I understand that now that I'm hearing it with the dialogue, it feels very fast. Why don't we pull that, there's a hi-hat stem. Why don't we get rid of that?"

And they hear it and, "Oh, yeah, that's much better."

If that track wasn't split out, I wouldn't be able to do that. I've gone to the dub stage in the last 10 years, I've delivered something to a dub stage probably 400 times between my television and film projects. And I've only had a cue that needed to be rewritten once.

And it was in the first the very first months of my career. So ever since then, I have never had a problem on a dub stage that couldn't be solved ultimately by some clever editing, pulling stems out, by that flexibility that the mix stems provide.

To put it all in perspective, give me the quick rundown of the process.

I spot the show. I find out what my producers want. I come into my studio and I write. After that, once they approve, it goes into production with my team. It's orchestrated. It's copied. Sessions are prepped. All the ProTools sessions are prepared. I go to the orchestra dates. I conduct. I usually have sessions happening at the same time to get all the soloists and percussionists and guitars and vocalists. All these tracks from all the different studios come together for the mix. My mixing engineer preps it for the dub stage. And it goes to the dub stage.

This all happens very quickly, and sometimes there are very short deadlines to work with. How often do you see a billboard for a project you haven't finished yet?

There have been a handful of times when I'm driving around town and I see a billboard for a project that I haven't even started yet. I haven't written a note of music, and it says coming September 24th. Ah, it's terrifying!

But most of the time, it's just a funny reminder. I'll go out to lunch with a friend, and I'll be driving around town and it's like, "I know what I'm supposed to be doing."

Most of the time seeing billboards around town is actually is actually cool. Because it just kind of reminds me that people are going to see it, and they're going to experience what I'm doing. I admit there is a chemical high to knowing that if I write this theme and I do it really well, that millions of people are going to hear it. Few people that write music in history have ever had that opportunity.

So it is kind of exciting when you see billboards and things are becoming real. It's actually kind of exciting for me. People are going to get to hear it. We're almost at the point where it becomes real.

Sometimes, especially when I'm doing, premium cable shows, I will finish a show top to bottom before anyone even knows it exists.

So sometimes, it's the inverse, where I'll be pencils down on a show, and then like three or four months later it's announced, and then you see the first billboard, and people will be like, "Dude, have you heard about this show, Black Sails? It's pirates. That's cool." And I'm like, "Yeah, it's going to be cool. I not only did it, I finished it already. And I've just been waiting for people to know what it is."

So I don't know. It works both ways I guess.

There's a long history of pirate stories in Hollywood, and many of them have a similar sound. Some composers who have some pirate themes have mentioned it can be difficult to break out of the swashbuckling style. Did you have that issue writing for Black Sails?

Black Sails was a really unusual experience for me. I'd worked with the showrunner, Jon Steinberg, before, and we had done a very traditional style score. It was a Jerry Goldsmith, John

Williams kind of adventure score for a show called Human Target.

It was what you'd expect it to be. His next show is Black Sails. And he wanted something so strange and so unusual. He didn't know what he wanted. He just wanted it strange and not what you would expect for pirate music.

We had — for television — essentially unlimited resources. If we wanted to do a huge orchestra and choir, that would have been no problem, but we didn't. And we spent a lot of time talking. I spent a lot of time with Jon trying to figure out what should this sound like. What is the sound of pirates? And we came to the conclusion that the classic era of Hollywood — Korngold notably — put such a stamp on what pirate film scores sound like.

The Golden Era of Hollywood put such a stamp on what pirate movies are supposed to sound like, what swashbuckling adventure is supposed to sound like, that we immediately took it off the table. We didn't want to use anything like that.

And not just for the sake of it. Black Sails is a very gritty, adult, dark drama. It is not Pirates of the Caribbean. It's Deadwood, on the high seas. So anything remotely adventurous would have destroyed it. In the same way anything remotely fanfare and bombastic on Battlestar Galactica would have destroyed that because it was not the language of the show.

So I gave myself some parameters, because I need I need parameters. I can't just say it can be anything. So Jon and I talked about using period instruments that are small enough to fit on a boat. And that's how we started.

I started with the hurdy gurdy, which I happen to play. And had found very little reason to play. And a framed drum and animal bones played like castanets. Fiddle, although we ended up using viola because it was darker and scratchier. I did have a string quartet for some of the more emotional passages. That was the absolute most traditional Hollywood sound that we got. And some guitars. And it was so scratchy and small and bizarre. It sounds like an improvised score but it's not. It's very detailed in its notations just to make sure I'm hitting everything in the picture.

And the first thing I wrote was the main title, which I even amped up a little bit and brought in some electric guitars and drum kit. And it was like this weird heavy metal sea shanty thing. It's really weird. I was writing it, and just thought this is so bizarre, Jon is going to hate this.

But he loved it. And the hurdy gurdy ended up becoming the defining sound of that show. I wrote cues on the hurdy gurdy, which is the first time I've written on something other than the piano. So I was rethinking myself melodically, timbre, texturally, and the score to Black Sails I think is the weirdest and coolest thing I've ever done.

It was a strange place to be pushed so far out of my comfort zone with something that is so dramatically specific. But you know I started with trying to be historically accurate. I did a lot of research into the music of the 18th Century, the kind of folk music that became sea shanties. I didn't start with the sea shanties. I started with the popular and liturgical music that kind of got co-opted to become the sea shanties.

It really worked. I think the show benefitted from having a bizarre sound because it's a bizarre show. And I know audiences really responded to it. The Television Academy responded to it.

But it was ultimately a product of being pushed outside my comfort zone and working with someone close enough, my showrunner Jon Steinberg, that I felt like I could trust him enough not to freak out if I did something really weird. And he could trust me enough to know I wasn't going to destroy his show when we were trying to do something that really just hadn't been done before.

CHAPTER 10

TRENT REZNOR
& ATTICUS ROSS

RECORDING ARTISTS & COMPOSERS

KNOWN FOR	ACHIEVEMENTS	
PATRIOTS DAY (2016)	ACADEMY AWARD, ORIGINAL SCORE, *THE SOCIAL NETWORK*	GRAMMY AWARD, SCORE FOR VISUAL MEDIA, *THE GIRL WITH THE DRAGON TATTOO*
BEFORE THE FLOOD (2016)		
GONE GIRL (2014)	GOLDEN GLOBE, ORIGINAL SCORE, *THE SOCIAL NETWORK*	
THE GIRL WITH THE DRAGON TATTOO (2010)		ASSOCIATED ACTS: NINE INCH NAILS (EIGHT STUDIO ALBUMS)
THE SOCIAL NETWORK (2010)	THREE GOLDEN GLOBE NOMINATIONS	
THE BOOK OF ELI (2010) (ROSS ONLY)		

What are the limits of what film music can make us feel?

Ross: Well, I think it can make the audience feel anything. I think film music has the power to completely change the experience of the movie. I think it can actually — I'm not saying it can make a bad movie good, but it can make a good movie great.

You've talked about a film being like an album. Can you explain that idea?

Ross: Yeah, it's something that we do together. And it's something I know that we both definitely believe. Much like an album, to me a film is a series of scenes. But to approach a film as a series of scenes, to me, doesn't make sense in terms of making a piece of music, making a world that's unique to that story. To me, I think the music, it should be native. And it should feel native to that piece, and that you should be able to, the whole of the — that when you hear that music, disassociated from the film, you remember, "Oh, that's the music from that film." Because that much effort has gone into it, you know. And I think each story is different and will inform you. We usually start with the script. So we're reading the script and we're thinking in sonic terms and storytelling terms what would be the right world for this to inhabit. I think it's served well in creating a unified piece of music that can change with the story, and is certainly in service to the picture, but at the same time can stand as its own and live in its own space. I think that we've always been incredibly lucky in terms of the director wanting the music to be a character in the film. And I think that you need that to be able to take that route.

Reznor: I'll elaborate on that if you want. Our background is from primarily songwriting and arranging music, not for film, for our own endeavors. And I realize that the way I approach that process when I'm songwriting is I'll start with my own script. What's the message of what I'm trying to say? And then I work out arrangement-wise — I don't sit and strum it on a guitar and get a song together, I kind of start with the setting, and the soundscape that it sits in, and start to imagine how I would arrange that to emotionally support the message that I'm trying to get across with my lyrics or the feelings I'm trying to evoke. And in that way when Atticus and I crossed paths many years ago, we both were coming from a kind of sound design perspective where the sound, the place, the setting, the dressing of the set sonically was of great importance, just as much as the lyric or the melody or anything else — the setting. Because, at the end of the day, a listener's going to hear this thing, and what we want is an emotional action. We want to support whatever we're trying to say with the right setting. And hearing someone strum that on an acoustic guitar sounds a lot different than it being in some alien soundscape. If we're trying to evoke feelings of happiness or dread or anxiety, we have tools that we've used over the years from a sound design perspective to support that narrative. When David Fincher reached out and said I want you to score The Social Network, I'd always been intrigued to see if I was able to do that. It was exciting from a challenging perspective. I hadn't ever done that before. I hadn't studied the craft. I hadn't studied the procedures and the methodology behind how people score films, but I've seen a million films. I love seeing film. I know if I like the music in a film or I don't like the music in a film, but I hadn't ever worked in that format. And what we did was rather than try to crash-course to see how legitimate people do it, we went with our instinct of saying, "What if we take the skills we know," which I just described of setting place, "and rather than the narrative coming from me, now the narrative is coming from this piece of paper and these visuals that we're provided, provided with from David?" And we found that it wasn't that difficult to, when thinking about it that way, the transition into that was, was pretty natural. And we had a very supportive environment with David, a very encouraging one to push boundaries. So it was different in the sense that now I'm not concerned about what's sitting in the middle of the stage. That's this actor. We have to get it out of the way, much like in a song I have to do that arrangement-wise with the lyric and whatever I want your attention on. But the process came pretty naturally. And again, coming from a place where the guy in charge, David, wanted something that didn't feel conventional and was allowed to kind of turn into whatever it naturally wanted to turn into. What Atticus was mentioning, creating our own world, the language of sounds and the choice of palates in terms of instrumentation or what we use to create certain feelings, that's a thing that we spend a lot of time on initially. When introduced to a project, we spend a lot of time absorbing what it is, listening with David, we sit and try to extract from him how he's imagining it, the shape of it, the kind of feel of the sound. And then we make decisions in terms of, "OK, what would be the best way to kind of execute that? Is that pastoral and traditional? Is that completely inorganic and synthetic? Is it a combination? Does it feel mechanical? Does it feel acoustic? Does it feel robotic and synthetic? What is it, is it dissonant? Is it pleasing? Should it evoke anxiety? What's the best tools we have to accommodate that without any kind of leaning towards — without any concern about what's proper or improper, just what's the right tool to get the job done?" And because we come from a record-making background, what we're aspiring to do is have this piece of work, this body of work, which could be five themes repeated and adapted or it could be 500 themes repeated and adapted — have them feel like they belong in the same family. That's not to say they all sound the same, but they are related to each other and it sounds like a chunk of work. The same criteria we have when making an album, where we want this album to feel like it came, they're brothers, they're siblings, you know, these songs. They came from a singular environment. And the next album, hopefully, doesn't sound like leftovers from the last album or rehashed ideas, but we're in a new country and a new, a new set of, you know, a new set dresser. So when we kick into a project, it takes longer a lot longer because we're thinking through, "What's the fabric of the sound? Is it right for this thing?" And how can it support, ultimately, its only job is to make that experience of the listener or the viewer in the theater to be transported into that storytelling world. And whatever we can do to help manipulate that, that's what we're here to do. It's exciting. When asked about the role of music in a film, clearly I logically understand when you're seeing a film, what you're hearing underneath it affects you. But when we were first put in the driver's seat, and we read these words on paper with a bit of fear, like "How are we going to support that?" I mean now we've seen this scene that feels sterile because there's nothing supporting it. And there's action happening. And you realize this power we wield, in terms of how much we can shape it by trying new things and watching how radically different that film, that scene plays out. That was a real eye-opening, wonderful experience to see firsthand — not just know that that would do it, but to watch it happen and watch the power we had access to in terms of manipulating the way people feel. And how it all fits together. And that hooked us into the idea that this is something we wouldn't mind pursuing with the right types of projects.

Ross: And I'll just add one last thing to that that does relate to your first question. And it's something that Trent mentioned then.

On The Social Network, for instance, there's an overall view to the music. But, in the script, that first scene, it was an Elvis Costello song that came in. And I love Elvis Costello. But it was an upbeat kind of "We're on a college campus" kind of thing. And when "Hand Covers Bruise" went in there, talking about changing the temperature of a movie, and the emotional response of an audience — radically different. I mean, you immediately knew you were not in a John Hughes movie. I like John Hughes, but Social Network is a different kind of movie.

Reznor: I can tell you it wasn't overly thought through. We were making something that we didn't think was going to live in such an important place. And I wanted something that felt a bit stoic but flawed. And a bit bold, yet melancholy — aware of its own shortcomings. Not to sound too pretentious. But the simplicity of that kind of unsettling drone that got more dissonant as it went on just felt like a cool moment that we could use somewhere. And when we were shuffling the deck trying things that didn't feel intuitive. What's that sound like over the font? I can't do that. But as soon as, soon as you saw it for a second, it radically shifted your perception of the film. And in that important area with the very beginning when you're not sure what this film is. You just went through rapid-fire argument, Aaron Sorkin dialogue, into this kind of weird, unsettling kind of sad, not triumphant tone, the whole movie feels different after that. I think it feels like a much more important film than the kind of college-life tomfoolery that it could have been misled into feeling with the wrong music in there. When David Fincher called, "Hey, I want you to score my next film." Fuck yeah. "It's a movie about Facebook." I'd be hard-pressed to think of something that sounded less sexy, you know. Possible rom-com might have done that. But then you read the script and you realize it's actually a very compelling story.

Ross: And if you did mention to people at the time, "What are you working on?" "Oh, I'm working on a movie about Facebook." You could just see them (roll their eyes).

What kind of skillset does it take to compose for film compared to skillset required to record an album?

Reznor: I think my only real skill is being able to be honest and convey a kind of honest emotional connection to my work. And I've screwed my career in Nine Inch Nails up because there have been lengthy periods of time where I haven't put records out because I'm not, for whatever variety of reason, and they change over the years, I don't feel like I have anything to say. Or I'm not able to clear the clutter out to be able to get it into your ears from my head. And when David first approached me about Social Network, it was at one of those moments when I'd just finished touring for two and a half years. I'd promised myself I was going to take some time off to not jump into a new stressful work-consuming environment. I was getting married. A lot of things were happening. Not a bad time, just a time where I felt the idea of taking on something that I knew would be stressful and terrifying because I hadn't done it before. And I didn't want to learn on the job on something, you know — I have great respect for David and I didn't want to fuck it up by, "Let me figure out how to do your thing for you." And be the guy everyone is slowed down. So I was practicing the art of setting up boundaries, and I said, "I respectfully have to decline, because I'm just not in a place where my head can focus. It's nothing against the script or you, and I'm flattered, but I don't think I can do it right now. And I don't want to go into it feeling like it's, you know..." And then I got a few nights' sleep and I'm the type of person that that then nags at me, you know. So when I got the courage to call him up a few months later, I said, "Hey, just so you know, I want to reiterate that, that wasn't any question about the quality of the material or your, what you do. It was just I, I wasn't in a place where I could pull it off. And give me, if you — I doubt you will, but call me next time." And he's like, "No, we're still waiting on you to do this, so come down." So I called Atticus and later that day we were immersed in that.

How intimidating was taking that leap?

Reznor: Well, we were very honest. And Atticus had done some work so I was relying on his understanding of just the process. I didn't even know what dubbing stage; I didn't even know what that means. And I would say, "What the fuck's a dubbing stage," you know. So I wouldn't come off like a complete idiot. But we were very honest with David about, you know, we're not, this isn't one of eight films we're doing this year and it's an assembly line where we know what we're doing. And he's like, "Listen, I've got your back. And I'm going to create an environment where you can succeed here," you know. "If you've got questions or you need help, we've got a good team here." And he really does have a good team. I think any great relationship begins and ends with, survives with respect and communication. And that's something that other than this relationship in terms of creativity, that's been the best one I've ever had. The team that he assembles from the editors and sound design and everyone, we have a very open and collaborative relationship that is why those films turned out as good as they did. It wasn't this protective, "We're working on the score and you're doing this." It's like, "Hey, what do you think about all this stuff? What do you think if we put that over here? Oh, you think we should flip this on its head. I don't agree but let's try it," you know. And often we wound up in a place that was a lot, basic collaboration, which for me is a kind of new concept.

Ross: And it's a very small team. That's the other thing. And I think that we're all friends. But it's literally us, David, Kirk, and Ren. And that's, you know, we're all in permanent communication.

Reznor: And we're enjoying the luxury of the hard work that David has afforded us by all studio interference, everything, we don't have to even, I don't know who the people are. It's the four of us bouncing ideas around. And he's the one off sword fighting to make sure that we're allowed to do what he feels is the best move, you know. And collectively, we never feel compromised by, "Testing shows that it might be better if…" We don't hear any of that stuff. It was a bit daunting for a number of reasons. One, I had no idea how to go about even executing it. Secondly, it's essentially a ton of dialogue and people talking in rooms. So it's not, it's not dragon battles and space serial killers. It's just

guys arguing basically. It didn't leave a lot of clues as to what
the role of music would be. Is it just a little texture here and
there? Because you had to stay out of the way of this barrage of
dialogue pretty much throughout the whole film. So we'd look
for clues from David as to what he was looking for. "Did you
want something kind of orchestral? Did you want something that
kind of disappears into the background? Are you looking for the
Star Wars theme to somehow fit its way into that?" And what
we were able to extract from him was, "I want it to feel kind of
electronic. I want it to have kind of its own personality. Don't be
afraid of trying anything. Don't worry about it being too much."
In the process we were encouraged to go further than we kind
of conservatively started approaching it initially. At first it was
kind of — I'm speaking for myself — "Let's not fuck this up.
And I wonder if we could put a thing over there." And I realized
that I was thinking way too "in the box," and David was the one
pushing us to say, "What if you colored way outside the lines?"
And we managed to color too far outside the lines at times to find
the boundaries of kind of what worked and learning about him
in the process. But sonically the choice became, and this was just
our interpretation, we didn't think, "OK, what would be accurate
music that would be playing in that era?" But in general, the
feeling of, and this is based on I just turned 50, so to me, computer
labs and college-age and — in my world — relates to mid-80s.
And the excitement of what you could do with these machines.
And it kind of retroactively feels a little bit synth-poppy in a sense,
you know. And that translated into music that had arpeggiators
and analog synths versus digital synths. Not a lot of samples. Not

the soundscape of say Dragon Tattoo, where we were focused on icy, cold, digital, much more impressionistic soundscapes. This was more about, "What's the sound of a good idea? When you have a good idea?" And I got a "How could I write it down or type it in code or catch up with it?" And it wasn't overly thought through. It just kind of lends itself to that kind of sound. And then there was a couple things where we got into some chip-tune sounds that were retro, not time-specific. But I think in a lot of people, particularly of my age, it triggers a nostalgic sentiment that didn't feel inappropriate to do.

Ross: And it is a computer chip, ultimately. But to me, they're references, but it doesn't feel like an 80s score or anything to me. You know what I mean? I think that there's, like Trent was saying, the idea of arpeggiator or, the idea of motion in the story. But at the same time, there's an incredible depth — that character, the loneliness. The it's certainly a three dimensional piece.

Reznor: Well that, again, with Gone Girl we started with listening to the kind of movie David was trying to make. And he described it to us as, "I want it to be funny, in a way, when you laugh you're not sure if you should be laughing and you feel strange if you're at a theater that maybe I shouldn't have laughed at that." And I didn't know what he meant at first. and I'd read the script and I'd read the book. And as I started to see scenes start to come in, I understood, it made more sense to me where it's absurd and dark but at the same time it needs a humorous element in it at times, because it's so uncomfortable. And the situation is so absurd. And David introduced the idea of, "What if we had music that felt like the music that tries to make you feel OK, that you might hear stuff that you might hear in a doctor's office or a shop or a spa or a place...but not authentic." And we've all had a massage or something where there's something playing that if you tune into it for a second, you think this couldn't have taken more than five minutes, real time, to make this piece of shit track I'm listening to. Have it have that inauthenticity. Have it experiment with some themes that feel like we're trying to manipulate you, the viewer, into "Look how OK this, this facade is," which then mirrors the facade the characters in the movie are displaying towards each other and also towards the outside world. And that was an interesting starting point that I don't think we would have come up with on our own, had David not said, "Try something." He didn't say, "Do these things." But, "Try something that evokes a kind of saccharine insincerity." And a series of experiments that we started led us down a path that created a cool element. The whole score wasn't based on that, but there were moments where I think that worked really well. That was a great example of us being led into a place we never would have wound up. And I think David was excited by the results that were better than he had, his initial idea, the seed was planted and something grew that was interesting and not what he expected.

Ross: I mean, there was, I think it's a known story, but it certainly —he was in a chiropractor in New York and heard this super-shitty record, which he sent us as an idea of that facade of everything being OK. And it was funny, when we got it up and he, OK. But I think what's really successful about that score, and I mean this with humility, is that those pieces that start in that very insincere way, if you tune into it, those reccur in different incarnations and curdle as the story does and become something that's much more dissonant and dread-filled. And I was proud of how it could start in this one way and end up somehow completely different.

Reznor: The way we generally work is, if you consider what we're coming from, like here's what I wouldn't know how to do: Here's a 12-second scene of someone walking down the hallway with a knife coming around the corner. I don't really understand how to think in that little snippet as a composer. So what we do is create four to seven minute exercises and compositions that expand on a theme. So if that, let's say there's a guy in a hallway, that terrible idea I just threw out there, we will create a piece that evolves from and it might be a repeating phrase, but we'll arrange it in a way where you could listen to it and it wouldn't sound out of place on one of the Ghost records that Nine Inch Nails had put out. But it evolves and it changes and it goes from uncertainty to creeping dread to full-fledged terror to aftermath to "I'm not sure what I should have done" to whatever it might be. Right? To silence. And we arrange it in a way that explores every variation that makes sense in that color palette. And then we'll take a snippet of that and we'll put it back in the picture and send that to Kirk and David. But we also give them the other five and a half minutes around it that allows them, because we trust them. If you want it a little greyer, go that direction. If you want the version without the tension, it's earlier in the track. If you like it but it doesn't need that melodic thing, that's probably later in the track. They can kind of hone in on the section that they think is better. And that comes back to us. Sometimes changed, sometimes unchanged, and we'll then start to explore it and fit it specifically to that scene with the right collaborative back and forth. But what it leaves us with at the end of the day, so we're creating a lot more music, because we do that for every little snippet. But the bonus of that is, at the end of the process when the film is done and now we all feel great about it — now, we've got a ton of stuff over here. Our next collaborative, or our next creative endeavor is to make an album, a listenable soundtrack album. And instead of trying to expand, "How do we take that 12-second thing and make it into something that makes sense to the listener other than just a collection of soundbites?" We've got a whole, we've got too much stuff to put into an album. And then we try to segue that into something that's listenable as its own piece of work. And that's fun to do. That's something that kind of goes unnoticed for the most part. But we're very proud of the albums that we've put out because we're aspiring for them to be something you put on and listen to just like a great album. Then it is reflective of the film, but it's not just the film playing with no dialogue all pushed together.

Ross: It's not the crash down; it's a new process that's started. The most insane of those being our five-one mix of The Social Network soundtrack, which we thought, "Yeah, well we've got, we've got the album finished. Well we could do a five-one mix, that'll probably take two or three days." Five weeks later...

Reznor: Three people have heard that. There's no real format you can even listen to it anymore, but it's there somewhere. But we did it, and that's the part that matters.

Ross: And we didn't do it for Dragon Tattoo.

What are you feelings about originality in film music?

Ross: There's lots of films where I'm blown away, you know what I mean? Something like the Incredibles. That's a film which I — there's no possible way I could do that. But when I listen to the score to it. It's incredible to me, not to overstate the word. But generally speaking, there is an aspect where you can feel, like Trent mentioned, where it's the same thing recycled. I'm surprised it's not just library music. And I don't mean it with any malice towards anyone. But I think that, in a sense, it's that thing of — I mean I guess our position has always been quality over quantity. And I can understand you want to make money. You do as many films as you possibly can. I don't know how many great ideas you can have a year. I mean not every film demands the music to be a character. But one often leaves — I've often left. There have been some movies I've seen which I'm definitely not going to mention where I've felt, "Wow. That could have been a great opportunity for the music to really play a role. And it would have made the film a lot better." And in fact, I think that the music has harmed the film.

Reznor: Sure. And when we start a project, and that could be a film, that could be a song, that could be anything that we're up to, generally it starts with not overthinking it but making sure we're headed down the right path, because we have options available. And a lot of times that initial strategic decision is one that is very important. So we'll think through what's the general approach. What instruments do we think we want to use? What do we imagine this thing's going to sound like?

We'll arrive and agree at something as a starting point. And then generally it's me sitting with instruments and Atticus recording, and we'll go in bursts where there might be — it's improvisational at first. And we've worked together long enough that we have a kind of language where we can know if we're honing in on something. He's making notes of what parts of it seem good. And then we might do 10, could be a couple things, it might be 10 instruments in a row of a kind of arrangement that's in our heads. And I'll leave and let him sort through, and he does the arrangements. And it's beneficial for me to be away from it so that when I come back in the room a few hours later, it sounds fresh. And it's beneficial for him to stay and arrange because I've just done it and now it's fresh in his mind. When I come back it's like, either my short term memory is shot — it sounds like I've never heard it before — or it might just be way better than it was when I actually played. And then it starts the kind of collaborative volley back and forth of honing in on what do we think it needs. Is it right, is it great? what's wrong? Let's try more things. And that process per track might happen a couple times, it might happen a hundred times where we just refine things. That's the general way it works. But it's a good back and forth where we maximize our strengths and play off each other. Because I'm not good at the arranging part.

Ross: On Gone Girl, because in some ways there are traditional themes and stuff, but to me that was in the studio the most experimental. Partly because a number of the things that we were using were kind of impossible to play, like some of that. There's a lot of homemade electronics involved in that one. And what was interesting about is what that we might be in a key and a tempo but there was no MIDI or anything like that. So it would literally be like there was just sound coming out of this table we set up differently. We'd get these kind of, I don't know what you'd call them. Performances. But it was a different kind of performance than say a guitar performance because of the nature of the instrument. I feel like the kind of collage quality that came out of that — I particularly feel like that one came to life in a sort of unusual way.

Reznor: It was fun through the whole thing. I mean we started off with a number of starting points that were ideas. The relaxing, fake, insincere music was one path we went down. Another path was this sense of the wheels are about to fall off the cart. How do we keep it together? What does that sound like? Not literally a wheel falling off a cart, but how does that sound like — something that has momentum but feels flawed inherently and it's going to get worse and worse until it can't stay together. That led us into some approaches that weren't the way we'd normally do it where he'd, as he was saying it was all live performances without any clicks or even concerns about tuning, putting the burden on him to make sense to, to adhere into some sort of whole. But once we started to hone in on that approach, then it takes a life of its own. And if the film stopped, we would have taken the music and made an album out of it because it never felt like we were — it's great when you're working on something where you know it's great for its real purpose, which is making the film the best it can be and being in service to the picture. But at the same time, incredibly inspiring to you as a sonic architect, and emotionally it's exciting in terms of "Well, we haven't done this before and we're right in tune," and you feel like you can't wait to start work every day. It had that feeling, too. It never felt like we were just doing music for a film. We're doing music that excites us. It happens to be for a film that we're excited about that's exciting the people making the film on that end. Alright. That's the best of all worlds.

Ross: That is the fun. The art, just speaking for myself, the fun is the artistic satisfaction. Being able to feel like that's the best we can do. That's fun.

Reznor: I personally like to go to theaters and watch films. And I think part of it is just to get away from being me for a while and escape, turn off the things that I'm churning through in my mind. And being able to disappear into a story and narrative and get lost for a minute. And I'm thinking about this through the eyes of someone who makes music for a living, and when I grew up, you looked forward to that time to put a piece of vinyl on and then sit down and put your headphones on and look at the lyric sheet and disappear into the song. And as access changed and everybody has access to everything, and now music is something that you listen to through two tiny little shitty speakers on your laptop while you're doing something else. The value, the importance of music has changed. Its role has changed. In a lot of ways, and not for everybody, but to a lot of people it's just a thing in the background. And it just dawned on me when we were working on Gone Girl, one of the few places I can think where people have full attention on something for an hour or two or a couple hours, is in the cinema. And during that time we've got their attention, even though it's part of the whole. It's still an interesting thing to think about in today's distracted, bombarded, over-informationalized world, that there's still a format where music can thrive. And I'm not giving up on any other arena where that might happen. But just the thought that crossed my mind sometime, you know. It's all about the experience and the care, I think, that goes into it. I'm motivated by excellence and aspiring to be the very best work we can do. And that matters. And I've learned a lot of that from Atticus in terms of, at the end of the day, there's practical needs that need to be met. But what matters is making yourself feel happy. And what I've found makes me feel happy, and I know makes him feel happy, is to give up at the end of the day saying, "That's the best fucking work we can do." And if you like it, great. If you don't, you don't. But it wasn't "good enough," And it wasn't "acceptable." It was fucking excellent.

SCORE: THE INTERVIEWS

CHAPTER 11

BRIAN TYLER

COMPOSER

KNOWN FOR		ACHIEVEMENTS
THE MUMMY (2017)	*THOR: THE DARK WORLD* (2013)	EMMY NOMINATION, MAIN TITLE, *SLEEPY HOLLOW*
THE FATE OF THE FURIOUS (2017)	*NOW YOU SEE ME* (2013)	
POWER RANGERS (2017)	*IRON MAN 3* (2013)	EMMY NOMINATION, MUSIC COMPOSITION FOR MINISERIES OR MOVIE, *LAST CALL*
HAWAII FIVE-0 (2011-16)	*FAST FIVE* (2011)	
SCORPION (2014-16)	*THE EXPENDABLES* (2010)	
AVENGERS: AGE OF ULTRON (2015)	*FAST & FURIOUS* (2009)	TWO BAFTA NOMINATIONS
	RAMBO (2008)	
SLEEPY HOLLOW (2013-15)	*THE FAST & THE FURIOUS: TOKYO DRIFT* (2006)	
FURIOUS 7 (2015)		
TEENAGE MUTANT NINJA TURTLES (2014)	*CONSTANTINE* (2005)	

What is special to you about film music?

My love for film music went back before I can even remember. The first time I even saw a movie, I loved that kind of music. Somehow those two merged and it made perfect sense, since films are seen so much worldwide. Music is the one thing that we all understand that we don't understand. If an alien civilization came to me and was asking me to describe a sound, that makes you feel, I don't know why — no one really has any idea why. How our neurons fire to make it seem like we have this universal understanding of "this makes you happy," or "this makes you sad," or "this makes you feel tension," or "this makes you laugh." Yet somehow it crosses all cultures all borders throughout time in memoriam, so it is really a cool thing.

Since I'm terrible at languages, that the idea of being able to speak one language that everyone can understand is pretty cool. And to create music that kind of crosses cultural divides made it so my need or my love of being able to show people the music I'd written made it so there were no barriers to that. That's part of why I love what I do.

Your love of music began on the drums. How does that affect the rhythm in your scores?

The drums being my first instrument was kind of an accident. There was a drum set there. It's not a very normal thing — a drum set just to be hanging out in a house, but I believe correctly my dad got it because he thought it looked cool. They were thinking it would be for my older sister. I was really young, I was like 4, and I would hear Led Zeppelin playing on the system, and my dad playing a record, or whatever it would be — Rush — and the drums appealed to me. I started getting on there trying to copy the records. Now, with the drums, I do tend to incorporate it, but I don't sometimes. Certainly a drum set is something very specific and will only be incorporated in certain kind of films, but I always try to sneak it in there, just because it's the instrument that got me my start in film music. The genesis of writing a piece especially for a film is, there really is no rhyme or reason in terms of what instrument there is.

You've done a lot of superhero movies, but the criticism is many sound similar. How do you make them sound different and reflect the characters?

Hero themes are more varied than I think people realize. Even within the DC Universe or the Marvel Universe. You almost have to step back — and I was really scared, by the way, at first when I had multiple movies. I was thinking, "How do I do sting shifts?" There's kind of this certain vibe to superhero melodies and everything. But within that, the distinguishing factor is the fact that they have made pains to distinctly draw these characters, so they don't just seem like all the same. Just dialogue, the way they talk, their character, and I found going from Iron Man, which is really this guy Tony Stark that is snarky, charming, clever, billionaire, playboy, with a mechanical suit. He's really a guy that's invented something. So his theme had to almost have that feel. He's very human. And then Thor could actually not be more opposite. He's a demigod that kind of can do whatever he wants. He's royalty. So you have all those — this blue-collar guy that then made it big by being an inventor, and then this demigod that's related to the lord of the universe. It's when you're writing that kind of music, they just don't have a lot to do with each other in terms of like the vibe, other than you want some triumph. It doesn't write itself. Nothing writes itself. But in a sense at least the map guides us, guides me. And that being the character. Anytime that I've been brought into a franchise or something when there's been previous score, — I've been lucky enough to follow in the footsteps of my heroes, Jerry Goldsmith, being right there at the top. So when Rambo came along, and I got the call from Sly, he wanted to make sure that my stamp was on it. And at the same time he loved the original score. "Like, how do we do this? Do we do both?" That was the question to me. He was like, "Brian, do we use the original?" And I was like, "Absolutely, must incorporate the original Jerry Goldsmith theme, and then create something new around it." And to me, that's always the way to go. Because you want continuity, and having just finished The Avengers, it was important for me to incorporate Alan Silvestri's Avengers music in there, as well. I love Alan, but at the same time I think it gives a continuity that using your own Iron Man 3 theme in those movies as well. Certainly, in something like Rambo, you're talking about a series that would have been continued on by Jerry Goldsmith if he hadn't passed away, so I think it's even a heavier mantle, stepping in his shoes. There's an homage and respect for what he did. You want that musical DNA to continue on.

What's it like working within a director's vision for a film?

This is something that I've always felt pretty strongly about. Movie directors, some of them are musical and have a musical background. Joss Whedon, in particular. He's really a composer himself. But on the whole, directors speak movie. They don't speak music; it's a whole different language. I grew up loving films and how they were made. I got really interested in the process of how you make a film. How they work with color timing and editing and lenses and lighting and all these things, and I would shoot films myself, little shorts and whatnot.

So I didn't even realize at the time my love for that, and learning about storyboarding and every aspect of it. By the time I got to working with a director, all of a sudden I found I was using that knowledge more than my musical knowledge. It doesn't really help to be, you know, "Should we do a heavy demi-semi-quaver on clarinet?" None of that kind of gobbledygook. It doesn't really make any sense to most directors, and it's totally pointless and you're going to get nowhere. So if you really want to connect with a director, you want to be able to say, "OK, I notice you're doing a tracking shot here, and you're pushing in, so maybe we should have the music swell," or do something that enhances that shot. And to them they're like "Ah, oh, that's what I want. They get it because you're speaking their language.

Then I think it's really important, especially new composers coming up, to not just learn the musical craft, but really learn the craft of filmmaking as well. I don't know if it's an advantage, but it gives you an arsenal, a common language that helps communicate. It's really helped out, especially with directors that are new to the process, where music is seriously scary to them. I can't tell you how many times I've talked to a director, and they say "OK, Brian, I can direct, I can write a scene, I can write dialogue; I cannot even try to begin to know how to begin a score." The fact that it's such a mystery for them, it makes them more comfortable. If I can say, "Hey, let's talk about the scene. What do you want from the scene? What didn't you get when you were filming the scene in the first place? Was the actor maybe giving the wrong performance, and you want the music to kind of do a magic trick to make it seem like he was feeling this, or whatever it is. Those are the things that they need as directors for their film.

You have a whole team you work with. How hard is it to give up some aspect of control to others and trust they can execute your creative vision for the music?

I think the beginning of my career there was a certain sense of reinforced self-reliance that maybe got over reinforced. Where I became a control freak, because it was how I knew how to do the films.

At the beginning of the films, you would get like a dollar to do the film, and I would do everything. So I would write the score, I play all the instruments, I was the mixer, I was the recordist, I was the engineer, I was the music editor, I would master it, I would deliver when everything was done. And I did this for many movies in a row. And when I started doing bigger films, and I started actually getting into the studio system, I didn't want to change the way I did it, because it worked. I didn't know any music editors. I don't know if they are going to touch my music, I don't want someone to mix my music. "What, someone else is going to mix my music, what are you doing?" "You can't, no don't touch, what are you doing?" It's absolute terror. And so for a long time I held onto things that I shouldn't have. Literally, there are films that have credits on them that are not people. That's because I was embarrassed that it said, like, "mixer Brian Tyler, music editor Brian Tyler, composer Brian Tyler." it was stupid.

Now, eventually, time being a temporal straight line that goes in one direction for us, I would run out. These big, more and more movies, they're getting bigger and bigger, the demands are stronger. And I had to learn to delegate, at great consternation.

And so over time, I have now learned to really rely on these few core people that I trust. Orchestration is something that I didn't want anyone to work on that or mixing or any of these things. And now I have a good team of people that I can feel slightly comfortable about. Now if you ask them how comfortable I am with this process, they would probably say that I am not, and because I do go in and — evidenced by just the two movies that I just finished, I did completely go in and end up doing my own mix. But it's gone through a process of at least having someone gone through and combing through it and finding the right takes, and kind of doing their pass, and then everyone knows that I'm going to jump on and do an entire new mix myself anyway. So I have left some of it behind, but I still have the stamp of my lowly origins, and I can't quite shake all of it. That's why I am a workaholic, as some would say.

Here's another thing. On some other movies, I would know of a friend of mine that wanted to get in to do something. And so I would be like, "Hey man, do you want me to put you down as the mixer or music editor or something?" And they are like, "Yeah! Yeah, it's great that would be awesome!" And I'm like, "OK." And so they would appear and they will have never even seen the film, and — this is my early days; I hope I am not getting anyone in trouble. Someone probably got their union card off like five movies that I did.

I just was that much of a control freak, so I have now reduced at least one to two tenths of one percent down from "complete control freak" down to like, here. Most of the things that I was working on, that I would do everything on, they are the early movies. And the strange thing about it is, just in this last week, also they are doing a reissue of some of my early scores. Two of them. So I am going through my old scores again for the first time and listening to them for a while. And I thought I would be horrified, but I am not. Actually, there is sort of something to it, where I want to be able to bring some of that guy back. There's something about that. I would do things musically that almost surprised me now, because I think, "Yeah, you know what, I didn't know this rule about music that maybe now I apply." "Why not break it again?

So in a way, it is fun to go back and listen to your old stuff because you can sometimes realize that there's something to it. There's a lot of stuff that I don't like about it too. But certainly this is part and parcel to the process overall. Strangely enough, I wouldn't change a thing, looking through my history. Because all of those weird processes and strange ways of doing things have made me what I am today, and so they all kind of make sense in a bizarre way.

Do you feel limited by the constraints put on you by a director or a studio, or by the temp score used when you first watch a film?

I don't think it's so much that the studios or any directors look at you too fit into a box — except that sometimes you do encounter, sometimes it's more of an executive, studio executive, or a producer. Definitely not at Marvel, because they are creative types, all their execs. At other studios, I have encountered where they tell you they want something different, and then when you do it, they say, "Well, why didn't you do it like the temp?" There is this box that they try to jam you into, and I've always been really box-resistant or temp-resistant. Even now, when most of the movies I score, it is temp from my own music, from my own movies, which is kind of one of those things that throws me. Because of course I know exactly how I wrote every note, and I don't want to repeat it. So I just kind of don't listen to it unless I'm in a screening.

Do you strive for perfection when recording a film score you've written?

I think when you do something wrong in music, it can be the coolest thing. If everything was consonant and perfect, music would, it would be terrible. it would be like putting auto-tune on Etta James. It would just take all of the soul out of it. And honestly, that is why orchestras sound beautiful. Because you have many, many players, trying to play the same note, but no one can. Everyone is off by microns of a percentage, which gives it that chorusing effect. Or even just choral, you have people singing. And if everyone sang perfectly, it would sound like one person, just singing somehow together. It would be the opposite of that communal, "there is a lot of people doing this beautiful" kind of thing. So I think that goes along with it. Not only does music rely on micro mistakes or errors in the music to make it beautiful — not singing the note perfectly, not being perfectly quantized in time, playing percussion behind the beat, the downbeat, or playing around vibrato on the piano. All those are technically, if you really think about it, errors.

It's imperfections. And so certain kind of rules of orchestration or harmony or structure in music that you are taught in school — if you abide by every one of them — you are going to fall into the same camp as everything that has been done before you. And there will be nothing original. So I think there is this going right outside the edge; those moments are when I think music becomes alive and original.

How important is it to you to create music that is shared?

That is the genesis of all of this really. From the time I kind of figured out how to create my own pieces because I think doing piano lessons and working on all that — I loved it, but it was just a natural progression to start to tinker with other things. Make variations, and then all of a sudden it was just coming up with all sorts of musical ideas as I went. The more I got into it, for some reason, there was the sense that I wanted other people to hear it, besides my family and my friends. It just kind of grew. It was almost one of those kind of inner conflicts I think composers have. Can you write music just for yourself? You write it to be of your own liking. You want to write something that you enjoy as music, but for some reason there's this urge and need for someone else to hear it. I felt like somehow it was being wasted if people weren't hearing it, so it really drove me to avenues and situations where I'd be playing live, where I'd be able to do music for something else.

Talk about hearing your music in other places, aside from the film. Do you ever anticipate it will be used outside the film?

As you write them, you don't even really think about it, but there's a very high likelihood that it is going to be used somewhere else. There have been all sorts of interesting and cool ways that my music has made its way into other avenues.

I wrote this long extended take on the Universal Pictures logo music, which I had redone, reworked Jerry Goldsmith for I think their 100th anniversary. That is the music that you see when you see the globe and all that. And I also did that for Marvel's logo. I wrote their logo music. And both of those logo music have found their way into theme parks. Now, they are longer suite versions, but also I have found that people will tweet me or a friend will give me a text saying, "Hey, I am in Indiana walking into the theater. The music that they are playing as we are sitting down is the Marvel theme logo music."

Theme parks, Universal Studios Florida has my music playing before shows. It's just interesting. I find these things out later. Of course, movie trailers get repurposed. Often I don't know that until I go to the movie theater, and I'm watching the trailer, and I'm like "Wow, this music seems familiar." And then I realize it is my music from another movie.

Certainly, concerts are the most fun. I love conducting concerts and getting out there and being able to hear it live in front of an audience. And it has been a blast over the years; countless times, seeing orchestras and choirs perform my music around the world when I'm not even there. They will send me a video and — college marching bands down to a teenager in his room that split screens nine different parts, and he's playing all the different instruments to some piece that I did, and piano versions of a theme.

There are just so many different avenues, and all of it is fun to watch. All of it is crazy, and flattering, and something I just never thought I would ever have seen — people doing covers of my music.

Talk about the secrecy of modern films and film scores.

There are a lot of these — more and more — when we do these films that are shrouded in secrecy. Anything especially that has a built-in following.

If you are doing something that has a comic angle, like a Ninja Turtles or an Iron Man or Avengers or — you name it — anything in that kind of milieu, you have fans and now very smart fans that know how to hack things on the internet and get into emails and whatnot. So you have to be really careful about these things.

There was the one time when I remember reading an Iron Man 3 script. One, I was super excited as a fan, and I wanted to know what was going on with Iron Man. So I went in there, but I knew I had to read the script and kind of take it in, because I was going to meet with all the Marvel people and the director and everyone, and kind of give them my take on what I thought the music should be.

So when I was reading the script, and it's this locked room kind of. It wasn't like armed guard, but it was practically — you are in the room, you don't have your mobile phone, there is nothing in the room, and you are just sitting there reading the script.

Well, the thing I realized is that everyone — I had talked to the producers ahead of time — and then as I opened the script I'm thinking, "OK, they know exactly when I talk to them, they know when I went in this room. If I don't read the script fast enough, they are going to think that I am a slow guy. I'm just a little bit slow."

And so, "I better read it fast, but if I read it really fast, am I going to miss things? And then get the script wrong?" So when I am talking about it, I'm like, "Yeah, you know when Iron Man fights Godzilla, wasn't that an amazing part?" Or whatever.

So it was this race between — and it just freaked me out, and I think I skipped a couple pages, and kind of focused on certain areas. But anyway, it all worked out.

One of my weird skills is that I can speed read. I can actually go through books, and it is something that developed in grad school, I think, for always procrastinating and running out of time. And so I actually can read really fast. But I think the nerves of it completely got to me. So it was interesting, but I am glad I didn't completely blow it in the meeting.

The secrecy behind — I remember working on Eagle Eye with Steven Spielberg, his company. All of his things are super locked down. Of course, when they send me the movies, like the Marvel movies or any of these, every frame of the movie has my name emblazoned right across the picture, just in case it ever gets out, of course, they can all say, "Hey, Brian Tyler."

And the scripts all have my name across it. There is a very high degree of security now with the way films have leaked.

I was involved with a film, Expendables 3, that leaked right before it was released, and it hurt the box office quite a lot. So now we do things like, we put drives into lockdown thumbprint fingerprint ID massive safes at night, when we are not working on them. Things that you would have never thought of years ago. Cameras, night vision cameras and IDs, thumbprint stuff on the studios, and all this stuff. And it's just become that way to make sure that the movie makes it to the theater before it makes it to a hard drive and uploaded to the Internet.

There is like an invisible signature to the print or the version of the film that was leaked. So they have an easier time tracking it down, and they are pretty good with that stuff. I think they can get to the bottom of those things. And it wasn't me, so that was good. I am alive. (Laughter.)

CHAPTER 12
MYCHAEL DANNA
COMPOSER

KNOWN FOR		ACHIEVEMENTS
STORKS (2016)	CAPOTE (2005)	ACADEMY AWARD, ORIGINAL SCORE, LIFE OF PI
THE GOOD DINOSAUR (2015)	VANITY FAIR (2004)	
	HULK (2003)	GOLDEN GLOBE, MOTION PICTURE SCORE, LIFE OF PI
LIFE OF PI (2012)	ARARAT (2002)	
(500) DAYS OF SUMMER (2012)	ANTWONE FISHER (2002)	
MONEYBALL (2011)	HEARTS IN ATLANTIS (2001)	EMMY AWARD, MUSIC COMPOSITION FOR MINISERIES, WORLD WITHOUT END
CHLOE (2009)	BOUNCE (2000)	
LAKEVIEW TERRACE (2008)	GIRL, INTERRUPTED (1999)	
LITTLE MISS SUNSHINE (2006)	THE BOONDOCK SAINTS (1999)	

You've often talked about how coming from Canada has made you open to a wide variety of musical styles. What is it about your home country that enabled you to be exposed to different musical styles early on?

Much like America — but in a slightly different way — it's a country of immigrants. But there is a less prevalent culture. Well, there's definitely a culture, and I think everyone who comes there, just like everyone who comes to America becomes America, everyone who comes to Canada does become Canadian. But it's a country that — to compare it to America — was founded on compromise between French and English. And so that spirit — as opposed to rebellion — that spirit of compromise and that spirit of working with a mother country existed up until very recently.

207

It's just in the culture. It's just more open to thinking of the world through other eyes and experiencing it in different ways. So it's great for a composer, and especially for me. I think it's one of the reasons I am interested in music from around the world. There's so much of it to hear and even, you know, as a kid growing up, it was easy to be exposed to different cultures and different languages and different kinds of music. It was something that I was interested in right from the beginning and wanted to play with in film music.

You often travel the world to learn from musicians before embarking on a project. For instance, I understand that for the movie Ararat, you decided to travel to Armenia to meet with musicians and research that culture's music.

That's an interesting point, and it's a subtle difference. Here in Los Angeles, there's fabulous Armenian-Americans, so you don't have to go to Armenia to get a great duduk player or guitar player or kamancheh. They're here as well. But there is something about, from a writer's perspective, being in a place where the music came from. You understand, I think, not just the superficial musical language but also the relationship it has with the culture, with the people, with the soil it is literally springing from.

I think it gives you another deep perspective — a way of looking at and understanding the music, which helps you work with those players better and helps you work with those sounds better, too.

And you also like to record in places where the music actually comes from.

Yeah, and Ararat was one that was really interesting. In fact, this is the 100th anniversary of the Armenian genocide, so we had a concert with the Toronto Symphony Orchestra where they did a suite from that score. So I've been thinking a lot about it lately and what an incredible trip that was. And we recorded in a 4th Century stone church that had no electricity and no heat. We were there in the winter and we were literally recording this choir by candlelight, and I had a battery pack on my laptop.

You can't really get any more real. culturally, you're getting to the heart of it. Incredibly romantic. And it's really inspiring to have those kinds of experiences.

What's the purpose of putting so much effort into researching locations and finding musicians all over the world? Does it make that big of a difference in the end?

A big part of it is procrastination, to keep away from the actual hard part, which is sitting there and grinding out music. (Laughter.) Anything to procrastinate is a good thing. But you spend as much time as you can immersing yourself in the backstory. As a film composer, you're part of the storytelling team. So you really have to, in order to help tell the story, have all kinds of knowledge, not just facts, but also emotional knowledge and spiritual knowledge about what it is that you're telling. And the more backstory you have and the more knowledge you have, the better job you can do.

It's in there. And so when you're writing, something might be seeping through and it really helps to inform the music.

In the film Moneyball, how much of your decision to make that a traditional orchestral score was rooted in the idea that baseball is very much steeped in "tradition" of its own.

It's an excellent point. That's exactly the kind of analysis and conceptualizing that you do when you're writing a score. You wipe the blackboard clean and you say, "OK, this is America's game." It's, like you say, a game that's fanatically historical, and it's all about the history and the tradition. So yeah, having some sort of iconoclastic instrument in there would be against the spirit of that story. So that's the way you look at scoring a film. You have to look at the story and what, what the essence is of the story.

What about your music for the movie Capote? How did you mirror Truman Capote's writing style with your music?

In the same way, it's kind of black and white. I read In Cold Blood, of course, as part of my research. And just his style is so clean, and it's expressive in an economical way. So that seemed to me to be a starting place for how the music should also be working. And also, why would there be an instrument that he, that Capote himself, had not heard? Somehow it just seemed wrong. And believe me, I tried. We tried some things. And to the general hilarity of everyone. But I did, I did try. I had some other concepts, which I won't even run by you. But yeah, I was trying, "Hey, what if, what if we do this?" And we looked at it and went, "That's horrible." And, you know, it just, it's way over here from the story. So, eventually we circled this idea and came to the idea that it's just simple, clean, elegant, spare — just like his writing. So you end up with strings and piano as kind of black and white writing almost.

So you found yourself taking out a lot of the excess in order to finalize your score?

Definitely. A big part of writing is taking all the superfluous notes out, and I always, maybe everyone does, but I always overwrite. Writing is easy. It's the culling of all the stuff that needs to be culled that's hard. That one, the concept, we finally figured out what it needed to be. That was definitely the goal of writing. But we literally, we'd spend like days moving a note like four frames this way and then come back the next day and go, "No." It was that subtle of a film. And Bennett, that's the kind of filmmaker he is. It's the same as Moneyball. It's just really precise, pristine filmmaking. And the music has to be on the same page as that. And so, really, it's just amazing. You move a phrase a few frames this way and it just doesn't work, and you bump it back and blam! It's just magic. It's that weird chemistry between picture and music that I've been doing for a long time but still barely understand. (Laughter.)

Every movie has its own unique set of challenges. But Life of

Pi had to be one of the more difficult films you've ever worked on.

It was a very complicated process, that film, to figure out the sound of it. Again, there's so much writing that happened. And it might even feel right for a week or two and then you sit back and go, "It's just not feeling quite right." The song ("Pi's Lullaby"), ironically, kind of came easily. That opening sequence is just so kind of rich and clear. The song was probably the easiest part of the score to write. And it was fun, too. I can't really say that about the rest of the score. (Laughter.) Which was quite the struggle. It was really this balance between — he's a boy. He's got youth and optimism on his side, and he's in this incredibly perilous and difficult place. It's finding that balance between those two things, and having to tell the story without a lot of dialogue on screen. And the music had to kind of help us follow his emotional arc without overstating it, which is always hard. It's a lot easier to overstate.

Not many people felt as if the book Life of Pi could ever really be turned into a film. How good did it feel to prove those people wrong?

That was really the amazing arc of our journey on that. The filmmaking team and Ang. For months and months it really, frankly, felt like we were going to fail. We would sit back and watch it and listen to the mockups, and it wasn't working. And it really was late in the day that suddenly there was one screening that I clearly remember where suddenly, we felt it. For the first time, it felt, "Wow, there, like Pi, there's the shore! Finally, it's come over the horizon and we can actually see that it's there. We just have to crawl those last few yards of sand."

It was a tough journey. Any film where you kind of invent a new language like Life of Pi does — there isn't really a film that it's based on. It's a very original story and an original way of telling the story. So it's dangerous filmmaking. And Ang, you know, revels in that kind of danger. It's harrowing to work on, especially with so much at stake. But the satisfaction of succeeding after a great deal of hard work, it's really something.

You took home several awards including an Oscar for that movie. Do you consider Life of Pi to be your best score to date?

Not necessarily. That's a great answer. It could be. But you're asking a parent to pick their favorite child. It's hard to say. And it's so hard, too, because the experience is tied up in the music for me. So, I watch a film and I have no idea what the work is like until a couple of years after. I might have not seen it for a year or something, and then I'm flipping channels and "Oh, Moneyball." And then I watch it and often, you know, usually I feel a whole lot better at that point than I did when I just finished it. When you just finish a project, I think you're really aware of all the ways that you've failed — all the ways that you did not hit the marks that you wanted to. So you kind of are blind to the places where you did succeed and the ways that you have, you know, accomplished something. So those things, those are the things that will hit you two years later. And it's consistently been that way. But it's also a matter of the fact that your emotional journey on the film is wrapped up in how you perceive it. So it's really hard for me to say. There are things that I think are good musically if you sit back. And again, in what context? Because in a concert context there's some scores of mine that I think stand really well as a piece of music. In the film, is it as good? I don't know. So, it's tough to answer.

You often collaborate with your brother, Jeff Danna. Who decides if you are going to tackle a project on your own or work on it with your brother?

Often one or the other of us is approached, and then when we're looking at it and we think this is something that would be great to work on together, for whatever reason.

And it may have to do with, you know, Jeff is originally a guitarist and plays all kinds of other plucked-string instruments. And I'm originally a keyboard player. So there is that. That expertise of being able to bring those different instruments to that table. But also, we do have slightly different skill sets. So, different strengths and weaknesses. There are some projects where I think this is something where Jeff would really be useful and this would be a great one for us to work on together. Sometimes it's made by us. Sometimes it's made by the producer or director, somebody like Terry Gilliam, who has worked with us before, you know. He would work with us as a team. That's just how it would come. So it's different every time.

Do you have any sort of sibling rivalry with your brother? Or do you put that aside when you work together?

I think there's a bit of both. I think that's a good thing. I think when we work together there is a sense of competition, and it's really good for the film. It's, "You wrote a pretty good cue. I'm going to try to write my ass off on this one now and come up to the level that you set." And I think both of us really admire the other one's work. And because we're slightly different, he can do things that I feel I can't, and I think it kind of goes the other way. So when he pushes the level up, then I try to push it up. So I think it's really good for the overall level of excellence. There is competition. There's definitely critiques back and forth, and there's arguments. I think we're used to collaborating with other people. That's what we do all day, and so collaborating with each other is really not anything new or difficult

We trade war stories about different bizarre and funny things that happen in this business. I think that is the other thing that's fun. When you're writing film music, it can be a really isolated experience. There's no question that the real work happens kind of between your own ears by yourself in the room with a deadline. So that's not all that fun really. But when there's someone that's kind of on that same journey and sharing it, it definitely makes the road more amusing. You can laugh about things that, if you were working by yourself, you'd cry about. So it's kind of a win-win situation.

I don't even know how many we've worked on together. I mean it goes back to when we were kids and played together in bands. And we played music together like all our lives really.

So, yeah, again, it's kind of hard to like say when it started. I brought Jeff into film music when I was kind of starting out myself, and I brought him to play guitar on a project, and then I said, "Oh, you want to try this cue?" and he kind of knocked it out of the park right away. So it's like, "Wow! You've got a knack for this, so let's do some more work together."

And then he got a TV series kind of very early on, and he moved to California. I was still in Toronto, so we were in different cities, and he had his own career. But obviously we kept collaborating maybe once every few years or something. And that's kind of how the rhythm has been. It's maybe every couple of years or something that we've worked together on a project.

You both seem to share a curiosity for music and how it works.

I am really curious. I love learning about it. I think it's just so cool how music is something that everyone understands, everyone on earth, and probably has for tens of thousands of years. And yet there's different ways of approaching it. I worked with this Native American flute player, actually on The Ice Storm with Ang Lee. And I would write a melody and I'd say, "Play this." And he would never play it the same way twice. And I realized that his way of looking at music was completely different. As opposed to notes and a key it was, "Well, this is the sound of a wolf. This is a wolf's voice. This is an eagle. Oh, you want the eagle? You want the eagle in pain?" It's like, "Wow! That's mind-blowing." I never looked at music like that. And yet, I just loved those moments where we're doing the same thing but just coming around from a different way of looking at it. There's something really magical and expressive that you can do with it, with that different point of view.

So film music must be the perfect venue for someone with an interest in all sorts of genres of world music. It is. When I first started doing this, it was definitely more uncommon than it is now. It's kind of the thing that everyone does now — work with world music in film and TV music. I think a lot of times it's without maybe the depth of thought and conception. Sometimes it's just, "Well, I have this sample library in my computer and it's got every instrument of the world and this one sounds cool." But without understanding kind of what that voice is and so on.

There is some of that but, honestly, it really has become kind of the language of media music writing, which is great. it's wonderful that that's kind of happened in the last 20 years. I think it makes the world a more interesting and a better place, now that we're listening to each other and learning about different points of view.

SCORE: THE INTERVIEWS

CHAPTER 13

TOM HOLKENBORG

RECORDING ARTIST & COMPOSER

KNOWN FOR

ACHIEVEMENTS

JUSTICE LEAGUE (2017) *RUN ALL NIGHT* (2015)

THE DARK TOWER (2017) *KILL YOUR FRIENDS* (2015)

SPECTRAL (2016) *DIVERGENT* (2014)

BATMAN V. SUPERMAN: DAWN OF JUSTICE (2016) *THE AMAZING SPIDER-MAN 2* (2014)

DEADPOOL (2016) *300: RISE OF AN EMPIRE* (2014)

BRIMSTONE (2016)

BLACK MASS (2015) *PARANOIA* (2013)

POINT BREAK (2015)

MAD MAX: FURY ROAD (2015)

ASSOCIATED ACTS:
JUNKIE XL
(SIX STUDIO ALBUMS)

How do you describe a piece of music to someone?

I mentioned that in a conversation, where we were talking about promoting yourself, or we were talking to an A&R person or talking to a director. You can say whatever you want about your music, but actually playing a piece of music makes so much more sense. Music is this universal language that goes straight to the heart and soul of everybody. Therefore, it talks by itself. Especially in meetings, when you play music for the first time for a director, which is the most important part of the process for me at least. Because then you can convince him of a complete concept of a theme or, harmonically, what you want to do. Sonically, what you want to do. Instrumentation, orchestration, whatever. That's a very important moment. And that's usually why I have a big chunk of music ready for the very first time that I meet a director, and we're working on a new film. Then at that point, it doesn't make any sense that I'm talking to the director. It's like, "Why don't you make yourself comfortable in a chair, and I hit play, and that will say it all."

You had a very successful artist career as Junkie XL which has crossed over a bit into your film scoring work. Hans Zimmer said he loved your artist name. Why did you feel it important to transition to using your birth name in film scores?

I really liked it, but I felt, over time, it was closing in on me. It felt like a straight jacket that wasn't comfortable anymore. It felt like a perfect tailored suit for many years, and then it turned into a straightjacket. With film scoring, I can now explore all these different areas that I used to explore, but I couldn't use it really in my Junkie XL artist career.

You've said you consider film scoring to be a more elaborate art form. What do you mean?

Why film scoring is a higher art form? There is a story there of two and a half hours, and you need to bring the best out of that story with your music, and you need to shift emotions, based on what you're seeing on screen, based on what the director finds interesting to pursue. That makes it, to me, a higher art form, because it demands way more from you than just being a cool musician. There are so many cool people in the world that make absolutely — and I mean that — really, absolutely fantastic music. But it doesn't mean they're great film composers, because that is, to me, a different art form, and a higher art form. You need so much more than just being a musician.

You collaborated with Hans Zimmer on Batman v. Superman. What is it like to be part of that iconic superhero series?

It's fantastic. The first time that Hans asked me to collaborate with him, on Man of Steel, I was so incredibly excited because it's one of those movies that are bigger than life, bigger than what we are. There are certain themes, too. It's not just something like Superman; it's also Blade Runner, it's also Alien, Cinderella. All these movies will be remade over time, over time, over time. So the only thing that you can do is just really invest all your energy and time in it and make it your own, and do something that is your own, because there will be some other composer who will do it again. So I think it's misplaced arrogance to say, "What I'm going to do, I'm going to define this character for the next 500 years." That's nonsense. It defines it maybe for the next two years, but after that somebody else will take over and do something else. I think that's the beauty of it too. But the superheroes — especially the superheroes — everybody recognizes something of themselves in that superhero. So whatever interpretation that director takes, whatever interpretation the composer takes by making that flash of reality, for that specific film and point, there will always be a group of people that embrace it, and a couple people who will be appalled by it. And that happens, for instance, on all the Batman movies, and that happened on all the Superman movies, and all the Spider-man movies. There were people that loved it, and people that hated it. And sometimes that group is really big that loved it, and really big that hated it. That's the interesting thing with these superheroes.

Do you feel any pressure?

Absolutely no pressure. there's a lot at stake, but I think that's a lot of what all these guys did too. They looked at it, and with all their best intentions they did the best that they could at the time that they thought was perfect and suitable for a character like that. And at this point, that's the same as I would do.

It was actually really funny because I think what sets me apart from I think many of the other guys that Hans works with is that I had an established artist career, and I had hits worldwide, and I worked with people like Madonna, Coldplay, Britney Spears, Chuck D. The list of people that I worked with was pretty long, so when Hans first asked me to join Remote Control, I said no. "Sorry, no interest at this point." And Hans, in his most friendly, German way — he's like, "I like this guy already." You know? Because I said no. I don't think he's used to many people that stand up to him and say, "No, I'm not going to do that." And Hans and I always stayed in touch. he called me out of the blue saying, "There are a lot of people that tell me I should be talking to you, but I have no idea who you are." And that's when we met, and we talked and I immediately was charmed by how he is as a person. He's very nice to be around and to work with. But then I started working step by step on very little things with him.

I did a remix completion of the Inception score, and then we did something similar on Sherlock Holmes, and then we worked together on Megamind, the DreamWorks film. I did a little bit for that. And then with Madagascar 3, I did way more, and it got more elaborate. Then after that was The Dark Knight. I did a little bit for that too, and then it was Man of Steel, and I did a lot for Man of Steel. And through that I got 300: Rise of an Empire. And then I got Divergent, and then I got Mad Max: Fury Road, and then Run All Night and now I'm doing Point Break and Batman v. Superman. So my career went really pretty quickly once that all worked out like that.

Did you every plan to get into film scoring, or did it just happen?

Well, when I got to L.A. in 2003, I wanted to get into film scoring, and that was my goal at that specific point. And I had my artist career already, since the late 80s, and all the way to 2002-2003. I moved out here, and I knew I wanted to be a film composer, but I knew I wasn't ready for it. And I knew that I had the musical background, and I knew I had the technical skills, but not the managing skills and not the overseeing skills. What is required to do a film score? Just purely on a technical level, with whom do you work, who do you need on a project, how do you manage your assistants — because, let me be clear, it's very hard to do a movie without assistants, because there's always so much stuff that needs to be done, especially at the very end of it.

That I saw with Harry Gregson-Williams by assisting him for a year and a half or so, or two years, on various projects. And then I started doing alternative films in Europe by myself, and then some of those films got more successful, and then I started doing well as a composer there. And then I talked to Hans. So it was a very slow rise and a lot of the things now come in handy that I did in the past.

I mean, I started as an engineer, then I became a producer and a mixer, and then I was a multi-instrumentalist and I started working with computers that I completely had all the control, and synthesizers and then it just went on and on and on. So all these tools and all these bands and artists that I worked with now come in very handy when you do film scoring — when it's like, "Oh, we need some of this, oh, I know how that works. I did that back in the day. This is how we do that."

What are your favorite parts of the film scoring process?

One is the very first time in the studio when you make something and you feel it comes together. It's like, "Ah, it's coming together." And that's awesome. And then the next time is when it's mixed, and you hear the mix for the very first time and you get chills from how it turned out. And then, for instance, if it's a film score, it's played by the string section, and you stand in that room and you hear the strings now performing the thing that you wrote, and you get chills again.

And then there's another moment where you go to the premiere of the film, and the sound is all perfect, and you see the final result and it's a kick. Or in my artist career, when I was done with a song and I would play it for the first time to the audience, and they would then embrace it. That's a kick like no tomorrow.

There's a similarity between film scoring and what I did live. The scariest thing is when you play a piece of music for the first time to somebody else — whether it's the audience, whether it's the A&R person of your record company that comes to the studio to hear the first two or three songs that you've recorded, whether it's the director who comes for the first time, whether it's somebody from the studio who says, "Hey, can you send me some scenes, because we want to know what you're up to." That is a super, super special moment, because you can always compose yourself as somebody else throughout that whole process. You can talk on the line, and you can say, "Oh, I'm so on it, I'm so inspired, I know what to do and it's going to be great," and everybody's like, "Oh, that's great to hear," and you hang up the phone, and you're just like, "What the hell am I doing, what am I supposed to do?"

And then you can get really nervous, and then that's a very sensitive time period. And then when you play it for the first time, you basically just put your soul out there. It's like, "OK, you're ready." But that's the thing I learned over the years. In the beginning, when somebody would say, "Oh, no. That's not what we want," my world would just completely fall apart. Now, when I'm done — like with Run All Night, a suite of 50 minutes, 52 minutes — when I gave it to the director, I've already abandoned it. So if he says, "I don't like it," it's fine. I'll do something new. But it's very hard to get to that point in your life when you can actually do that. It took a lot of practicing, but I went though this so many times that I just got better at it.

You mentioned getting chills from music during several stages. What does that tell you about the music you're creating?

I don't care what music it is, but if I make a track, it has to give me goosebumps myself. I don't say that to be arrogant, but if it doesn't hit me in the stomach as being a great piece of music, I cannot expect the audience — anybody out there — to have a feeling that it hits the stomach. Then it obviously doesn't come from my heart and soul; it's a fabricated piece of music that sounds great, that sounds like something else but will not hit anybody's stomach. People will say, "That sounds cool," but they're going to leave it at that. But if you make a track that is life defining for you, maybe out of the seven and a half billion people on this planet there's one person that feels the same way.

Where do you usually start in the scoring process? Do you want to read a script before you see the film, etc.? How early can you get a sense of what a film score should be?

I usually like to talk to certain people about what the movie is, whether it's the music editor or the director or somebody from the studio. And potentially read the script, and then leave it at that for a little bit and then my mind goes wandering. Everybody understands this process even though they're not working as a film composer. When you read a book and it says, "There's this great dark forest, and this beautiful woman came out of the forest," everybody pictures a forest. None of these forests will be the same. None of these beautiful women will be the same. It's exactly the same with music. So I read a script, and I get all these ideas in my head musically, and you can ask 15 other composers to read that same script. They will all have different musical ideas. Now, the interesting part is once you see the film, and once you start working on a cue level, that fantasy gets brought down to a smaller range, because now the movie is dictating your musical ideas. So my most musical ideas for a film come after conversations with people and reading the script. Then I see the film, and then I say, "This idea is not going to work. That idea is not going to work." But usually, those ideas, I don't get when I'm working on a cue level. Let's say I'm just watching a scene of seven minutes. Then to perceive those seven minutes as open — as if you do just after reading a script — is very hard. So that's why I usually make a lot of music beforehand, so I can surprise myself with ideas that I have.

I know there are composers that start at the beginning of the movie and work their way through the end. I have a super high admiration of people who do that, but I just absolutely can't, because throughout the process I have new ideas. I go back to the beginning and fix it, and then in the middle and in the end, so forth. In that perspective, it's important to pull the two major group of composers apart. I'm in the second group of composers; the first group of composers are the old school guys that I admire so incredibly for all the things that they have done and still are doing. And by old school, I don't mean the guys that are old;

I'm talking the way of writing music. Some of them are just pencil and paper. Some of them just sit behind the piano, and then orchestrate it later, or work with orchestrators. Now, in this scenario we're just talking about musical notes and harmonies and how it's arranged for an orchestra, and how it's orchestrated, and the special effects you have with that. That's the first group of composers. The second group of composers where I see myself being part of. Where there's a lot of production going on at the same time, and the orchestra has a role in the final result, but it's not the defining role. Actually, all the movies that I did have that in them.

So if we look at Mad Max, I spent at least seven months producing the score, trying this, trying that. Different types of drums, different types of guitars, different types of processing, certain types of things and just putting them in. Constantly working on the mix. How am I going to use the surrounds? How am I going to use the fronts? These are usually questions that a traditional composer doesn't deal with, and that saves time. So when I work on a movie, and I've written all these rough demos, they are sparked by just a script and conversation with the director. Or maybe seeing the movie only once, just like that, and then just forget about it for a second.

Talk about how you start to plot out a film score from scratch. How do you begin?

I like to put in the markers in the film. This is very important; I've got to nail this. And then I need an arc that eventually lands there. And then there, and then we go out. I try to focus on those first, and then I try to go to sub-markers. It's like, "OK, within this marker, what's the tension that I need to bridge, and where do I need to go there?" So the first arc that I have now becomes this, and it's like, "OK, I've got to do this, and I've got to go that, and then that." And now, let's go to the second marker and do the same thing, and then let's play everything back until the end of the second marker.

So that's what I do a lot, constantly playing back the whole film with all my demos in it, so I get a sense of what my arc for the music is.

SCORE: THE INTERVIEWS

CHAPTER 14

HARRY GREGSON-WILLIAMS

COMPOSER

KNOWN FOR		ACHIEVEMENTS
THE ZOOKEEPER'S WIFE (2017)	THE CHRONICLES OF NARNIA: THE LION, THE WITCH AND THE WARDROBE (2005)	GOLDEN GLOBE NOMINATION, ORIGINAL SCORE, THE CHRONICLES OF NARNIA: THE LION, THE WITCH AND THE WARDROBE
THE MARTIAN (2015)		
THE EQUALIZER (2014)	KINGDOM OF HEAVEN (2005)	
TOTAL RECALL (2012)		
THE TOWN (2010)	MAN ON FIRE (2004)	GRAMMY NOMINATION, SCORE FOR MOTION PICTURE, THE CHRONICLES OF NARNIA: THE LION, THE WITCH AND THE WARDROBE
THE TAKING OF PELHAM 1 2 3 (2009)	PHONE BOOTH (2002)	
X-MEN ORIGINS: WOLVERINE (2009)	SHREK (2001)	
	CHICKEN RUN (2000)	
THE NUMBER 23 (2007)	ENEMY OF THE STATE (1998)	
DEJA VU (2006)		

Tell me about how your background and how it informs your music.

Like, who the hell am I? (Laughter.) No, I studied music since I was very small, since I was 5 or 6. And I went to a really strange little school in Cambridge in England, which was set up by Henry the 8th for 16 boys to go and learn music and sing their hearts out. And it's still going, obviously, and then I went there.

This is going to take me some time. In the late 60s, early 70s. So I could read music better than I could read English, at one point.

I was already learning several instruments, but my main instrument was my voice. And so I had a really good foundation — a good education in music. And I'm often asked by young film composers or people who would like to follow that path, "What's the best thing I can do?" And my answer is always the same, which is to get a really good, firm musical education. I think some people think they can jump into film music with technology as it is. You can definitely make musical noises, blips and blurps. But to have some really good understanding of music and the power of that, and be able to harness that in terms of scoring a film, I can't think of anything better than to have a really good musical education. I mean, presumably, if you're going to be an electrician, you've got to learn about electricity first, before you plug anything in. It's the same thing. So I was very fortunate to have that, but I didn't know that I was going to be a film composer. I wasn't even aware of film music, as a small boy, and I didn't follow that path at all. So I went through music scholarships, and then went to music school in London, and after that I turned to teaching music. And it was a little unconventional. Most of my path has been, actually, when I look at it, in so much as I didn't go to teacher training college and learn to be a teacher. It's hypocritical already. I decided to be a teacher without learning to be a teacher.

I wanted something more than just the classroom situation as a different challenge. I went to teach music and sports, actually, in Egypt. In Alexandria — it's obviously quite rough there at the moment, in Egypt. But it was a beautiful place, and it was an amazing place to learn to teach. So, during my teaching of music, I would write things, write music for the kids to sing, play, act. And I wasn't sure whether I necessarily wanted to be an actor or a musician at the time.

I knew where my forte was; it sure wasn't in acting. And also, I got a couple of acting jobs, and realized that really sitting around on a bus waiting for my time to walk on and then walk off again was just not my cup of tea at all. So I took this path and after a while of teaching, I realized I really wanted to stretch my music in a different direction. I wasn't quite sure what that was, and I was really fortunate to be introduced to a fabulous composer in England called Richard Harvey. I called him — someone gave me his telephone number — I called him and said, "Look, could we meet up?" And he said, "Well, hold on a second. Do you play cricket," which is basically your baseball, OK? "Do you play cricket?" And I'm like, "Yeah." "Do you eat curry?" So I said yeah. He said, "Great, you're in my cricket team. Can you come on Sunday, we're playing against some other musical team."

And it turned out he had a studio in a really cool part of London, which I couldn't afford to live in. In fact, I could hardly afford to walk in it. But he had a studio there. It was awesome. He was doing a lot of really high-end TV projects, and a few films projects, and I learned an awful lot from him. And I hung out in his studio in Chelsea in London and learned the ropes. And during that time, I was kind of the guy who made the tea in the studio, and ran around after people.

And there was a directive, suddenly, to clear everything out of one of the studios. So I said, "Well, what do you mean? Like the couches?" "Yeah, everything." "You don't mean the mixing board?" "Yes, everything. We want that room absolutely empty." Now, this was a recording studio, so why would anybody want it empty?

"Yeah, there's this German dude coming over from Los Angeles. He wants the room. He brings all his own gear. Believe

me, this can be a lot of gear. Clear out all the crap in that room."
So we did, and sure enough Hans Zimmer arrived.

I was fascinated by what he was doing. He put all his gear down. He was just finishing The Lion King. He was about to do Crimson Tide, and asked me to do the choirs on that, because he knew that I'd been a choirboy as a little guy and I knew something about choirs.

He assigned me a very attractive Russian translator, and Abbey Road Studio 1, and a bunch of big, bearded sad little Russian sounding men, and he wanted this sort of male voice choir integrated into his score for Crimson Tide, so that was the first thing I did. We became fast friends, Hans and I.

It was from that meeting that I said, "Man, I've really got to follow this path." And after a while, he left this room in London, came back to L.A., and I felt really sad, like an opportunity had passed me by, and then the phone rang. He said, "Look, Harry, I can tell you really want to come and do this," you know. "Dump that crappy car you were driving. Just leave everything as it was, get a one-way ticket, come to Los Angeles, and work with me on The Muppet Treasure Island. Because you know all about kids, you've been teaching. I think this could be your genre." So I was on the next plane.

That was in 1995. So here we are in 2015, and nothing much has changed. I don't make the tea for him, but I came out here on a whim, really, to see if I could make a go of being a film composer, and I was kind of an apprentice. And back then Hans had me as his composing assistant, and a fine composer called Nick Glennie-Smith, who was kind of the outgoing me.

He'd been Hans' composing assistant and was just spreading his wings and about to get his own movies. So there was kind of a gap to be filled, and I moved right into it. And I worked with Hans over the course of a few years, writing the odd cue. I was there if a crumb fell from his table. I was there to pick it up, and to catch it and run with it. And an opportunity did come up, and another opportunity came up, and that's really how I got my start.

What did you learn from working with Hans?

The main things that Hans taught me, have nothing to do with music, so I thought that was nonsense to begin with. And then the more I was able to observe him — the thing is, as an up-and-coming composer, what could be more invaluable than to be in meetings with Tony Scott, Ridley Scott, Jeffrey Katzenberg, but not be the fall guy, or not be the guy on the hot seat? But I was in the back of the room, observing, listening. I was a part of the conversation. Hans was very inclusive in that way. When the time came, I was able to use a lot.

Hans could sell a two-minute silence as an action cue, if he had to. If his life depended on it. He's pretty good at selling his own music. And he's got a great way of understanding his role as a film composer. As to what he could bring to a film, I think I learned a lot that way. Musically, we don't really cross over that much, me and Hans. He has his thing, and I think I have my thing, and perhaps there are some influences I have taken from him.

But come 2 o' clock in the morning, in the car park outside his studio back in the day, in the late 90s, I'd be there fretting about how am I going to get this cue written for a little movie that I'd got. And he would be in the car park, dragging on a cigarette, exactly the same thought going through his mind.

It might have been Gladiator or one of these big things, but the same neurosis occurs whether you're a very successful, Oscar-winning composer as he was or someone starting out as I was. And we kind of used each other. He'd also often drag me into his room, "Harry, listen to this, man. Listen to this theme. I think this is the tune I need."

And he'd listen if I had suggestions. He'd tell me to go away and jump if he didn't like it. But similarly, he would come into my room and give me confidence and give me some positive feedback — something to hang onto. "Harry, I think you need to rewrite that, but I think this part of this is really good." You know? I didn't necessarily have to listen to him, but it was really good starting out to have someone I could look up to.

I always think if I'd have been a sportsman — which I quite would have liked, actually. I was into sports; the English ones: rugby, cricket and football — or soccer, as you call it. Those were the sorts of sports I was into, because they're team sports. I wouldn't have been a tennis player or a golf player. It's kind of you against the world. That sort of slightly narcissistic thing, it's not really my thing. But I like being a part of a team, and composing is a solitary job by its very nature. Hans showed me a way of being quite inclusive.

In fact, one of the main things that he taught me musically was how I could include a director. If I were to ever be the composer on a decent feature film, how I could include the director and

producers in my process. And that was by having all these banks
of samplers that would imitate the sounds of orchestra, so that
I could sample up. when I first came to L.A. in '95, I don't think
I owned a computer, let alone used computers and music. I had
been taught to use a pencil and paper. But Hans was completely
the reverse. He's only had one piano lesson in his life, and that
didn't go well. By his own volition he uses the white keys. black
keys are kind of off limits for him. That doesn't mean to say that
his music is all in A minor.

Listen to Thin Red Line, man. His music travels through many,
many keys and he had found a way of getting these imaginative
thoughts he had out of his head onto the film, and his way was
through these machines. And he showed me that and I've taken 95
percent of that on and run with it.

How do you like to start on a film project? Where to begin?

If we take it down to real basics, you've got to believe in your
product. So for my own part, all I can say is that I generally start at
the piano, because I'm comfortable at the piano. And nothing gets
in between me and the piano like electronics or computers. I'll
find something — a harmonic shift, harmonic sequence, a theme,
a melody that means something to me — that means something
to the film. I'll start with that, and when I'm fairly sure I've got
what I want, then I'll move over to this station here and I'll start
sequencing that music. I'll start arranging what was piano for a
guitar, some drums, and a bagpipe if I want. It's unlimited, the
amount of sounds that one can generate from these samplers,

so that's where the imagination comes in. I always think that if I've had any success in film music, it's because I've been able to harness a small — a nugget — maybe a small theme that probably millions of people could write, the same thing as me. But to take that and make it useful, in terms of the film, and arrange it in such a way that it becomes an integral part of the film, and how it touches the film, how it hits the film, at what moment it starts at the speed it is. The pitch it is, and the keys it runs through, and the emotion that it brings. So as a composer, one's always looking at the characters in the film and what kind of emotional arc they paint and how musically you can track that.

Is it nerve racking to play music for a director for the first time?

Well, yeah. one's watching out for many things when you play music for the first time. Often a director's body language will tell you what's going on. I mean I remember playing the main theme — or I thought it was going to be the main theme — for Shrek in my studio. I was still in Hans' studio at that time.

The G-spot in my studio was a really comfy couch, which was behind where I program and stuff, and Andrew Adamson was sitting there quite sort of benignly and listening to this.

And he suddenly recoiled up, and both feet came up onto the couch. I was like, "Ah, man. He didn't like that." But actually he loved it. He just got excited for a moment. Something touched him. And, yeah, you can read a lot into a situation by someone's body language, not just from a composer's point of view.

You conduct your own scores, whereas many composers do not nowadays. Why do you believe that is valuable for you to do yourself?

I decided early on I was going to conduct my own scores. It's six of one and half a dozen another, you know. If you speak to John Powell or Hans Zimmer they'll say they prefer to be in the control room, not conducting, because that's where everything's fed through. They have more control. Basically, we're all going after the same thing. We want the best result, the best performance for the film.

So my way of getting that is to be in amongst the musicians. It helped that when I got my first few films, Smilla's Sense of Snow, The Borrowers, these films sent me back London to Abbey Road and, hello, in the orchestra were a lot of people who I was at music college with.

And I like being in amongst them, and I feel — what's the difference between conducting in a session as opposed to on a concert platform? In a session, as you know, they have headphones and they're going to have a click track, so they have the beat. So it's completely unnecessary for a conductor to be all rigid and — you know, what? You're giving them the beat twice? No. Absolutely, I find my role will be much more body language, and much more expression and eye contact and bringing performances out. So I think if you watched my conducting in a studio, you'd think, "Wow, they're not going to play very well in time if he gets up on the concert platform, because you won't be able to detect much of a beat." But I don't see it as my role. On the concert platform obviously, they're depending on you for a downbeat, so it's got to be much clearer, much clearer.

Do you ever find the process to wear on you? Perhaps if you're doing a film you aren't quite as passionate about?

I don't find it a grind. I've transformed the way that I go about. Two or three years ago, I got to a point where I was doing probably too many movies a year, and I'm doing much fewer movies now, and I'm trying to do them better, and I have my studio at home which I'm happiest with. So I've changed how I work completely, so I'm a happy guy. I'm very happy with my lot. It's a lifestyle. It's more of getting up in the morning and my first thought is, "What cue am I going to attack today? How can I move the project forward?" So it doesn't feel like work at all, but it is. It is hard work, but it doesn't feel like something I don't want to be doing.

CHAPTER 15

STEVE JABLONSKY

COMPOSER

KNOWN FOR		ACHIEVEMENTS
TRANSFORMERS: THE LAST KNIGHT (2017)	*BATTLESHIP* (2012)	FIVE BMI FILM MUSIC AWARDS
DEEPWATER HORIZON (2016)	*TRANSFORMERS: DARK OF THE MOON* (2011)	THREE BMI TV MUSIC AWARDS
TRANSFORMERS: AGE OF EXTINCTION (2014)	*A NIGHTMARE ON ELM STREET* (2010)	
LONE SURVIVOR (2013)	*TRANSFORMERS: REVENGE OF THE FALLEN* (2009)	
ENDER'S GAME (2013)	*TRANSFORMERS* (2007)	
PAIN & GAIN (2013)	*THE ISLAND* (2005)	
GANGSTER SQUAD (2013)	*THE TEXAS CHAINSAW MASSACRE* (2003)	
DESPERATE HOUSEWIVES (2004-12)		

Tell me about how your career composing for film music began, because you started in computer engineering.

I'll correct you a little bit in that I didn't specifically want to go into film composing, actually. It was more that I got really bored with the computer engineering. My friends, there was a specific day I could remember now like it happened yesterday, that we all came to class after this project, this big project we had to do, and they were all so excited about the way they'd done it. And they were like, "Look at this, look at this." And I was just miserable, you know. I just didn't want to do it. I was bored. And that day I kind of decided, "Yeah, this isn't for me." And I had already taken a bunch of music courses throughout my college career, because I was into music, just playing clarinet and things in high school. So

I said, "Let me just switch to a music major." So it wasn't a specific decision, "I'm going to now pursue film composing." It was more of, "What can I do, now that I've become incredibly bored with what I thought I was going to do in college?" And that was the most logical thing.

I actually thought I was going to be more of a recording engineer, because of the sort of electronic computer background. I had a little studio at my house, so that was what I thought might happen. Film composing was — I don't know that it was even in the picture at that time. It's just music in general was kind of it.

You've found your passion. Do you consider it a job, or is it a hobby you turned into a career?

I tell people all the time that I don't really have a job, because I would be doing this anyway. Before people paid me to do this, I did it anyway, you know. I had a little keyboard. I would sit at home and just orchestrate my own music and, you know, the crappy sounds that I had. And had a blast doing it. And the work part of it comes in when the schedules start to tighten, and sometimes on a project, picture might be changing. The cuts and the edits are changing right up until the last second, so you're just trying to keep up. And you don't want the music to suffer through all these edits that happen towards the end. So it can get a little crazy, and that's when you just have to say, "Alright, we've made sure this gets out to the public, and in the best way possible. And we're just out of time." But, just coming up with the ideas and the music and working with these directors. These are really amazing people in this business — amazingly creative. I learn something every day from these people. So I'd say 90-percent play, and 10-percent, at the end, is when it's really, "Oh, shit, we've got to get it done."

Tell me about your "next-day test" for cues you write.

That's a good test, the next day, if I finish. I often will finish a piece of music — you know, I'll be writing at 11, 12 o'clock at night, having worked on it all day long. I'm like, "This is crazy, this is really exciting, this is it, this is good." You come in the next day. I can't really explain it psychologically; I don't know how it works. But so many times I've come in the next day, and go "Boy, this sucks! What? How did I think this was any good?" Sometimes I will come in the next day and just wonder what was I thinking last night. And it's just because you get into a flow and a roll, and you think this is great, and I don't know, you get so excited about what you're doing. And you lose perspective, I think, is really what it is. So I hate having to write something right up until the moment I'm going to play it to the director or producer or whoever, because I don't have that buffer of "let me get away from it for at least an hour, or a couple hours, preferably overnight, so that I can come in, and sometimes I'll always want to change something, a mix. Maybe it's just a little bit of a mix issue: this is too loud, this is too soft. Because, by the end of the day your ears may be a little shot. But sometimes, you really just, "I don't like it anymore." And I delete it and start over. So that's, that's really for me personally, because I have to like something for at least a couple days before I'm going to show it to anybody else. I'm my own biggest critic. (Laughter.) I listen to this stuff hours and hours every day, and if you do anything for hours a day you're going to kind of lose a little perspective of what you're doing, at least creatively. You get into these things so emotionally, you're so emotionally invested in this music and maybe you're having an off day. But all kinds of things can affect, affect how you're, you know, approaching the music that day. So the next day test, for me, is getting a good eight hours away from a piece of music, coming back to it, opening it up, and giving it a listen from start to finish. Don't think about anything; just play it. And if by the end of it I still like it, then I know, "OK, I can proceed and play this to the director." Or I can finish the idea. Or expand on it. Or make a little mix change here and there.

Sometimes I'll listen to it and I go that's just not right for this movie, and I'll put it away and maybe use it somewhere else. But it's just that, it's a good, for me personally, I don't know if other composers do this, but it's, it's my personal test of if something is worth pursuing or has merit or is right for this particular film. Because my workflow is sort of organic, like I don't have it all in my brain. I have a basic idea of what I want to do with the piece of music that particular day, and depending on what happens in a process, I might go get off on a tangent and it turns out that tangent felt good at the time, but after sleeping on it, I can see that it's just not right.

I think that's a big part of the job, just knowing you have to be very aware of what works and what doesn't because if you, if you keep throwing things at the filmmakers that just don't work, they're not going to want to work with you any more.

So you have to have a good sense of what's appropriate for each scene and be able to police yourself as a composer and stuff like that. I may have spent three days on this but it's just not right, so just throw it away.

With more and more CGI in films, often not on the early cuts you have to score the film to, is it harder to find the right sound?

Yeah, on CGI-heavy films, that's almost always the case, where the first cut I get has little or no CGI in it. Like Transformers specifically, the characters themselves, like Optimus Prime, for example, when they're filming a scene and the actors have to look at Optimus and talk to him, the way they work that on the set is they have a pole, you know. I don't know, a 25-foot pole and a guy standing there holding it like this. And on the top of the pole is Optimus Prime's face, just a cardboard cut out of his face. And the actors, I don't know how they don't laugh, but they're like talking to this face on a pole. And, just so that eye line is correct and they're all looking at the same place.

So that's what I get. I get people with poles, and I get an action scene like — (laughter) — it really just is panning shots of nothing. Occasionally, a car might explode and you go, "Oh, something must have happened there." And then a car will suddenly go flat and you go, "OK, somebody stepped on that car." And I will constantly have to ask either a guy like Michael Bay or I'll call a cutting room, and I'll say, "OK, what's happening right here?" Because I can't tell. And half the time they go, "You know, we're not sure, we're not sure either."

Really, that's part of the issue with these films. Up until the last minute, because computers are computers and you can change anything to the last minute, they often do. And even dialogue, you can change a mouth up until the last minute. They go, "Oh, we don't like those lines anymore. We're going to have Optimus say something completely different." So there are a lot of variables. And I personally try to avoid major scenes that are completely CGI, just because I know there's really no point in me doing it. And I have, because I have done it. I've scored scenes the director might say we really need the music to know what the scene is going to feel like. So I go, "OK," and I just worked to nothing and almost every time I need to a certain extent, re-do it. I mean the emotion might be right, but all the timing is off.

So it's difficult. That's a difficult thing to deal with, because music is kind of about flow and rhythm. And if suddenly there's a new shot there, and you go "OK, but that flowed so nicely before, and the rhythm hit this perfectly." So now I have to figure out how to insert two and a half seconds in there. And it becomes kind of technical. There's a little bit of math involved to make it all sort of fit together. But it's part of the job, especially now. A lot of CGI is where it's at.

Do you like to read the script of a film before watching it?

When you read a script, you imagine a version of that film in your mind. And the odds of that being the same as what the director shoots are pretty much zero percent. So every time I've imagined a film, and The Island is the example I always give, because that's sort of the last time I let a script give me any kind of direction. The scripts are good for basic story. Basic plot points. I know I'm going to need a hero theme. I know I'm going to need action theme, and whatever theme, love theme. But for tone and pace, I don't find them to be very useful, because really — and most directors will, when they shoot, the script is sort of a starting point. The film evolves out of that, in my experience. It's never really the script anymore once it gets on film. The basic lines are there, the basic story's there. But I've found a lot of producers and directors, when I call, I'm about to start a film and I call and say, "Can I get the script?" "Well, you know what, just let us show you. It's not going to help you because we've changed it so much since, on the set, during the filming, during the postproduction, editing. It's not going to help you."

So, I think, like I said, the script is good for the story and the basic points. But I need to get the tone, the real tone, which is where I come in. The feel, the sound of the film. That comes from meeting with the people, getting their ideas, and seeing footage if there is footage to see. And so that's where the real process I think takes place.

Tell me about working with Hans Zimmer and Harry Gregson-Williams.

Everybody, I think in general, thinks Hans kind of gave me my start. Which, if Hans didn't have Remote Control, I probably wouldn't be sitting here. But when I first got to Remote Control,

I didn't really know. Film composing wasn't my goal. I was just such a huge fan of Hans that I thought if I'm going to do recording engineering anywhere, why not at Hans Zimmer's studio, where I love what he does. And so I started interning there. And that's at the same time when Harry had just arrived I think from London, maybe a year before I started.

And he had just acquired all of this gear. He had been working in Hans' room. He had just acquired this huge stack of samplers and computers and things, and he needed someone to help him set it up. And the studio manager at the time, he knew I was — as much as I appreciated the work — I was tired of picking up cables from the cable store and getting coffee. And he said to me, "Do you want to help Harry?" Because Harry needs help. He can't just set all this stuff up. So I helped get his studio going, and got to know him. And at some point he just hired me. I was spending most of my time with him anyway, even though I was technically, still an intern for the studio. I was mostly with Harry. And he would let me sit in while he was writing, and I would see what he was doing. And eventually he just started paying me, and I stopped being an intern. But I learned a lot from watching him, not only to write. I learned a lot of technical things, just seeing how he was using the computer and the different samples. And just a lot of technical stuff that I didn't learn in college, certainly. Because my music education was more general. It wasn't film scoring. It was just sort of general music composition. We didn't get into electronic music at all. So everything with that regard I learned just on my own or at Remote. And just watching Harry work was really cool and informative, and kind of exciting. I could see what he would do with picture, and I was paying very close attention. And that's actually probably when I became more interested in composing music to picture versus just being in the music field and doing whatever — hitting record on the machine. I think that's probably when my interest in film scoring specifically came to be. I grew up in L.A., so I was a film fan since I was very little, so I always appreciated films and film music. But I never thought I would be writing it.

How did you move up into a role as a composer?

Harry would make it clear that it was OK if I wanted to use the studio when he wasn't in there. And it was I think during a film called The Fan, which is a Tony Scott film. He was working on that with Hans, and there was a scene that I — when he left one day — I said, "Oh, let me just try." I don't know what exactly possessed me to do it, but I said I'm just going to mess with that scene. And I scored the scene. I don't remember what I did. It was probably terrible.

But the next day I was still messing with it. Harry hadn't come in yet, and I think one of the studio people walked by, and they're like, "Oh, what's that?" "Oh, I'm just screwing around here." and I played it, and they said, "Oh, that's pretty good." And Harry got word of it and he listened and he's like, "Oh, it's good." And he kind of showed me some things. And not that long after that, he asked me to write a scene for real. It wasn't that film in particular, but I think it was the film he did the following project.

So it started with a little cue. And then I would work when he was gone, so I didn't have any life. I would work with him during the day, and he would leave, and I would work at night. And then I would come back for my day job. And then getting the feedback from him on what I had done that night was really helpful. It was a great learning experience, you know. He gave me a really great schooling as far as film scoring. And just from the basics to the emotion you kind of have to feel it or you don't. But there's a lot of other stuff that goes into it.

I really appreciated Harry's sort of guidance through all that. And Harry really spoke well of me to Hans. Once I started writing more for Harry, they would talk a lot, and Harry would say, "Yeah this guy, this guy's good." And eventually Hans started asking me to write cues for his projects. And it was just sort of a snowball thing. It's all a blur now. I don't even barely remember it. I just know I loved it so much. I was having such a great time that I never really left that building for, I don't know how many years. I was just there all the time. And I guess it paid off, you know. I learned a lot and they, a lot of opportunities came out of that, just being around these people. Watching them deal with the top people in the business. Watching Jerry Bruckheimer come in and sit there and Harry has to play him the cue, and get this feedback from him. And that's a big part of the job, obviously, is you can sit there and write music all day that you think is great. If the filmmakers don't like it, then you could save it for your own CD someday. But you're there to serve the film. You're not there to just write music. You're there to help the film be as good as it can be or help the filmmakers achieve what they want to achieve, just emotionally. Hans and Harry were really great teachers.

That's what Hans seems to have fostered in a number of young up-and-coming composers at Remote Control.

Well, I think Hans has created a really cool environment for composers and I know the world knows that. Hans has a building, and there's a bunch of composers in it. But that's only the beginning of it, really. It's like a small community. When I started, it was actually a very small community. Now it's sort of expanded, and he owns almost the entire block in Santa Monica, I don't know. But when I started it was just a couple of buildings. For instance, I'd be writing a cue, say, later in my career, I'm working on a project. And I'm writing a cue and Hans comes in just to say hi. And I go, "What do you think of this cue?" that's quite a luxury to have to be working on something and have Hans Zimmer come in and give you tips on, "Is it working, or what do you think about this sound?" And so he's created this environment of people helping people. And it all comes from him being just a really generous guy, I think.

I think a part of the reason why he has so many people involved with him is that he just likes to see people like myself start the way I started with him and Harry and then slowly work through this system that he's created. To the point where you're ready to do your own films. Before working with Hans, I couldn't have worked on a film like Transformers. I wouldn't know what the hell to do. And not even musically speaking; it's just dealing with the intense pressure of a $200 million film. The music's a big part of it. I take my job very seriously. And there's a lot more to the job than just writing the music. You have to deal with a lot of things, that it's just too boring to go into, but it's a lot of personalities and people and scheduling and changing things. But personalities being the big one. Watching Hans work with people.

So, it was hard. But thank God it was hard, because now you can throw anything at me, and I've seen it all pretty much. And I'm ready for it. Nothing's going to faze me, because Hans really — whether intentional or not — he really puts you through your paces and makes sure that you don't get off easy. It's a real learning experience. And I think it's genuinely because he wants you to become better.

CHAPTER 16

JOHN DEBNEY

COMPOSER

KNOWN FOR		ACHIEVEMENTS
MOTHER'S DAY (2016)	ELF (2003)	ACADEMY AWARD NOMINATION, THE PASSION OF THE CHRIST
THE JUNGLE BOOK (2016)	BRUCE ALMIGHTY (2003)	
DRAFT DAY (2014)	SPY KIDS (2001)	
JOBS (2013)	THE EMPEROR'S NEW GROOVE (2016)	THREE EMMY AWARDS
PREDATORS (2010)		SEVEN EMMY NOMINATIONS
IRON MAN 2 (2010)	INSPECTOR GADGET (1999)	
GEORGIA RULE (2007)	CUTTHROAT ISLAND (1995)	
CHICKEN LITTLE (2005)		
SIN CITY (2005)	STAR TREK: THE NEXT GENERATION (1994)	
THE PASSION OF THE CHRIST (2004)	HOCUS POCUS (1993)	

Why is music so important to you?

Music, to me, is and was really the first art form that I really responded to. The thing that felt like home — that was most appealing to me.

When I was about 6 years old I started to play guitar, and therefore music has been a part of my life really form the very beginning.

It's truly my lifeblood. It's the way I express myself. It's really everything to me.

Did you always know you wanted to work in a collaborative art form that included visuals for your music?

I loved the idea of music with visuals. I do remember, specifically, that I was really fascinated, probably as a young kid, by the sound with the picture. There was always a connection there for me.

I probably didn't really realize that until much later. Probably, as I started to study music later in life as a teenager, and into my college I think that I gained an appreciation for music and what it can do for a film or a television show. I remember watching The Man From U.N.C.L.E., the original series, as actually a kid, and loving the sound of that music. And fast forward a little bit, and we get into Star Wars, in '77, and hearing John Williams' fanfare for the first time, and realizing that, if you turn the sound down, it's a whole different experience. So somewhere in that area I started to realize that some of these films or TV shows would be very different without that great music.

How do you describe the role music plays in a film?

The role of music can be different from moment to moment. And I'll give you an example. Music sometimes has to carry a scene. Yes, that's true. I think there have been too many directors over the years that have asked me, "This scene isn't so effective, so maybe you can do something with it?"

Other times, its role should be to really not intrude. If something is working, I always feel that the music should not intrude, and it should just be sort of another emotional color in there, that maybe isn't affecting you, or pushing you into a certain emotion, but it's complementing what you're seeing on the screen.

Other times, you just have to be unabashedly glorious, and sometimes you have to really, really make a scene or a sequence work. I find that most often in the opening titles of certain movies. Sometimes the opening title has to really establish what the movie is about.

Often times, I think a good main title, musically, can really transport the audience into the film. So at different moments, it can play different roles, I think.

Do you get a good sense of what you want to do from the idea, or from the script?

Really, once I'm on a film or a TV show, it always is an interesting process to me because I never that sure of what type of music is going to be appropriate for the given show, and there are surprises along the way.

Sometimes you think by reading a script, it should be A, B or C. I've found most of the time that it ends up being a D or an E or an F. It sometimes is very elusive, and the things that you think obviously are appropriate sometimes aren't.

And sometimes you really want to consciously play against what the obvious would be. It's always changing, and that's one of the beauties of what I do, is that I'm never sure where the path's going to lead me. You hope for the best, you hope that's it's going to be appropriate for the film, but you can never plan that going in, at least for me.

You're talking about counterpoint.

Yeah, exactly. I'll give you an example. I just did a show called Houdini for The History Channel. A very big movie series starring Adrien Brody.

Going into that, there were many ways we could have gone. We could have gone very period, very traditional, but this was a moment where I felt that it would be interesting to try to play against the period aspect of this thing and go somewhere else — go very contemporary and go very aggressive. And that's what we did. And I think it worked really, really well because you're musically playing against what you're seeing in the sense that you're not normally hearing very aggressive electric guitars, and heavy synth pads and things like that with a turn of the century character like this. So it was an interesting idea and I think it worked to great effect, playing it against what you'd normally think.

How much control do you find you have over the music, especially compared to directors, producers, etc.?

As composers, we are at the service of the director and what he or she wants. And it really is our job, our crucial job, to establish the tone of what it is that they're thinking in their mind.

What has changed a lot in the last 20 years is our ability to communicate what that music might be. Meaning, when I started out as a young guy, I was on pencil and paper, with a piano. And we really didn't have the great ability to demo the work as we do now. Back then, it was more about playing a theme on a piano or playing a couple of pieces on a piano and hoping the director likes the direction. It used to be, "Bye, see you in four weeks on the scoring stage." And they'd be hearing the music for the first time. It usually was a pretty good experience for them, but there are times when they're hearing things for the first time, back then, that they might be a little bit taken aback — that, maybe it wasn't exactly what they thought.

So nowadays, we really have the ability to, in a very sophisticated way, give them a snapshot, or a pretty good black and white or semi-color snapshot, of what the score will be, and that's really helpful. Because then we can work here in my room to finesse it, and we don't have to wait until the scoring stage to have a surprise.

Do you ever have really strange musical requests from a director? How do you work with them?

They come with those requests all the time. Meaning, there are always a lot of creative chefs in the kitchen. Obviously, the director is the most important chef, but you will have networks, you will have film companies that have a certain idea of what they think it should be. And the seasoned composer can kind of navigate that. You have to learn how to navigate it. There are things that you might try that I might inherently think aren't appropriate, but try it. You hope that if you give it a really good shot, and people see it, that they may realize it's not the way to go. But you're always going to have that. It's a collaborative effort. Film has always been that way. I think actors, actresses — they may feel what way a scene should go, but maybe they get input from the director and people as to how to take a character. So it's the same with a composer. You really have to have a pretty good handle on how to deal with people in a positive way and try to keep those ideas, try to manifest them. And if they aren't right, hopefully the room will know, and we'll kind of navigate that. But you have to always try things, to the point of, if it doesn't work, it doesn't work. But you have to try.

There are a lot of crazy things that you have to sort of score. You have to kind of intellectualize them, and you have to ask yourself, "How am I going to do this?"

Probably one of the harder things that I've ever had to do or figure out was The Passion of The Christ. And how do you intellectualize or try to put music to this story. And some pretty difficult scenes to watch. So it's always sort of a process in that regard.

What do you consider to be your process?

You always try to find that thing. I always look for in every film, that moment when I feel I've unlocked the key to something. For me, invariably, I learn if I'm on the right track with a score when — if I don't get tired of something I've written after a couple of days, and I revisit it and I start to go "Mm, maybe there's something there." That's sort of my process.

The other part of that equation is when I get the director in for the first time, and I can play them a couple of ideas. Invariably, that's when you know if you're on the right track or not. And, by the way, sometimes they don't go that well. (Laughter.) Sometimes you're completely off. But you know that quickly, and that's part of the process. And that's, to me, as valuable as hitting a home run the first time out.

Once you get some feedback, you sort of know which way not to go, and then you try another way. And over time you find that direction, and you actually unlock what does become that score.

How can you know you're maximizing the musical effect, without overpowering a scene?

That's a pretty critical and crucial subject that composers have to deal with. I'll give you an example: The actor/actress metaphor again. I think that's where the director can come in and say to the actor, "You're being a little broad. Let's pull it down a little bit." Same with a composer.

Sometimes, we think we've just written the most beautiful piece of music of all time. And then when you're sitting with the director and you're sitting with the creative team, sometimes you realize "This is really too much. It's saying too much. It's really taking over the scene." And you kind of find that out by being in the room with the director. It's something to be very cautious about, because if you fall too much in love with your music, you're going to think that every moment your music should be on 10 and the dialogue should be on 1. It just doesn't work that way. There are times when the music should have its moment, and there are many times when it shouldn't.

I'm one of those people that react to music when it's too loud. And a lot of times I'll go to a dub — a dubbing stage, where they put all the pieces together for a film — and if I feel the music's a little too loud here and there, I'll say it. And that's sort of my mantra. I'm usually going toward erring to subtlety, as opposed to big sort of overtness of the music.

Let's talk about conducting. Why do you like to conduct, when so many other modern composers don't?

I conduct today because, first off, I enjoy it. It is to me the culmination of the process. Sitting in front of a keyboard for 12, 18 hours a day, 14 hours a day, is not my ideal of a good time. (Laughter.) What my idea of a good time is making the director happy — that makes me feel great, if I've done a meeting, director's liking the direction of the music. That's the first thing. The second thing would be being in front of the orchestra. Being in front of live musicians. It could be one, it could be 90. That's, to me, where the ultimate creation happens, because it's not until those musicians take a hold of the notes you've written, and impart life to it — it's really just nothing. It's just something you made up on a keyboard and who cares? (Laughter.) Who cares? So I live for that.

Did you ever get a request to save money by not using a live orchestra?

Well, they all ask. The new reality in Hollywood these days

is that every studio and every production company has gone through cost cutting periods. But composers have also felt that, and we've had to rethink a lot of how we do things. There is always that element of, "Can we do this more cost effectively?" There are always ways to do things more cost effectively. But it makes our job so much harder when, let's say a director wants a big orchestra and big orchestral sound. If the budget isn't there for that, it becomes very difficult and we end up trying to create that in the box. And maybe we use a smaller ensemble to sweeten it to try to make it sound like a big orchestra. So there are challenges these days, and that question of can we do it somewhere more cheaply invariably comes up.

My pushback to that is that I hope, at least in my career and working life, that I don't ever have to deal with the idea that there are no live musicians on a score, because that would be really tough to handle.

My life, my livelihood is based on having great musicians come in either single or in a group to really birth the music.

We're in the middle of that. And sometimes you win that battle, and you can do something creatively that you feel is appropriate, and other times you have to deal with it. Depending on the situation.

How close does a score sound on a scoring stage? Does it sound better or worse than what you've mocked up in a computer?

For me, better. There's still no substitute for real players, just to be honest with you. it's getting really sophisticated — all of our sample libraries are getting very sophisticated — and that's good. Those are tools that we use to try to represent the music in the best way we can. But there's still no substitute for a great string player, great guitar player, thankfully, great horn player, great flute player.

Now, I do complete synth scores that are very contemporary, and that's great too, but if I have a choice, if I'm going to do a great orchestral score, there's nothing like having the real musicians. I'm going to keep fighting to have that.

What does it feel like to be in front of an orchestra conducting as they're playing your music?

It's a pretty wonderful experience. To those composers who don't do it, I would hope they'd give it a shot. Because, to me, there's nothing more immediate than standing on a podium and giving a downbeat to a piece of music that you spent a long time crafting, and hearing it for the first time. It's — I guess it's like seeing your child for the first time being born. The joy, the emotion of what that is.

I did something recently — I had to go to London, which is never a problem because I love London — but had to work over there, and worked with the great musicians over there. And again, hearing your music for the first time being played by really quality musicians, whether it be in L.A. or London, whatever. There's nothing like it. It sort of invigorates you. It's scary, if things aren't the way you thought and you have to make changes. But it is truly. I think I get the best performance for the music when I'm on the podium.

It's sort of like if an artist is sketching something, and then somebody else comes in to fill in the color. you may or may not get what you want. But if I'm on the podium, I'm going to get exactly what it is, because I know in my head what it should be, before they're even playing it.

The first time through, for instance, I know immediately what I want to change, what I want to do, what I want to make a volume change or a note change. To me, it's an incredibly important part of what I do.

Speaking about the orchestra in terms of colors — can you explain the concept of color, and describe the different colors, or voices, or textures at your disposal when using an orchestra?

Really, the instruments in the orchestra are colors. The oboe is a great example. Oboe is always thought of with that love theme, or that really sad theme. Directors a lot of times will ask me, "What's the instrument?" That's the oboe, or that's the clarinet. And they'll go, "I don't like it; it's too sad."

Bassoons are sort of the comedians of the orchestra, for animation especially. They're always that funny sound that you hear that's sort of low. Color can be a lot of different things under different circumstances.

It's so much fun to think of instruments and what emotion they evoke. We mentioned the oboe, which is sad. The cello is angst-ridden and passionate. The high violin could be kind of silly in the sense of an over-the-top love scene. The trombones, they're the jokesters. They always hear a joke and tell a joke. Then they're playing something like the Imperial March. They're the meat and the guts.

The french horns are just the heroes of the orchestra. Most every big theme — and love — has probably been played by a french horn. The harp is the magic; it's the little fairy dust that does things during transitions in music. It's kind of the utility instrument of the orchestra because it can do so much. Some of my other favorites are things like saxophones. It's jazz and sex but can be really silly, too.

Flutes are the birds of the orchestra. They make you feel high like a bird flying through that air. That's a flute. So each instrument has its own thing. Timpanis are sort of classical drums. Certain instruments have difficulty being something they're not. It's like people. You are who you are. You can't take a flute sound and process it electronically so that is something that isn't a flute anymore. They're not the trombones.

CHAPTER 17

TREVOR RABIN

RECORDING ARTIST & COMPOSER

KNOWN FOR		ACHIEVEMENTS
MAX (2015)	*NATIONAL TREASURE* (2004)	ASSOCIATED ACTS: YES (FOUR STUDIO ALBUMS)
GRUDGE MATCH (2013)	*BAD BOYS II* (2003)	
RACE TO WITCH MOUNTAIN (2009)	*REMEMBER THE TITANS* (2000)	ONE GRAMMY NOMINATION, *BEST MUSIC VIDEO*
NATIONAL TREASURE: BOOK OF SECRETS (2007)	*GONE IN 60 SECONDS* (2000)	THREE ASCAP AWARDS
SNAKES ON A PLANE (2006)	*DEEP BLUE SEA* (1999)	SIX BMI FILM MUSIC AWARDS
COACH CARTER (2005)	*ENEMY OF THE STATE* (1998)	
EXORCIST: THE BEGINNING (2004)	*ARMAGEDDON* (1998)	
	CON AIR (1997)	

You come from the hugely influential rock band Yes. How did that inform the way you approach film scores?

As far as Rock & Roll, I actually didn't start as a rock player. My father was the leader of the Johannesburg Symphony Orchestra, and I studied classical piano, and I did that for years. I started with a great guy, the head of the university in Johannesburg. I studied privately with him, orchestration, arrangement, formal analysis, composition. And then at about age 12, I got a guitar as a gift for winning a piano competition.

Having studied classical music, and then gone into rock with a pretty classically oriented band, Yes, it wasn't regular kind of Led Zeppelin kind of stuff. But very much doing shows, and preparing and choreographing shows, and making albums where the sequencing in those days years ago was very important. I think that helped in the entertainment value of the film. You can't just write wallpaper music and let it lie there; it has to complement the film. And I think coming from that performance side of this really helped enhance the performance of the actors, hopefully.

How is a film score like a song?

The most important thing, for me, with film scoring is theme. In that sense, it is very much like writing a song. If you have a theme that people can remember, hum to themselves. if someone is walking out and is humming the melody, and you ask them what is that, and they say, "I don't know" because they've sort of just unconsciously enjoyed the theme, and has tied that theme to the various characters. But I think theme is really the important thing. Obviously, the style of the movie, the genre and what you're doing for the instrumentation is pivotal and vital to what you're doing, but I still think theme is the most important thing, and coming from a songwriting perspective, I think that helps.

When writing a pop song, you do have to get to the essence of what you're selling pretty quickly. With film, you have more time to develop and if you don't give yourself time to develop, you can paint yourself into a corner, and half through the movie, you're done. But I think it's really important to try and give a suggestion of theme the music's going to be early on. So I don't believe you should give yourself too much time before you get into thematic elements of the film. And talk about the difference between penning lyrics to a song and writing something for a film that is purely instrumental.

If I write a song and then put the lyrics to it, the lyrics are sometimes a bit of a task. Whereas when I write a song where the lyrics come first, it's easier to write the music to it. I find it harder to write lyrics to music than music to lyrics if that makes sense.

Writing film music doesn't burden you with lyrics. Although I like writing lyrics, I can really concentrate on the essence of the music.

One thing I've always found kind of strange about film music is the guys who come to it from an orchestral point of view, and then — I don't want to mention names, but there are people who, without an orchestral background, and give it to an orchestrator to do. And a large part of what that film score becomes is from the orchestrator. If you look back at the greats, you would say to them, "Oh, I like your orchestration on the fifth." It's part and parcel of the whole thing. When I'm writing music, I'm writing the themes, but the orchestration is very much part of that. I remember doing something once and it was transcribed, the french horn part was put on a trumpet because it was too high. It wasn't too high for a great horn player; it was fine. And I remember getting in a fit because it'd been given to the trumpet part, to the trumpet player, and I said, "No, I want this on the french horn. I want it to struggle. That's part of why it's on the french horn."

Why do you think orchestral music is thought of as being "less cool" than pop or rock music?

I think if young people just gave themselves the chance to

listen — maybe there should be a short list of really cool things to listen to, because if you have to go through 100 symphonies, you're going to get pretty bored, you know.

It's an interesting thing. My son, who's in a band called Grouplove, and they're doing very well right now. But many years ago, his friend came to him and said, "Oh, I heard this band, The Beatles. They sound just like the Electric Light Orchestra." And it was just because they didn't understand that every note Jeff Lynn ever wrote came from The Beatles, and it's not the other way around. And a lot of John Williams scores, and other people, these great melodies, you can hear have been inspired by some of the late greats.

For kids who haven't heard a lot of orchestral music, and they hear John's score to Star Wars or something, it's like "Oh, that's really cool, that's really great," but nothing new has ever been done. It's all been done before.

Again comparing rock with orchestral film scores: How do the sounds you can write differ?

One of the first things my professor said to me was, "You've got to remember, the orchestra has no pedal." And that was one of the earlier things he said, but just the color. There's so much on the palette for the orchestra, which you don't have in a rock setting or a jazz setting, unless it's specifically done to that end. If you listen to a great overture with an orchestra, there's just so many colors and so many avenues to go down, light and shade, which you just don't have with a modern day rock band, or dance music, or whatever you want say.

I was going to use the word finesse because, the ability to light and shade an orchestra is just so extreme, and it's just so rare. Rarely do you hear that in the Rock & Roll world. The orchestra can have just a powerful presence, and then go down to such a tiny presence. you have an oboe with a tiny melody only to be enveloped by everything.

Tell me about the schedule for composing a film. What kind of time do you get to make it?

If we're talking about animation, that can take sometimes years to get done. But if it's just a general movie, someone comes to you just roundabout post, or even if you're hired beforehand, you get involved somewhere around post. It's usually around six to 10 or 12 weeks of time you get. It has gotten worse and worse, because every time someone sets a precedent of, "Oh, this is great, he got to do it in six weeks," the next guy who comes along is like, "Well, scores take six weeks," and then the new person gets five weeks, and pretty soon you're getting very little time. Or less time than it used to be.

I think eight weeks should be a reasonable amount of time to get a film done. More is better, but I've gone on to projects when they haven't liked what's been happening, and want to change the score, and I've had two or three weeks to do it. And I know some guys have had less than that. I think as much as you try and as hard as you try, you're not going to be able to give the same time and energy and commitment as if you had 10 weeks.

The first week is always a terrifying week, because I spend the first week usually just watching the film, without really looking at it, just letting it run, and start writing themes, and then if I get to a theme and, "Oh, that suits that" then I'll just have a skeleton, and another skeleton, and it'll just be this mess over a long thing of watching the film. And then I'll start developing those themes, and then there'll be one or two of those themes that I just haven't come to terms with. And it's always kind of terrifying because I've got to start scoring this movie, but I don't want to start doing it until I have the themes.

How do you overcome that?

I usually would do what I fondly describe as an underture, which is underscore, but an overture meaning all the themes, trying to write just about all the themes hopefully, and have them interact with each other and work together and play this long piece of maybe a five to eight minute piece of music for the director. Because, if he hears it and likes some of the themes, when you apply them to the picture, temp-itis kind of disappears.

So I like that, but sometimes if that underture is taking too long, I'm starting to move into the territory of leaving myself five weeks to do this, and four weeks.

That, to me, is the terror. Getting all the themes written. Once that's done, then it's just sort of getting it done in the time period you have. And then the movie gets cut, so you have to take that into consideration, and then, weeks in, the director will come in and say "I like that theme, but maybe we shouldn't use it on him.

Maybe we should use it on him, and use the other theme on him." And it's not a jigsaw puzzle; you can't do that. It all has to be re-written. So there are many things that cause detours.

Sometimes there's the movie where you have very little time, and there's quite the support, or the budget, so it's nice when there's a good budget.

When you hear a finished score in a film, how often do you still have the urge to keep working on it and refining it further?

I have not written a score yet, out of close to four dozen movies, where I haven't thought at the premiere, "Ah, I'd like to do that again." So I think the idea of, if I had endless time — I'd never finish. Deadlines are really good for me. I need them, and they help me get things done, because every day is a new day and every day you kind of got to come in and do it. There's no day off. Actually, weekends don't mean anything to me once I'm on a film.

Where do you usually begin in terms of uncovering the right sound for a film?

I like to start by reading the script first and foremost, and getting an idea of what these people look like, and then getting maybe a rough cut. And I really like to do that before I get to spotting. So by the time I get to spotting, I've got a idea of some of the themes already. Now that's not necessarily always how it happens. Sometimes you're booked for a movie and the next day is spotting, so that's harder. I always like to see the film before spotting so I have some input into the spotting.

What do you look for in a spotting session with the director?

Spotting, to me, is really important, because it gives me an idea of what the director's looking at and what he's looking for. When I watch with the spotting, they play the temp score with it, so I get an idea of what he wants to do. Once I start scoring, I very rarely listen to the score. My ambition is to get to a point where the director doesn't care about the temp anymore. "Oh, you've brought something that gives us something that enhances further than what the temp does." That's important to me.

How much music are you usually writing for a film?

The amount of music going into film, generally? We'll say that in the 50s and during that time, there might be 20 minutes or 30 minutes. I remember Psycho; there was very little music in it. But the music that was there was incredibly important, and really worked. These days it seems like there's a want for as much music as possible. If a movie's an hour and a half long, or an hour 40 long, I've done scores where you've written 90 minutes of music for the film. They end up taking some out. I would say it's usually at least an hour of music, for a full-length picture. And if you've written an hour, you've probably written an hour 40, with all the stuff that's been thrown out. Action movies tend to have more music than a romantic comedy, because the action needs to be played at all times. And it's quite difficult to do, because part of the time with an action movie, you're fighting with the special effects. So where you take the special effects out, and just watch the picture with the dialogue, and you think "Wow, this is really exciting." But you put the picture with the dialogue, and there's just not enough room. So you have to scale back on it and write it differently. So it's very important to take into consideration the special effects. Now, the special effects you are often using on a film, it's not the final special effects. They just kind of like a working track of special effects, but you get an idea of what they're going to do in the final film and how much space they're going to take.

Your music from Remember the Titans has been used for many things, including sporting events around the world and the 2008 election night victory speech by President Barack Obama. Do you ever think about whether a cue might be used for something else?

The score for Remember the Titans is one of the scores I was very happy with, which doesn't happen very often. But the movie came out, and the movie did very well, and because of that movie, I was asked to do the theme for the NBA, which I did, and it's been playing for the last 15 years or something. Sounds very different from Remember the Titans, but it's because they liked the theme from Remember the Titans.

But I'll never forget this as long as I live. When President Obama was at the acceptance speech, which I think was in Denver in a big stadium or something, I was watching it. And the phone rang, and it was Joel McNeely, who's a friend of mine and a great composer, and he said, "I'm at the convention, and Remember the Titans" is playing as loud as a Kiss concert. Fireworks were going on, and it was quite a moment. And I thought it worked. I thought it was written for it. So that was really enjoyable. Titans was also used for the last seven or eight Olympics, the last Olympics, it's always been the Titans score. So it's quite interesting, watching it being used for something completely different. Sports as it may be, and in Obama's case, politics. It's a very different placement with how I used it with Titans, but I think it worked, I think because it's very stirring. I went for a very stirring piece of music for that, and it worked.

Joel said to me, "Are you happy about this," and I said, "Well, I wasn't asked, which I'm not happy about, but I'm very happy it was on Obama's speech rather than the other guy."

Did you ever get paid for that being used publicly?

No! No, you don't get paid for that. It's looked upon as news. I wasn't asked, and I don't think I got paid for it.

It's funny, particularly on Remember the Titans, the music, for me, was written so specifically for that. I never really thought about whether it could be used elsewhere, and then to hear it at Obama's speech, and it worked so well. I kind of got a lump in my throat. It was quite amazing. It might have been him, but I like to take credit for it. Yeah, it was all me, it had nothing to do with what he said. (Laughter.)

CHAPTER 18

PATRICK DOYLE

COMPOSER

KNOWN FOR		ACHIEVEMENTS
CINDERELLA (2015)	*BRIDGET JONES'S DIARY* (2001)	ACADEMY AWARD NOMINATION, DRAMATIC SCORE, *HAMLET*
JACK RYAN: SHADOW RECRUIT (2014)	*GREAT EXPECTATIONS* (1998)	
BRAVE (2012)	*HAMLET* (1996)	ACADEMY AWARD NOMINATION, DRAMATIC SCORE, *SENSE AND SENSIBILITY*
THOR (2011)	*SENSE AND SENSIBILITY* (1995)	
RISE OF THE PLANET OF THE APES (2011)	*A LITTLE PRINCESS* (1995)	TWO GOLDEN GLOBE NOMINATIONS
ERAGON (2006)	*MARY SHELLEY'S FRANKENSTEIN* (1994)	
HARRY POTTER AND THE GOBLET OF FIRE (2005)	*CARLITO'S WAY* (1993)	LIFETIME ACHIEVEMENT, WORLD SOUNDTRACK AWARDS
NANNY MCPHEE (2005)	*DEAD AGAIN* (1991)	
GOSFORD PARK (2001)		

You've talked many times about the concept of gesamtkunstwerk. Can you explain what that is and why it's important?

It's really an expression that Wagner used to describe his life and the world of opera. Because he felt — and the same applies to film, in my opinion, it's to me a no-brainer that — all the elements in film make up the whole. So each of the disciplines in film are as important as the other. Sound, score, costumes, makeup, lighting. The phrase means, "total art."

And really, it's about arts, all the arts in the film. So I suppose I think operatically, in terms of the harmonies I use and the way I approach a score. I concentrate very much on the narrative and the characters.

You began as an actor and moved away from it. How did that change the way you thought about music in film?

I was a long time ago. I do the odd thing now for fun, but yes, I gave up the acting seriously almost 30 years ago now. My work as an actor definitely informs the way I write, without a doubt, because I see certain performances and sometimes see inherent weaknesses in this performance. Where the director has been able to, or the actor wasn't able to provide what was required and the music in certain circumstances helps a lot in terms of injecting certain elements that are missing there. So it definitely informs my work, without a doubt.

What do you consider your goal, when it comes to scoring a film?

Well, the ultimate aim is to create a strong theme for a character. The leading hero in a film like Thor. And this theme in fact I wrote — really, it was based on what could be a little tune from perhaps the Norse countries and the Scandinavian world that became a sort of homeland theme for Thor being estranged from Asgard and on earth, and that's how that theme came out. And it has this element of heroism and pathos in it. It has this sort of homeland thing. It's like a folk tune. That theme is much more choral. But if it was played accompanied by a guitar or a little folk harp, it would become quite a different folky sound. But it has an element of strength in it, as well as pathos and heart. And that's what that character had in abundance.

And also in Cinderella, I suppose. One of the heroes is the character, the prince. The high rising sort of figure gives you a sense of space and air and testosterone and it's sort of youth and joy. Those are the things you look for. Again, coming from a character-based root. Really, it's about the journey of the character. Where is the character going? What's he or she like? Why are they like this? What are the striking elements in a character like Thor? What's his dilemma? The father element. The connection with his father. There's the massive sort of ego they both have, and the eventual splitting of the father-son relationship in terms of power. One wants power. And the other one is wiser. The other one's younger, more impetuous. All these sort of elements — they get mixed in your head before you embark on writing a theme.

How do dialogue and sound effects interact with music and does it limit your ability to do anything?

Well, dialogue does reign supreme. You have to hear what they're saying. (Laughter.) You have to know what the film's about and what's the narrative. So it's important to write around the dialogue, and for the dialogue. And there's an interesting case of the music and dialogue. If there's a voiceover in the film, generally speaking. You play the voice over. You don't play the action behind it. You play what you are hearing. And they're always tricky for a composer to do, because immediately, voiceovers are there giving information. They'll be setting up the film. Either for very good reasons, or for lack of filming or lack of clarity to a story. Or throughout, in the case of Cinderella, it's just really for this sort of nice, charming, tradition of, and episodic chapters where Helena Bonham Carter would say, "And so, Cinderella found herself alone and blah blah blah." So these are, these are nice sort of comforting little pieces of conducting for the younger people, and part of that tradition. And so invariably you play the voiceover.

Really, your job is to weave in and out. And I pride myself in — even at the height of some action pieces of music and in orchestrally coming down for an important piece of information to come back up again. And also, it makes the music interesting as a result. People say, "Are you bound by dialogue?" No, that's what makes it interesting. You have to be far more inventive. you can't cut to cut to cut.

You've written so many memorable and powerful scores over the years. What do you consider your proudest achievements in the art form?

Fortunately, I'm still in many ways a cynical person, or an older person. Well, not cynical meaning wise. I would say that at times. But I'm aware of how the world works. But I still haven't lost my joy in listening to good music, and the joy of writing it, and the great satisfaction of hearing people play music, and the great privilege it is to have people play your music.

I'm working with a group of young students in Scotland on a new program we're trying to get going there, and it's doing well. They're performing a score of mine for a silent movie, and they're doing it live to picture. It's from my home shire in Scotland.

No matter how much older I get, I still haven't lost my joy and love of music and listening, and the joy of listening to music and to writing music. And I have the great privilege of people playing music. I never ever take it for granted. It's always an enormous pleasure. It's always very exciting.

For me, it was thrilling to see these young people writing, and you take your instructions and your guidance and suddenly they're paying leaps 30-percent, 40-percent forward. I mean and I've been working with these kids on and off for over a year and the difference from a year ago to now is unbelievable. And this program I hope continues because it's the first time in schools they've had children playing live to click with a picture.

Film is a massive thing, and now for everyone it's a huge thing in the world. And to be part of this program and see kids enjoy music and drama and what it's doing for them, and for myself.

Your battle with cancer changed the way you think about music. What happened and how did it help you beat it?

During my illness, I remember my wife put on a piece of music — in fact it was a piece of Mozart — and I had been suffering from, I suppose what's called clinical depression. And instigated by the chemo, and at this point I was actually in a very dark place. So when I hear people talk about depression, I think, "Well, I hope it wasn't the depression I experienced," because depression was — my brain was blacker than the lacquer on this piano.

And so when I heard this music, it was listening like

digital chips you see landing in front of me. It was like brittle, meaningless. And, in fact, my wife did realize finally that actually it's compounding my despair, because I thought, "Oh, my God, you don't have the wherewithal, there's nothing there left to rationalize. The rationality in your psyche has gone, because what's left is a husk really." You don't have the rationale to say, "Oh, well, this is just the depression, the result of the chemicals. And you will get better and you will experience music again the way you did before." And that doesn't even come in. You're just in that place, that's it.

And then they gave me antidepressants, which I actually resisted because of a bizarre Calvinist sort of upbringing that I've had. (Laughter.) I somehow or another wasn't dealing with it. They're like, "What are you taking?" Chemo and this and that thing, and if you use an antidepressant. And then I realized, of course, I'd have to take that advice. And then miraculously, it was within a couple weeks, I could listen to music again. It was quite an emotional thing. So that has an impact for the rest of your life.

But, bizarrely, I was in the middle of an animation film, and because animation is a locked, is a locked picture. There are no changes really, once it's established. Way better than live, it's a locked picture, so you're not having to deal with the vagaries of changes that are absolutely commonplace these days. And the director at Warner Brothers gave me an extra month, so I said I'd give myself three weeks.

So I sat down one day, and I started to doodle, and my music editor would send a blank manuscript. In the old days, instructions, all the actor's instructions, were in it. And so I had it in my room, so I just started writing the old way, by hand. And I wrote about 30 seconds, and I thought, "Well, that's not bad." I did look a bit like Tom Hanks in Philadelphia, sort of was my thing.

Anyway, my brother rigged up a video machine and my TV was on the fridge. And in the old days, you had the remote control at an angle, and the cassette in those days, they'd beam it from the little rig. He built me a little rig made of melamine. And I wrote on this rig. In fact, that was part of my process every day. I would clean it myself because I was neutropenic — I had no defenses so you were completely neurotic about having your room sterile.

So I took it upon myself to give me something to do — to clean it every day. I cleaned this part of my room every day as part of the getting up and doing something process. But I don't know how I wrote music, to this day. I have no idea. The professor came in one day, and had a long chat. They give you so much freedom to do anything you wanted to enable you to get through this process. At least that was the protocol at this hospital. Some other hospitals are quite strict.

But they were very relaxed about this sort of idea, if it made you feel better. But he asked me, "How could you do this? Because I've never seen any kind of intellectual pursuit during this horrific process." And I said I have no idea. "We were all fascinated at how you could do this, because I myself — and he's a leading specialist in leukemia research — spent two days one time with an illness and I was going stir-crazy. I couldn't even read a tabloid newspaper." And I said, "I wish I could give you an answer. I have no idea."

It could inform your playing, retrospectively, but at the time there's some part of your brain, I discovered, a composer's brain, that is totally and utterly detached from the rest of reality. It's a strange thing, and I'm here to prove that. The quality of the score I think it was as good as anything I've ever written. And all the same, the same detail that I like to inject into a score is there. But in terms of the work, the process, the craft, it was totally unaffected by that situation.

So the process of being a composer, I don't think that you can say Mozart felt this, or Haydn felt that. No. If the bombs are dropping around you, a composer can write. There's some part of the brain I've discovered that's uniquely separate from everything else. So, it doesn't matter that, it's just that everything switches off. And it's inexplicable.

I think there's something there in the makeup of a composer or maybe even a writer.

Do you think a composer's brain thinks in terms of music? Do you hear music in your head?

I constantly think music. It's just a bit of a curse — or a blessing. It's just endless. It's endless. Tunes are endless. Tapping is endless. Rhythm is endless. You hear sirens, and I can write when we go on holiday to France. We're lucky to have a place in France, I could have the kids running around, bouncing balls, throwing things, screaming at each other in the old days. But the minute someone starts to tap — "Don't do that!"

But in terms of the artistic process, whenever I read things I think, "No, that's not true. Mozart didn't feel that. Beethoven didn't feel that. Stravinsky did not feel that." He could just do it. Stravinsky could write on a plane. He just loved traveling to avoid tax. He wrote on a plane. You could write. I mentioned the noise of the kids passing, I don't hear it. I'm from a big family, 12 brothers and sisters, so I'm used to noise. But the minute there's a tap or a rhythm, that part of your body that's completely wired to rhythm and sound and the combination of all those things, it becomes an issue really.

If someone's tapping, don't do that. They could be throwing balls past my head. Don't hear it. I read about an alpha state, which we all inhabit. We all go into an alpha state to write. And I totally buy that because people meditate and search for this alpha state, because things happen. And your life changes when you reach that. That's why Buddhists meditate. I believe all that. I think it's a very powerful, powerful thing.

SCORE: THE INTERVIEWS

CHAPTER 19

MERVYN WARREN

RECORD PRODUCER & COMPOSER

KNOWN FOR	ACHIEVEMENTS
JOYFUL NOISE (2012)	ASSOCIATED ACTS:
DREAMGIRLS (2006)	TAKE 6
(MUSIC ARRANGER)	(TWO STUDIO ALBUMS)
HONEY (2003)	FIVE GRAMMY AWARDS
MARCI X (2003)	10 GRAMMY NOMINATIONS
A WALK TO REMEMBER	SIX DOVE AWARDS
(2002)	10 DOVE NOMINATIONS
THE WEDDING PLANNER	SOUNDTRACK PRODUCER,
(2001)	BEST-SELLING GOSPEL
STEEL (1997)	ALBUM, ALL TIME,
	THE PREACHER'S WIFE
THE PREACHER'S WIFE	BY WHITNEY HOUSTON
(1996) (SOUNDTRACK)	

At it's best, what do you think music can do for a film?

Film music takes the viewer on a journey, or at least it supports the journey that the director is taking the viewer on.

When it works well, film music helps to take the viewer on the journey that the director wants the viewer to go on. The music has to be interesting, and yet it has to be unobtrusive. And it can make you feel things that you might not feel if the music weren't there.

Do you think people react to music in different ways?

I think it's just human nature. I think we all react to music in some way. People refer to it as the universal language. Part of it, of course, is what we've been exposed to and the kinds of music we listened to growing up. That sort of thing.

But most humans respond to music in one way or another. And I think that's why the score is so important in a film, because it really can help the viewer feel what the director wants him to feel. That sounds like manipulation and in a small sense it is. But I think that's an important part of the art piece, is to help the listener and the viewer feel something, along with those pictures, and to go along on that journey, and to have an emotional experience, and be drawn into that story. I love the process. I am a songwriter and record producer as well. And that's a very different almost part of the brain. I don't want to say left brain-right brain, but it's a different process. And both I find enjoyable. One is a shorter-length process. Film is a longer process — several weeks typically.

And it's very different than just writing music that you just want to hear that isn't attached to a picture. When the music is attached to picture, it takes on a different character, and can actually become a character. And I really enjoy that entire process. People have asked me, "Which do you prefer? Do you prefer film scoring? Do you prefer producing records?" I really enjoy both and can't imagine doing one to the exclusion of the other. So I can't imagine not doing film. It's just hard work. But it's a lot of fun.

How should music interact with a picture in a film? In what ways do you try to add meaning to it?

Well, you have a scene in a film. Of course, in a movie you're going to have many. But, to answer your question, you have a scene, you're watching that scene, and you're trying to come up with music that supports the scene — that helps to tell the story, helps to support the story and complements it in an unobtrusive way.

So, depending on what you're looking at, there's math involved, because perhaps there is something that happens at one point, and then there is something that happens exactly 11 seconds later, or 44 seconds later. You have to sort of map those things out. And depending on the style and depending on the director's taste and your own, you may have to figure out a way to musically emphasize events that were not done with a click track. All of a sudden, there's something here, and here, and you have to mathematically figure out how to punctuate those moments musically. So there's so there's math involved. Of course, there are computers that help us now. And back in the old days, it was all done manually, and with calculations. Computers help but still we have to you know sort of figure out the best way to approach all of those moments.

I wouldn't say it's daunting, but it is exhilarating. You've got this clean palette to use a cliché. And you've got images. When I see images, I hear music.

It may not be the right music, but I hear music. And so it's at the beginning. Part of the process is determining what I think might work well. And then collaborating with the director, showing him some things, getting his feedback, finding what he or she likes. And sort of coming to a consensus in terms of the direction.

The first few cues are often sort of an exploratory period, once you're sort of setting the tone. Especially, if I haven't worked with that director before. I'm sort of learning what he or she likes. And then after a while you sort of settle into the style of the piece, and then you can sort of go from there. But you're starting out with nothing, and it's a matter of figuring out what is the style, what is the tone, what is the direction here. And how are we going to best support the picture.

Most composers get a different sense of the music needed for a film from its script than from the picture. Do you notice that as well?

Oh, it's night and day. Depending on the type of movie, I sometimes do read the scripts in advance. And it's we form our own pictures, and it's just like reading a book or a novel; you form pictures in your mind. But until you actually see footage, you don't know exactly what the director has in mind.

Often, what I end up seeing is very different from what I thought it was going to look like. So that's actually sort of an interesting phenomenon. You read words and see images but when you see someone else's interpretation of those words, sometimes they are similar to yours and sometimes they are very different. And that's sort of a fascinating study. When the director says he likes it — not to be silly — but that's really when you know. Because I think there can be multiple approaches to a scene, whether it's a song or score. We've all had — when I say "we" composers, or perhaps people who have studied film — have had experience of looking at something and trying different things, trying different pieces of music against the picture.

And sometimes they all work, but they all do something different. So there may not be a right way. And there isn't a one right way or a one wrong way to do something. There are a lot of approaches, and it's a matter of figuring out what this director likes.

What do you do when an approach you take just isn't giving you the music needed?

Well, it's important to be able to go with the flow. Things change; directors may change their minds. I think it's also important to be able to take a step back from your own work. We all love what we do, and you might write something, but you might take a step back and say, "That tempo should be brighter, faster." Or maybe you did and there's a little bit too much percussion. I think you have to be willing to look at your own work and not be so attached to it that you're opposed to critiquing it and refining it and improving it. Whether or not that direction came from the director or whether it comes from yourself, I think that's important. And also just being able to get along with people and sort of go with the flow, because things get hectic. And you've got to keep it together and just keep plowing through.

SCORE: THE INTERVIEWS

CHAPTER 20

JOHN POWELL

COMPOSER

KNOWN FOR		ACHIEVEMENTS
JASON BOURNE (2016)	*THE BOURNE SUPREMACY* (2004)	ACADEMY AWARD NOMINATION, ORIGINAL SCORE, *HOW TO TRAIN YOUR DRAGON*
PAN (2015)		
HOW TO TRAIN YOUR DRAGON 2 (2014)	*THE ITALIAN JOB* (2003)	
	THE BOURNE IDENTITY (2002)	
RIO (2011)		GRAMMY NOMINATION, SCORE FOR MOTION PICTURE, *HAPPY FEET*
HOW TO TRAIN YOUR DRAGON (2010)	*SHREK* (2001)	
	CHICKEN RUN (2000)	
BOLT (2008)	*THE ROAD TO EL DORADO* (2000)	THREE BAFTA NOMINATIONS
KUNG FU PANDA (2008)		
HAPPY FEET (2006)	*ANTZ* (1998)	SIX WORLD SOUNDTRACK AWARDS NOMINATIONS, COMPOSER OF THE YEAR
ROBOTS (2005)	*FACE/OFF* (1997)	

What does music bring to a film?

Emotional manipulation. It was invented by Leni Riefenstahl for Triumph of the Will. By the end – the time the end – you get to the end of this giant sequence with Wagner playing, I think it's "Parsifal," and you just are so absolutely behind those Nazis.

Nothing else can do that. obviously the imagery and the cinematography and the beauty of the construction of the shots was a big part of it. Words were clearly nothing. And then the rest of it was done by music. So the ability to be able to manipulate people, really. It's the ultimate propaganda tool.

So I mean I think that's absolutely the pinnacle of its achievements sometimes.

Talk about the importance of musical influences.

Some great music is being made for films by great composers. However, if we all continue to just listen to film music, we're all basically just — where are we going to go from there?

I always try to encourage people to get out and listen to some other music. And film music is getting narrower and narrower and narrower, as it's getting temped and temped to the Nth degree, and the composers who come in and write that music are following the temp so closely that we're getting to a narrow point where there's hardly anything interesting coming. And when you do hear something interesting, it comes from a totally different direction.

It comes from people who work a totally different way, where a composer will be hired to write music without seeing the film, or a director likes a person's album and gets them to write some music with nothing seen at all, and then edits the movie to the music, and that's when it starts to get kind of different.

But then that will become the new standard, and then everybody will listen to that and temp that and then it kind of gets more and more narrow.

So I just try encourage people to try and find — there's a world of music. There are thousands of years of music.

Obviously there's 600 years of western music, plus everything else. There are hundreds of years of incredible pop, American pop music. There's so many different things that we could be listening to, and why listen to film music?

You've said you're a film composer because you like making lots of different styles of music.

Well, that's why I do it. That's the only reason I've ever done it really, is to get a chance to make music – was really all I've been interested in since I was 7, since I heard Mendelssohn's violin concerto.

Then I spent a while trying to play that Mendelssohn violin concerto, and realized that playing is really hard, so I went into a much easier part of it, which was writing music. The easiest part is writing music for film, because it can be pretty crappy music sometimes, and they still give you all these great musicians to play it. And they give you studio time in the best studios, and they pay you for it, it's great. I mean the downside is you have to make it fit in the film.

And you use a computer to write music. Why is that so important and do you ever feel limited by it?

I'm musically dyslexic and intellectually stunted, apart from being, you know, emotionally disabled. So I need a computer to basically remember all the things I can't remember. It's like a constant companion, sketchpad. It's paper, but it's just my version of paper. Or my version of being able to remember what I've just played. Or my version of being able to actually voice chords correctly.

I can go back and fix all these things that I can't really do with my fingers and my brain. I can use the computer in these kind of supportive roles.

But the idea of being able to sort of have it all flow out in one go — it just doesn't really exist in my world.

Anything can mix. Somebody can make anything into an instrument. you can make a giant cow turd into an instrument, if it's kind of arched the right way, and dries in the right temperature, and has a nice kind of cone to it or something. So yes, in the same way that there's some of the worst music that's ever been written has been played by the London Symphony Orchestra — it doesn't matter what the tool is; it's the idea.

There's lots of shitty music done on a computer, so obviously that's the whole point is that everybody gets the chance to mess up on computers. That's why I like them as well. It allows me to quietly, in the privacy of my own room, make a lot of mistakes over and over and over again and then work through those mistakes and eventually try and swim up and find some interesting thing.

If I had to do that on paper, straight with an orchestra, I'd be making so many mistakes I think. I don't think anyone would hire me.

It's become the most important thing, and it's really economics. And you know there's a creative aspect to it, but most of it is economics. It just allows us to not – you know. If I had my druthers, I'd obviously write with a computer, but I wouldn't necessarily play everything to the directors. I'd maybe want to then take it to the orchestra and play it with the orchestra to the directors. But obviously we can't afford to do that, so we try and play it.

There are two ideas really in the computer. There's writing, which could sound awful to everybody else, but if it achieves what I'm hearing in my head and helps me achieve what I'd like the orchestra to sound like, then great. But unfortunately I also have to play it to people, because they want to know what it sounds like before we spend all this money on an orchestra.

Obviously, this is saying orchestral music. So much of what I've done probably is this combination of music that is creative in the computer, and is computer-created in the same way that rock and roll and pop music are created. But then just to mix it up with the orchestra, because the orchestra makes everything sound expensive.

Tell me about how you came up with the music of the Bourne Identity and the Bourne series. Specifically coming in late to add those string rhythms.

I had an electronic score that was kind of working, but it just didn't have any cinematic reference. So I think Doug was feeling something was missing, probably couldn't figure out how to say, "How can we make it sound a bit more cinematic?"

And we'd deliberately gone away from the orchestra because he'd sort of tried that, and I knew that that was not working for him, and so right in the last minute we just did a quick U-turn, went back and called up a bit of the language of cinema. At the same time I tried adding brass and things like that, and he didn't like any of that. See, he didn't want it to sound Bond.

He wanted something new for the same kind of character. And

in every aspect of the film he was looking for a different way of telling that same kind of story, really. So allowing me to go as far as I did without strings, and judging it that way, and then just at the last minute, just add this element that gave it a little bridge connection to what we kind of expected from a film — a cinema sound. I think that's what it did.

What Hans has certainly done on The Dark Knight is obviously blur this line between this giant symphonic sound and electronics, and you're not quite sure where one ends and the other begins. With Bourne, honestly I was kind of coming away from a place where I loved Hans so much for getting me to that place, and I was trying to figure out how to get out from under his shadow.

Because he's such a strong voice in Hollywood, being associated with his organization was incredible and gave me everything but limited me to a certain point. So Bourne was really a reactionary score. It was just trying to do everything that we'd never normally do if you had to sort of fit into (that) sort of sound.

So everything that we would normally do that sounded ambient, I'd make dry. Everything that sounded big, I'd make small. It was literally just 180° on everything, and it made it easy in a way.

And from that came sort of an approach that was based on my interest in minimalism. And then join that with a bit of the stuff I was listening to, you know, Bjork and Massive Attack, at that time. So you throw those together, and then that makes what I was trying to do with that score. And then that changed everybody else a little bit, and then they started heading that way, and then that developed into other things.

Can you explain the concept of minimalism in music?

Well, again, electronics in film scoring is economics. We don't have the money for a big film score, so obviously early on it was very deliberate. Talking about Forbidden Planet and how crazy sounding that was because it was all electronic. But that suited the story very much, so a lot of these things are economics playing into the creative, and the creative is often not as important sometimes as the economics.

But often big steps forward are made by the creative choice, so having electronics is often about the fact that we can't afford an orchestra, or we don't want it to sound orchestral, and that's a deliberate thing. Or, can we have a bit of orchestra, but make it a bit more hip.

So anywhere along that sort of sliding scale of kind of how to make something that everybody expects, but just a little different, or a little cheaper.

Tell me about your first really big film, Shrek, which you scored with Harry Gregson-Williams.

Basically — and DreamWorks knows I love them — but the problem was, it was a knife-edge film for them. It was a very important film for them. Things had not gone as well as they had hoped up until that point. It was a real deciding film. It was a real unusual film, and that's when everybody kind of goes crazy and they're not really sure if they're doing the right thing or not.

I think Harry and I had to search high and low and make sure that every single place had been looked in, and that's the kind of thing that made it difficult. The film worked. The film would've worked without music.

It's a good film, you know. It's a great script, great performances, and great animation, and a unique time – a unique piece of timing on the kind of fractured fairy tale. So it was all about just making sure it flowed right.

They had some really interesting musical choices that they had already made, between The Eels and the "Hallelujah," and things. And so it was already placed very carefully, and everything was working really well already, and so the score just had to — again, sometimes it's just, "Don't fuck it up." And that's all you need to do. You just need to make sure you don't draw attention to yourself. You support the emotions correctly, you don't push too hard, you're not too vanilla, but you're not too flashy.

So it was just kind of getting it to the perfect spot. It's just always hard, really. When everyone's nervous, that's all.

You've talked about your appreciation for Carl Stalling on the old Looney Tunes cartoons, and the speed at which the orchestra plays. What do you adore so much about the Stalling orchestra?

Some of the greatest music, I think, that's actually been written in the history of music is by Carl Stalling, because he was an amazing brain who just sucked up all of this fantastic music that he knew as a kid, and figured out this way of comedically making it fit.

I love funny music. I do like music that's funny. And there are not many people who can do it, and Carl Stalling did it naturally. What was brilliant about it was that you could watch the cartoon with the music, and it was funny. And then you could totally disassociate yourself from the actual images, and the music still had incredible wit as well as incredible verve, life, emotion — whether or not it was deliberately overemotional.

It was incredibly sort of referencing millions of great classical music, and pop tunes, and the thing that we don't appreciate it, watching it now, is that there's a lot of lyric gags going on.

I mean, Questlove got in trouble when he started playing — I can't remember the name of the song — "Lying Bitch Woman," or something, when some ignoramus politician went on the show. We don't realize that Carl Stalling was doing that a lot.

He was quoting songs, and quoting the lyrics from songs just instrumentally, while things were happening as well. And so if you look at some of the research people have done, you can see that there's a lot of commentary going on. And that might be an intellectual conceit, but I find that to be just – that's the peak achievement — one of the peak achievements in film music, really.

Do you try to work in similar references to film as well?

Well, it's dangerous to wink, and I hope I haven't winked too much. What is important to do sometimes is soften the effect of things, and that's a sort of an example in animation is that you can have quite an intense scene, and the music can make it more intense, or you can keep it exciting and it's to do with rhythm as well. Basically, if you have a drum kit — and this is a thing that everybody gets. If you have a constantly moving rhythm, it gives you a comforting expectancy. In other words, a drum groove going under an orchestra.

The orchestra can be sounding like it's, you know, Stockhausen, but if the drum groove is there, it totally stops the Stockhausen, that sort of desperate fear of the music. And it allows you to balance it with something that's kind of known, and more importantly, cyclic.

And the cyclic part of a drum groove lets everyone know that things are stepping forward in a very ordinary way. That's why you might get a great effect from a score that doesn't have that, and is kind of lots of crazy meters. Jerry Goldsmith was the master of that, and that was one of the things he did. He kept you on tender hooks, not knowing where the next beat would be.

Or he would give you a sense of where the rhythm was going, and then he'd pull that rug out from underneath you, so the ability to be able to kind of soften, as it were, the effect of dramatic music with rhythm, that's one of the big balancing acts you play, in certainly animation and then in certain other films as well.

It's really about whom it's for, so you wouldn't think of the audience without kind of trying to tell yourself, "Is this audience, is this visual, is the story more dramatic or less dramatic than this audience wants it to be?"

And if so, I can pull or I can push on it. I've never really done a horror film. I did a couple of shorts before I even got to Hollywood that really — I'm sure people would be horrified, because they were really — I mean it was like, there's a dark side that anybody can really find.

And it was in such an intriguingly crazy piece of filmmaking by a couple of French brothers, and they used stop motion and it was truly upsetting, and I had fun doing that. But many horror films, I just find so — I didn't enjoy the idea of them.

So I couldn't really find it in my heart to find the right music for them, so I think I would've probably used too high a Stalling factor for them.

I'm a big fan of great composers writing music for film. I'm not a great fan of shitty composers writing totally good, appropriate music for film.

Say whatever you like, but John Carpenter changed film music by writing a very limited musical vocabulary that worked incredibly well for his films, and I like his films very much. And I like them including his scores, but the music itself is not designed to be anything other than this perfect support for his films.

It's also no coincidence that he is the guy writing the music for his own films and 90 percent of the composers that would've come along would've been overwriting all the time for him, and that's probably why he gave up and did it himself. And it's very easy to overwrite because you feel you have to do something, because you're a composer.

Maybe some of the best film music has been made really by people who perhaps get to a level where they realize that they're already a good composer, and they need to calm down, and they don't need to kind of push so hard. They don't need to prove anything, so they kind of pull back and then suddenly it kind of just slots right in, because it's not that they're not trying, but they're not having to show off musically. They really are supporting the film much more than they might have done earlier in their careers, when they were a little bit more immature. I think I'm talking about myself here.

How selective are you in choosing what kinds of films to work on?

We're all a bunch of tarts, really, and we need the money. And it depends really what you're talking about as far as when it is in your career, as well. I can honestly tell you, at a certain point, that almost all composers would have done that ISIS recruitment film if they were offered. And then they get a bit of money and they think, "Well, I don't need to do that now, because that's not — people will think." So it's a question of, you can only make that decision if you don't need the money at a certain point. But when I came out of college I went and started to do advertising music, which is kind of a bit questionable as to whether or not it has a morality, a moral purpose in the world. Again, it's about manipulating people into buying things so there's not really much — there are no high horses for that one.

But I thought, "I'm not going to do cigarettes, I'm not going to do nuclear power, and I wont do anything for the military," because it struck me as that we shouldn't be selling those things to anybody. They're bad for us, generally. "So just try and avoid that, and then we'll be alright."

But I remember in England, I did the privatization of the water, which at the time I thought was a crazily bad idea by the conservative party, and I still do — you shouldn't have utilities privatized.

But I did it. I needed the gig, and I did it, and it was — yeah. So I can't really talk from a very high moral standing here, but then as I've gone through Hollywood, I have tried to choose things that were at least pernicious.

It's not that I've been very good at doing music for films that are uplifting and important historical films, or changed people's opinion on subjects. But I've just taken the approach, which is that if I can be part of entertainment, and I can help manipulate them into a place where they enjoy the storytelling, that's great. So I've tried to stay off the more egregious films, and as I get older and as I get more money, I kind of don't need to do the ones that I really don't want to do, and those are basically ones that are just constantly fighting. I don't like things that make heroes warriors. I prefer things that make heroes people who can think their way out of a problem, rather than beat their way out of a problem. Even interesting films and TV — immediately, there's always somebody who gets tortured to get the information we need to save people, and you can have a question of the direct link between our behavior as a society and the propaganda, to get back to Leni Riefenstahl. The propaganda that we can help, as composers, manipulate.

We have power in our hands, and I think it's important. And I have certainly spoken to other composers and tried to persuade them not to do certain things that I thought they were too good for. And also I worried that they would be too good at manipulating people in a way that, when they're telling stories, that really don't do us any good.

Probably best that I don't name names, but Hans and I are always talking about that sort of thing. I think he likes the fact that I take the kind of more extreme position on some of the films, and there are films that he's done that are incredibly important.

I helped him out on The Thin Red Line. That's a war film, and in my opinion it does not take a position that is anything other than important about war. But other films, I feel that he was helping perhaps make those films more palatable. And that surely isn't — I mean I'm sitting here a few weeks after American Sniper has done a huge load of business, which proves that there is an audience for people who want difficult subjects to be made much more palatable and easy, and to fit in with their view of the world.

I can't say that I'm much of a beacon of righteousness on this, but it's been one little thing, since I've done adverts, I've tried to sort of set myself.

Tell me about how you first encountered Hans Zimmer and his studio.

I met Hans when I was in — it was in Vienna, I think, and it was about three in the morning. And it was a brothel, and he was coming out. He'd just finished his shift, and I was going in to start my shift, and — (Laughter.)

No, I met Hans by helping him out over a Christmas gig that he did, where he had to change a whole score over Christmas, and he pulled various people in, and I was there to help. One of them, who was kind of more of a paper-and-pencil guy — great, great composer, but Hans wanted it kind of knocked into computer shapes that he could comment on.

So I went in, and I think Hans saw that I was interested in nerdy things, and that I was willing to work over Christmas — I mean literally all day Christmas day. I didn't have any Christmas. And that I had a sense of humor perhaps, so he enjoyed that, and then I'd see him occasionally when he was back in London. I was in London all this time, and he'd say to me, "Oh, you should come out." And I didn't feel ready at the time, and I was finishing up something. Actually, the main thing I was finishing was an opera I was doing with a friend of mine, composing an opera to be performed in Germany, and we finished that. And then I kind of got to the end of that, and the idea of going back to doing advertising music was just too difficult to swallow, so then I thought, "Maybe I should go."

I just came over, and I took a place for a year in Venice Beach thinking, "I'm going to sit and have a break, I've been working on adverts for 10 years," — no, it wasn't that long, about eight years.

I thought I'll just watch and see what happens, and once Hans found out I was here, he kind of dragged me in. And the first thing I did was help him on song arrangements on The Prince of Egypt, and so that's when I met DreamWorks.

He was supposed to do that. They wanted him to do it, and he basically pointed it at me and said, "This kid can do it. And if he doesn't, I'll help fix it." So he kind of gave them a guarantee. So I wrote a load over a weekend, I wrote a load of tunes, as we do, themes, and just try them out a few scenes from the movie. And they very kindly pretended that Hans had written them, and Hans denied. So there's this kind of fun thing. And then they hired me, and I generally didn't fuck it up, so that was OK.

Composing is often a very solitary job, but how was it working with another talented composer like Harry Gregson-Williams?

We didn't push each other deliberately, but he's a very good writer, so the natural jealousy of two young composers that have been not forced together but have been – it was Jeffrey Katzenberg's suggestion that we do Antz together. He worked with both of us on Prince of Egypt, so he said, "Why don't we try that?"

I think Hans was against it, actually. And Jeffrey said, "Let's try it." And so Harry and I didn't really know each other, so we would sit there, and we thought, "Well, we'll go and write tunes and see what comes up," and he'd write ones, and I'd go, "Shit, that's fucking gold, what am I going to do?"

So then you'd be pressured to go back. We'd go back to our rooms, and try and write something kind of trying to up your game because — we're friends, but there's a jealousy at that point in your career where you see the other person being really good writing, and you think, "I've got to best that. I've got to best them." So I think that probably pushed us. Maybe Jeffrey knows that. It's a bit Hunger Games maybe, but from there we developed a very good relationship. I think we both realized after a few films that the difficulty was — if we weren't careful, we'd be formed into this pair, and then we'd never kind of have separate careers.

And even though I love the way he writes, and I think Harry

is this wonderful, bizarre sort of love of some of the odd things I do, he always complains about my brass writing and trumpets, but I think he enjoys it. The thing was that we were always very different. We never intended to have a career.

Harry was great about it. I think there was definitely this kind of fire under the two of us that probably made us really try, and we'd always write tunes apart, and together try things and look at the tune sort of backwards. Sometimes you kind of say, the tune had just gone through a bad meeting – in other words, Harry presents a tune, and Jeffrey says it's a piece of shit, "Why are you doing this?" And then go, "Well, let me try something, and turn upside down, and see if I can make it do something differently that might help." And the same with Harry. He works a lot with cues, and a lot of tunes in Antz were really created sort of as this weird mixture of throwing between us. And once that sort of started to work, then we would take off.

We'd split up the cue sheet, and we'd develop those tunes wherever. Whatever thematically they were attached to, we'd develop the tunes during that scene and try that cue, and then if you'd had three goes at that cue and it'd been thrown out, then you'd say, "OK, I cant do this one anymore." So we'd swap stuff around. It's a good way of doing it. And when there was probably 80 minutes of music for Antz, and eighty minutes of music for Chicken Run, that's great. But 38 minutes of music for Shrek was a bit embarrassing to take two of us. And it took about twice as long as anything we did for those other films.

SCORE: THE INTERVIEWS

CHAPTER 21

ALEXANDRE DESPLAT

COMPOSER

KNOWN FOR		ACHIEVEMENTS
THE SECRET LIFE OF PETS (2016)	*MOONRISE KINGDOM* (2012)	ACADEMY AWARD, ORIGINAL SCORE *THE GRAND BUDAPEST HOTEL*
FLORENCE FOSTER JENKINS (2016)	*THE KING'S SPEECH* (2010)	
THE DANISH GIRL (2015)	*HARRY POTTER AND THE DEATHLY HALLOWS* (2010)	GOLDEN GLOBE, ORIGINAL SCORE, *THE PAINTED VEIL*
THE IMITATION GAME (2014)	*FANTASTIC MR. FOX* (2009)	
THE GRAND BUDAPEST HOTEL (2014)	*THE CURIOUS CASE OF BENJAMIN BUTTON* (2008)	EIGHT ACADEMY AWARD NOMINATIONS
PHILOMENA (2013)	*THE PAINTED VEIL* (2006)	EIGHT GOLDEN GLOBE NOMINATIONS
ARGO (2012)	*THE QUEEN* (2006)	TWO GRAMMY AWARDS, SCORE SOUNDTRACK
ZERO DARK THIRTY (2012)	*SYRIANA* (2005)	

You've spoken about music having a certain depth it can bring to a film.

I guess, the magic of movie music is what brings out to your emotions and your sensations and is not yet in the frame — meaning it could be depth of field, to take an example, which is more physical; it could be the past or the future of the character so that's more emotional content. It's a movement that goes from A to Z, that direction for you.

And that's a flow, and music does have a movement from left to right. So the correlation of these three elements, I always felt them magical when I was going to the movies. I could feel all that happening and trying to render when you write a score properly and still with music, which has some strength and some content is quite a challenge that I'm still struggling with every day.

How did great film music inspire you to become a film composer?

Well, I wouldn't sit here today if I had not experienced music that stood alone and I must I must say that being able to buy the albums when I was in my teens of the scores I that I liked after seeing a film or sometimes before seeing the film was a real continuity to my passion.

So, of course, when I started composing for movies I always hoped that I could write good music that could stand alone. And actually, for many, many years, I was very shy about that because it took me a while to say I'm a composer. I used to say I'm a musician. My name starts with a D, like many composers that I admire — Dutilleux, Dudamel, that's for movie soundtracks. Debussy. And it was hard for me to imagine that I would have one day a CD, I mean an album at the time, then a CD, in the same section as these letters. But, of course, having the opportunity to listen to music away from the film is crucial, I think, not that you can always achieve that goal but I think I try.

How do you best work with a director on a film?

I'm no different from an actor or a set designer. I come with my history and my background and the fantasy I have of the storyline and of the film. So if the director calls me, it is because he wants another element that will complete his work. That's why he will choose this actor, this actress, this production designer, or this composer. There's a reason — he thinks that the puzzle will be a good match. Now, all the great directors I've worked with have the intelligence — all the human knowledge — that to have great collaborators you have to give them freedom.

You think of music as being 3D. What does that mean?

There is a three-dimensional — music is three-dimensional to me. Of course, when you read a score, it's two dimensional, but when I think about the music in a film, as I said before, there's a world in front of me, it's not just flat. There is a depth of field when you use a camera. The actors go from the back of the room, where they're playing, to the front. It's like being in a theater. There's the dimension that you can feel, and music has to follow that, I think. You can emphasize it. And the more I compose, the more I want to be part of this object and actually move inside this object and move into the three dimension of a movie without having 3D glasses. That's not the point, it's just that music can create so many things, you can widen the screen just by entering suddenly, very slowly, a full orchestra, where there was before just a few players.

Suddenly widens the screen. It can also widen the screen in the other direction with the depth of field. With the position of the instruments in the studio you record in. So, yes, there is a three-dimensional thing that I'm kind of obsessed with.

And the concept of communicating through vibrations.

Yeah, that's something that I spend a lot of time with. It's also one of my obsessions, because I compose with the picture; I have the picture there with me. I can try again and again and when I say vibration, again it's about this three dimensional sensation. Sometimes you write a piece, you hear it to a mock up, to the picture, and you feel it's flat. There's nothing. You're not bringing anything new to what is already on the screen, there's nothing magical about it.

Until you find, after many attempts, something where I feel that suddenly there's a movement in front of me, which is the music which certainly is part of what the film is doing, of the energy of the film, of the soul of the film, of its breath, the way it evolves on the timeline, and that's what I call the vibration — when I can feel the music is really in the face.

You know, it's like when two instruments are in tune or not in tune. When they're not in tune the vibration, the harmonics don't align properly and the sound is not pure. There's this thing I'm looking for.

Do you feel film music manipulates an audience's emotions?

I wouldn't use the word manipulate, I would say patronizing. Because that's the general idea. Again, with great directors, they trust the audience to be smart enough to understand things and to anticipate things and to be moved at the right moment without being pushed. So I try to follow that track, but when we speak of movies there's various types of movies. There are many types of movies in the cinema. If you write for a very intimate cinema verite type of film, music has to be of another caliber than if you do a fantasy movie. So I would say that it's impossible to generalize. Movies are all very different, and there's no rule that you have to follow. Actually, you shouldn't follow any rules because there's no truth.

You're very involved in a lot of your projects on different levels, including orchestration.

The process that I've always chosen was the demo everything myself. So all my mockups are done by me and myself in my studio, there's nobody there, it's just, it's a very little studio. There's nobody in my studio and I couldn't take it. I couldn't bear it I think, since I've been orchestrating. since I started to write music, and it's a passion, my demos are actually really precise, detailed, which allows me to give them away to somebody in Paris, or here, or wherever team I work with. But I follow that very carefully. I check it regularly and I make sure that it does match what I have in mind.

But yes, letting go of orchestration physically is something that I really miss now. I think I do in between films transcribe music, movie music, for a string quintet that I love and that allows me to go back to my pencil and eraser and it's a moment of great joy for me.

SCORE: THE INTERVIEWS

CHAPTER 22

ELLIOT GOLDENTHAL
COMPOSER

KNOWN FOR		ACHIEVEMENTS
PUBLIC ENEMIES (2009)	BATMAN & ROBIN (1997)	ACADEMY AWARD, ORIGINAL SCORE FRIDA
ACROSS THE UNIVERSE (2007)	THE BUTCHER BOY (1997)	
	A TIME TO KILL (1996)	GOLDEN GLOBE, ORIGINAL SCORE FRIDA
S.W.A.T. (2003)	MICHAEL COLLINS (1996)	
FRIDA (2002)	HEAT (1995)	
THE GOOD THIEF (2002)	BATMAN FOREVER (1995)	FOUR ACADEMY AWARD NOMINATIONS
FINAL FANTASY: THE SPIRITS WITHIN (2001)	INTERVIEW WITH THE VAMPIRE (1994)	THREE GOLDEN GLOBE NOMINATIONS
IN DREAMS (1999)	COBB (1994)	EMMY NOMINATION
TITUS (1999)	DEMOLITION MAN (1993)	THREE GRAMMY NOMINATIONS
SPHERE (1998)		

What's the most difficult job you've ever taken?

The most difficult job I had in composing, not composing but arranging songs for a movie, was Across the Universe, because there were 33 songs. And I was responsible for producing at least 20-something. Twenty-five, or something like that.

It wasn't the Beatles situation, it was thinking about those composers — George, John and Paul, not in any order — as composers who are like George Gershwin or something.

And there was quite a challenge for morphing it from a band situation, or a rock and roll situation, to a dramatic situation. And changing keys for adjusting a tessitura range for the singers, etc., was a huge, difficult task. It was daunting for me to be involved but very satisfying in the end.

What do you see as one of the bigger challenges of composing music for film as opposed to concert works?

I have a tough time enjoying something that I don't know the outcome of completely when I'm composing it. I understand volume, but it's hard to get a complete grasp on all the sound effects that are required for an action movie.

In some cases it works out great, really great. In other cases I say, "Why did I go to all that trouble composing and working on the orchestration and revisions and modulations and instrumentation, and now I can't hear it because there's a car chase happening?" So, you know, I enjoy car chases, but in this case, I can't anticipate what will happen. I understand turning down the volume. I understand getting rid of the music completely. But I have trepidation in composing something that a giant block of sound effects will be added to it. But it's where the challenge is I suppose.

What's your process working with a director to achieve his vision or your own?

It's a chronological process. I whittle down and whittle down along with the director in the situation, until I have something that hopefully the director can see, or revealing his or her vision. Because whether it's an actual pencil or whether it's a delete button, I've found the process of eliminating the extras revealing and very instructive to me. All the work, all the extra stuff, if I boil it down to the essential property of what I'm going for, what the director is going for. That's where the eraser comes in quite often.

You've talked about reflective music versus reflexive music. Can you elaborate on that concept and how it changes your approach to a film?

Reflective versus reflexive. That was referring to Interview with the Vampire, because I had approximately three weeks to write two and a half hours of music. So, therefore, I had no time to really reflect. It was just a reflexive process. "Go! Go! Go!" I relied on my subconscious, on my training and my various situations in other movies to rely on. I couldn't stop, I had to do it. Whatever it is, it's coming out on June 27th, you know?

And the scary thing is seeing your name — for example on Batman Forever or other movies like Interview with the Vampire — going down in the Subway in New York, and I'm halfway done, and seeing your name on the poster, and saying, "Oh, God," you know. I have a long way to go in two and a half weeks.

There's a lot of pressure on a big studio film.

And they get ferociously large here in L.A.

Tell me about jumping into the film composing industry as a young musician and orchestrating cues.

I started out for the first 10 years of my professional life orchestrating exclusively my own scores. And then I worked with, and continued to work with, a wonderful orchestrator who started as my assistant, and we both exchanged one page of his, one page of mine, until I wrote one page out, and he wrote 10 in the same amount of time.

So he was perfectly suited to work along with me in the film medium. He's a very gifted musician, and especially in film, it's something about the hours, and something about the grinding schedule. You absolutely, absolutely need someone to be your second heartbeat, so to speak. Or you'd just be dead. (Laughter.)

How is it different writing for film versus another musical work?

Well, it certainly it is. Ballet, opera versus film. Three situations. In ballet, for example, you are working with flesh and blood. So if the choreographer wants a solo for two lasting I don't know "X" amount of minutes, you have to put in built-in pauses, so that dancers have a chance to rest. In other words, you can't write a 20-minute adagio and expect the dancers to keep up the duet.

In opera, you chose your own clock based on flesh and blood, how much a singer could sing.

You brought up a very interesting idea about film music's role in a film, as it relates to time. How can music bend timing of a film?

It's very specific about malleability of time. You can bend time in such a way that a 20-minute sequence of the movie feels like 10 minutes by adding something that pulls you along, and some string that all of a sudden engages you, and 20 minutes ago, you said, "What happened? It felt like 10 minutes."

In the same way, you can make a millisecond seem like three minutes. And everyone says, if they're in a car accident or if they fall or something, especially in impact car accidents, you imagine things traveling in slow motion even though it took place in maybe a second and a half. That's the feeling. Not to be horrific or something, but take a kiss, for example. A composer can have a gift of making that kiss seem more significant, seem more temporally significant, seem longer.

SCORE: THE INTERVIEWS

CHAPTER 23

HENRY JACKMAN
COMPOSER

KNOWN FOR		ACHIEVEMENTS
KONG: SKULL ISLAND (2017)	BIG HERO 6 (2014)	BAFTA NOMINATION, CAPTAIN PHILLIPS
THE BIRTH OF A NATION (2016)	CAPTAIN AMERICA: THE WINTER SOLDIER (2014)	FOUR ASCAP AWARDS
CAPTAIN AMERICA: CIVIL WAR (2016)	TURBO (2013)	FOUR NOMINATIONS, INTERNATIONAL FILM MUSIC CRITICS AWARD
THE MAN IN THE HIGH CASTLE (2015)	CAPTAIN PHILLIPS (2013) WRECK-IT RALPH (2012)	WORLD SOUNDTRACK AWARD NOMINATION
PIXELS (2015)	X-MEN: FIRST CLASS (2011)	
KINGSMEN: THE SECRET SERVICE (2014)	WINNIE THE POOH (2011) KICK-ASS (2010)	
THE INTERVIEW (2014)	MONSTERS VS. ALIENS (2009)	

At it's best, what does music add to a film?

One non-verbal way of figuring that out is having the experience — which almost nobody who watches films ever has — which is seeing a film without music. (Laughter.) Occasionally that happens in a film score seminar and whatnot. But if you were to watch The Empire Strikes Back with no music, you would very swiftly find out the role that music is playing.

You can enormously enhance the characters and the storytelling and a sort of — funny enough, if it's the sort of film where a director will let you, you can actually enhance the structure, the narrative structure of the film.

I often feel like the best training for writing music for film actually isn't really film school or composition lessons or orchestration lessons or technology lessons. It's actually English literature analysis (Laughter).

That's an exaggeration. If you can't write music, then the best ideas in the world, when you come to write them, it's rubbish. So it doesn't mean anything. But if you look at a film, like a two-hour film, and actually have an understanding of the arc of what's happening and the character development and the story, then the most important thing will be revealed, which is why you're writing that piece of music.

You're essentially writing your music to someone else's vision?

That's really the main difference. If you're a concert composer, or in a band, you write a piece of music because it's cool, and people like your music, right? Whereas film music — if you're a producer and you had a choice between Stravinsky, who's one of the greatest concert composers who ever lived, who potentially might just ignore the film and write a fantastic piece of music that is world class concert music, but severely harming the film. Versus someone who's quite mediocre but has a phenomenal sense of picture and how to help the film, but the actually pieces might not be the greatest composition ever. As a producer, you would definitely pick number two not number one. Number one you'll end up with these amazing concert pieces that are of no use to you.

The picture is in front of you. That's what I do; it's just it's not really a problem. It's not really a fight. In fact, half the time I feel like once you're on a role on a film, it sort of asks you to do something. I know that sounds really hippie.

If you work with your director, and you've got themes that people can agree on, and you've got a general direction, then once you start writing cues, just by watching the picture carefully and then understanding the scene in relation to the rest of the picture, half the clues are there.

How important is raw experimentation?

I mean, you'll go down a few blind alleys, and it's always worth doing that and experimenting to see how far you can push something. Or it's actually valuable sometimes to do something, and discover that it fundamentally doesn't work.

Sometimes movies are very ambiguous, and have contradictions, and there are different ways to skin a cat, and you could feel like it's self-evident what ought to happen, but a particular director might have a very unusual way of looking at things and actually want to rub up against picture and be asynchronous. Or something counter intuitive or ironic, so there's always interpretation.

But exceptions aside, once you're sort of in harmony with the story and the director and the picture, I almost feel like the scenes kind of ask you what to do.

What specifically do you look for when spotting a film?

Good acting, people's gestures, especially their eye movement and camerawork. Suppose you're at a spotting session, if people haven't spotted the film correctly, and you feel like there ought to be music where there currently isn't, it just screams out at you. As you just sort of zoom into something I go, "Music! Where is it?"

I guess that's more the placement of it. But I feel like in the beginning, part of scoring a movie is an area where you're more likely to go around in circles, or try different things, which is definitely worth doing.

Do you ever think to yourself after the fact, "I did that cue perfectly"?

I'm quite suspicious, if you kind of launch in and just everything you do is version one. I'm not saying that there needs to be blood on the floor before you proceed (Laughter). But you usually ought to have a little bit of birth pain if you're on to something vaguely interesting otherwise.

It should never be the first thing you think of to get when you're starting anyway. I always think it's a bit suspicious when the first thing you think of is just working everywhere.

Actually, funny enough, with themes it's often the first is the best. I say the first, but that's because I spend a lot of time on themes. So it's a slightly misleading statement. But very often I'll work for a while on themes and then when I show the director, "OK, this here this is what I think," or "This is what I think of the theme" for Pixels or Big Hero 6 or Abraham Lincoln.

So, often that part will work. But then there's always how to arrange it, and how to orchestrate it, and how it all functions in the film.

Yeah, I just I feel like you can almost tell when you're fighting when there's a creative tension of an unhealthy type in what you're doing, versus the picture. You can almost feel it.

How can you tell when you're not in the groove?

When you're not quite in the groove, you can sort of feel it, because as you're writing and the picture doesn't feel like your friend anymore, in some weird way. It's not quite gelling. And when you sink into the groove, you have a very harmonious feeling. Which, hopefully that should come fairly quickly (Laughter). If it doesn't, then you need to think about writing completely different music.

What was your journey into a career in film music?

Well, I'm a bit schizophrenic, because I started off with the poshest imaginable musical education. when I was a little English chorister at St. Paul's Cathedral with my Elizabethan ruff.

I remember singing at the Falkland memorial service and in the middle of this big Latin Gloria or something, or whatever it was, I turn up to the left and literally in one row I remember seeing the Queen of England, the Duke of Edinburgh, Lady Diana and Prince Charles, Ronald Reagan, Mikhail Gorbachev, and Margaret Thatcher all in the front row 30 feet away. And I did classical music and all the rest of it, but just typical kind of teenage rebellion, and a meager computer and 8-bit sampler. The whole rave thing was kicking off in England, so I just jettisoned my entire classical background and just got messed up for five years much to the chagrin of my parents. But in fact what I didn't realize is all of that that bifurcation into staying out until four in the morning listening to drum and bass and rave stuff, and then going into pop music and working with people like Trevor Horn, was a great privilege. What I didn't realize is this is all priceless education for film music, because — not that it mattered. It doesn't matter. I don't think John Williams wakes up in the morning and goes, "Oh, dear, I'm a complete failure. I don't know how to assemble a dubstep tune." It simply doesn't matter. And even in today's climate, if you're a strictly orchestral composer, great. So what? there's loads of really great orchestral music, and if you only are on the band side in electronic, and don't really know how to make something sound a bit like Strauss, that also doesn't matter.

I'm just very grateful that kind of by accident I got a really strict classical education. The other part of going wild and growing my hair long and getting into all that other stuff is lots of musical rules which I thought were real just kind of evaporated. I remember hearing this inner-city tune. I remember when I first heard that I went, "No, no, no. You can't go C-minor, F-minor, B-flat minor, E-flat minor. That's like parallel harmony. You have to go C-minor, F-minor, B-flat major, F-minor. And it's because someone had a chord just sampled, so they're just going and it jarred my ear the first time I heard it, because I was in the midst about having to write essays about Bach chorals and all the rest of it.

And then I went clubbing, and why I love it. It sounds great.

So, in fact, it was actually actively useful to get involved in music that was often made by DJs and people who didn't give a shit — excuse my French — or didn't give a monkey about it. Now we have to be careful about our deployment of harmony. They didn't care about deployment of harmony. They've sampled a chord that sounds cool, and are moving it around and then slamming a beat up against it so they can have a good time, you know what I mean? And so that more intuitive approach to music, and also, you just get exposed to electronic production and engineering and a whole different way of looking at music that is often much more visceral, and how cool things sound and not about, "Hmm, how are we going to develop our first subject in the modulation section?"

Tell me about working in pop versus in film, and the types of music you can create.

I used to get frustrated even though I had the great privilege to work with people like Trevor Horn. I remember working with Seal, who's at the sort of classier end of pop production, where you get really interesting arrangement and everything. Ultimately, it's three minutes and 30 seconds within the vision and the aesthetic tramlines of a known artist. You can't sub me, and go, "Hey, why don't we sling in some 16th Century church music?" It'll just be annoying and you'll lose your fan base.

And so with the crazy eclectic musical background I had, I always was like, "Oh, wouldn't it be great to do this or that?" Blah, blah, blah. And the amazing thing about film music is you know what it may be called upon. Because the thing about film music is, "Oh, wow, this is a story set in 16th Century France and you're going to need something.

Or, "Oh, look, this is a movie set in 2014, and it's about a political conspiracy. The amount of subject matters there are for stories are so diverse that there's almost no such thing as a piece of musical experience or education you might have had that might actually be valuable.

In a way, that's probably more diverse than almost any other practice of music. If you're in an orchestra, you're probably going to play orchestral music unless you do film or work with a conductor. Or if you're on the classical side, it's not going to be that diverse. If you're in a band, you're probably going to play your music. I feel like with film music, you might be exposed to any or all of the above, whereas other musical jobs are just sort of necessarily a bit more confined. And that I just think is fantastic.

And now I don't moan as much. I used to moan all the time that music can be restrictive. But with film music, I don't feel that at all.

CHAPTER 24

MARCO BELTRAMI

COMPOSER

KNOWN FOR		ACHIEVEMENTS
BEN-HUR (2016)	*THE HURT LOCKER* (2008)	ACADEMY AWARD NOMINATION, ORIGINAL SCORE, *THE HURT LOCKER*
THE SHALLOWS (2016)	*3:10 TO YUMA* (2007)	
THE GUNMAN (2015)	*THE OMEN* (2006)	
THE HOMESMAN (2014)	*I, ROBOT* (2004)	ACADEMY AWARD NOMINATION, ORIGINAL SCORE, *3:10 TO YUMA*
THE GIVER (2014)	*HELLBOY* (2004)	
SNOWPIERCER (2013)	*TERMINATOR 3: RISE OF THE MACHINES* (2003)	
THE WOLVERINE (2013)		EMMY NOMINATION, MUSIC COMPOSITION FOR MINISERIES, *DAVID AND LISA*
WORLD WAR Z (2013)	*BLADE II* (2002)	
CARRIE (2013)	*RESIDENT EVIL* (2002)	
V (2009-11)	*DRACULA 2000* (2000)	
THE THING (2011)	*SCREAM* (1996)	

How did you first get into film music as a young student?

I came from a classical background. I was trained to write more concert music, but it's sort of disillusioning in a way to go through an academic background solely to be teaching in an academic setting. It's like what part of the background is missing? The human aspect. The condition with people. The audiences for new music are really small. I felt like you're working a little bit in a vacuum.

When I came out here, I didn't know much about film scoring. There were scores that appealed to me that I liked and so forth, but in terms of a job it wasn't even something I considered that much. But after I learned a bit about it, there was a program at USC that Jerry Goldsmith was running, actually, and I began to change. And I started working for Chris Young. That was my first job, actually. And I saw that you could really be innovative and do things in film that you might not be even able to explore in the concert world.

The first film I did was something you never would have seen. It's called Deathmatch (Laughter). Actually, I didn't have a studio at the time, and I came from a pencil and paper background, so I didn't really know about how to — well, I still don't know how to use computers, but it was even worse back then. So Christophe Beck actually helped me with it. He had a studio and some gear.

What appealed to you about film scores?

I just liked the process. At that time, I really liked being able to come up with sounds. One of the things that I was very interested in orchestrally and all was being able to push the boundaries of playing and extending techniques and timbre and interesting colors. And one of the things I found out about film composing was that you can do a lot of that stuff electronically, and it's not for a performance that has to be repeated night after night. It's for a singular performance. So you can use whatever devices you want to make it work, and that's something that appealed to me. I don't know if the first film I did, if I would recommend you go out and buy the score (Laughter). I don't think there is a score, even if you try to track it down, but it sort of got me. I enjoyed it.

Broadly speaking, what is the purpose or role of a film score to an audience?

It's sort of like their emotional partner throughout the movie; their emotional guide. It's been said many times by other people, and I've probably said it, too, but music shouldn't call any attention to itself. You shouldn't be aware of it, because if you are then it takes you out of the picture. And I don't fully agree with that. I think some of the best film scores, I am very aware of, and they heighten the emotional experience of the film.

I think at its worst, what film music is often asked to do is to provide something that is lacking in the picture. Like, it wasn't acted properly, so can you fix it? I don't think the music can be there to fix anything. The music should be there to provide either a subtext or an undercurrent or some sort of emotional journey that may or may not be said. It's to guide the viewer to a deeper level of understanding and involvement in the film, subconsciously.

Can you briefly explain how your approach might be different for different genres of film?

Stylistically, the techniques used to score a horror movie might be very different from what you do in a drama. Oftentimes in a horror movie, a lot of it is about the ride itself: leading people, keeping them in a state of tension and playing with that tension and release and anticipation. And that involves a certain way of doing anything, playing up to a certain point, having false accents, being quiet in certain areas that lead to more tension.

With a dramatic picture, I think the concern is less with the ride aspect and more with the emotional development: getting inside the characters and so forth. But in the end it's the same thing, even though there's a different process. Both are doing the same thing. Both are a way of subverting the audience to a particular point of view or a particular feeling.

Do you prefer more traditional orchestral music or more sound-design driven scores?

I like melodic statements very much. Having a chance to develop them, often times, at least in some comedies, I don't see that many movies to begin with, but I think you don't want to get caught up in playing musical sound effects, because it's too fragmented. There's not enough chance to develop ideas. I think in a drama it maybe allows for a certain kind of development of ideas that you might not be able to have in others.

For World War Z, the story goes that you wrote a score that was so scary that it bumped the film into an R rating. How did that play out?

Alright, you have to look at the picture as a whole. They shot a movie that was very intense. It was very dark, originally. It was a big-budget movie, and the studio, rightfully so, wanted it to be a summer movie that the kids could go see. If it's an R-rated movie, it probably hampers the box office so they wanted it to be a PG-13 movie.

When I started working on the movie, it was a very different film than what it ended up being. I think they re-shot about a third of the movie. And I responded to the images that I saw, and the music was very dark. Thematically, it was very dark, and the orchestration was very intense and gritty and dark. And there was some concern — look, it's about zombies. It could be a very intense, scary experience. It was riding that edge between PG-13 and R that whole time. Anything contributed to that, and the music happened to be one of those contributing elements they were very sensitive to. Actually, in the end, because it's still up to the end of that project, it was kind of a strange project because there were different factions. There were some people who wanted a dark, gritty movie, and others who wanted a popcorn movie. So I ended up writing two scores for it: one that would satisfy the popcorn moviegoers, and one that would satisfy the grittier, visceral, darker score. And I actually recorded them simultaneously in different studios in London. And in the end, it became a hybrid of both scores. Music — it has an impact. It affects the psychological impact of the film. If you put that music with other images, it probably wouldn't be a problem. But the way it was with the images they had, I think it may have just pushed it to the top.

If you look at the shower scene from Psycho, without the music, it's not that scary. You notice the cuts, you notice the process that's going on. But as soon as you put the music there, it takes that away, and you're stuck in the mindset of this psychotic killer and it's obsessive. And it's something you can't say or even show. But if you feel it, it makes it much more intense. So that's how it happens.

Do you like to work from the film's picture or from the film's script first?

I'm very visually inspired. And I have worked from just a script, but it's very deceiving for me, because when I read a script I create my own movie in my head, which invariably there are so many ways to slice it, right? So the actors interpret it, the director gives them notes, the way it's shot, the speed of the shots, everything has such an important influence on the movie that invariably I've been wrong when I've worked from the script, and I have.

People will say, "Let me give you a script, we're shooting this in a year, but why don't you start and get some ideas." And I'm thinking, "Great, I'm going to get started early and figure out what to do. And I always end up writing things that, when I see the movie, don't work for me, and it actually puts me in a harder situation, because then once you already have something established in your head, then to change or switch gears. It's harder for me than to start fresh and be on the right track. So from that perspective, I'd rather have something visual to work from. It is much more meaningful to me.

I would read to see if it's something I'm interested in doing, because the script is the foundation for the movie. You need to have a good script. It all begins with the writing. But the director is who makes the movie. And to work without that step is — I think some people can do it, but I can't.

Composers are often concerned about being pigeonholed into doing a certain genre or type of film. Do you have that fear?

The thing is that music — and I'm sure it's like this with many other things — it's more universal. It's more a conceptual thing that takes different facets. It's not like everything you write is in a specific genre. Your mind works in many different ways, and I think that's the beauty of it.

If you did only one thing, I think you might lose inspiration for that particular thing over time because, it's like you can't eat steak every night (Laughter). Maybe there are people who want or could focus on one particular thing. you can think of painters who specialize in a particular type of painting, and that's what they do. But then again, their subject matter changes even if the style doesn't change. Maybe there's a commonality of style, and you begin to create a voice for what you do. But it shouldn't be dictated by genre, but more by what moves you.

What moves you?

Just from curiosity and fun, the exploring what can be done and what makes music and what is musical, and how can you take familiar things and bend them is almost like sculpture. I think it's something that's really fun to me. I don't think that's anything new. The whole exploration of developing harmony in the past few hundred years is all about that. where else can we take this?

I think technology — something that wasn't available to people in the past — is something that's really opened up a world where you can explore things in ways that weren't possible even a short time ago. It almost lends itself to the creation of instruments that do certain things, and that's something that in this past movie, The Homesman, that became the whole thing. Seeing and being inspired by the film, and then creating something that would best sum up in the smallest possible way what the music was about.

I work here with Buck Sanders, he's downstairs. We spend a lot of time figuring out what the voice of the film is going to be, and what we need to do to achieve that.

Was that experimentation part of the motivation for building your own studio from the ground up in Malibu?

The reason I built this studio was that it was getting prohibitive to be renting studios to achieve some of the things. Here, we can do pretty much anything here that we need to do. Yeah, it's an important part.

Talk about some of this experimentation you've used in films.

In World War Z, for instance — and it's not just gimmicky. In World War Z, the zombies contract their disease by biting, and there was always a sense when I was watching the early picture, before it changed, where there was a big emphasis put on the teeth and the gnashing of the teeth and all that. And I was thinking that's a really cool idea, and it would be cool to use teeth as a musical device, as a rhythmical device in the film. And it was actually Tommy Lee Jones who suggested to me, you know, that in southwest Texas they have these wild pigs that are called javelinas that communicate with their teeth, their jaws. He said, "You should check it out," so I did, and we got some javelina skulls and put some contact microphones on them. And they make this cool rhythmical sound, because there's this scrape of the canine teeth as the jaw opens and closes and there's also the impact, so you have this almost complex rhythmical sound that you get from it. And that became really important as a rhythmical thing. And that inspired a lot of the rhythms that you hear in the movie.

Other things, like in that same picture, the other thing that struck me about it was the emergency broadcast signal. It starts off with the emergency broadcast signal, and that high-pitched sound that you often hear before they give public service announcements. I was thinking those sonorities would be cool to play with and use that as the harmonic beginnings.

I mean, the thing as a composer, I'm always looking for is what is the origin of the ideas, what is the fundamental root from which the tree of the music, the fabric of the film can sprout? So even when you're working on a particular cue that's some scene that's later in the movie, it all stems from some idea that's integral or organic to the concept. And then it provides some integrity to the score.

In The Three Burials there was a cactus that we actually plucked the needles from. It was a Native American thing, because they give off different pitches. And The Homesman, which I just finished working on, we worked a lot with Aeolian harps, which is basically when the wind blows you can tune the strings and get different sonorities out of that. We built a big Aeolian harp out of a piano up on the hill, where the piano wires go 175 feet up the hill into water tanks. I can show you that. It takes the music right out of the wind, because when the wind blows, it howls. You can hear it and the neighbors think we're a little crazy, because you can hear it a mile away.

CHAPTER 25

MARK MOTHERSBAUGH

RECORDING ARTIST & COMPOSER

KNOWN FOR		ACHIEVEMENTS
THE LAST MAN ON EARTH (2015-16)	HERBIE FULLY LOADED (2005)	ASSOCIATED ACTS: DEVO (NINE STUDIO ALBUMS)
VACATION (2015)	THE LIFE AQUATIC WITH STEVE ZISSOU (2004)	EMMY NOMINATION, MUSIC COMPOSITION FOR MINISERIES, QUICKSILVER HIGHWAY
PITCH PERFECT 2 (2015)	RUGRATS (1991-2004)	
HOUSE OF LIES (2012-15)	THIRTEEN (2003)	
22 JUMP STREET (2014)	THE ROYAL TENENBAUMS (2001)	FOUR DAYTIME EMMY NOMINATIONS
THE LEGO MOVIE (2014)		
HOTEL TRANSYLVANIA (2012)	HAPPY GILMORE (1996)	GRAMMY NOMINATION
21 JUMP STREET (2012)	PEE-WEE'S PLAYHOUSE (1986-90)	SEVEN BMI FILM MUSIC AWARDS
CLOUDY WITH A CHANCE OF MEATBALLS (2009)		

How much of a film's impact comes from the music?

Depending on the kind of film it is — if it's live action, it's probably only about 40 to 50 percent of the film. But if it's animation, it's probably about 75 percent or more of the film. Because you have a lot more heavy lifting to do in animation.

Animation — no matter how beautiful the animation is, it's impossible for animators to make the grass in the background growing, and to make blood pulse through veins properly, and animation requires you to do all this stuff. You bring life to it.

As a matter of fact, I think that's why people still stick with orchestras so much for animation; because in that, you hear it. You don't really hear it, but it's there on the soundtrack.

There's an orchestra with maybe 100 people in it, all their

hearts are beating. They just heard the conductor go "4-3-2-1," and then they start. And they're playing, and there's blood going through their veins, and they're breathing air, and the mics aren't right in front of their nose, but they're all in the room, and they're all alive.

An orchestra is such a living organism that it really helps out animation — that is, at its best and its most-computerized beautiful form. It's still not as complete as real life.

What does music written on a computer lack?

The living organism. It's missing the living organism, and yeah you get it with humans doing the voices of the characters, but an orchestra goes almost non-stop through animation films, if you watch them. A 90-minute film will have probably 89 minutes worth of music in it.

You're talking to somebody who is a sound and vision artist. When I started off in school, I didn't see a difference in in the different art forms. I just found them all as different ways of solving the same problems, or stating what you wanted to state in a more perfect form. So when I was in school, I was curious about performance artists, about people like Andy Warhol. I thought he was the coolest guy in pop culture, because he made films, he painted, he was a photographer, he printed, he did fashion design, he worked with the Velvet Underground somehow, which was in 1968, or whatever year the first album came out. I thought that was the best album that could possibly be made.

And he was connected to them, even if it was just putting a

banana on the cover. But it seemed like he was more integrated than that. And so I'm from the world of sound and vision being totally important to each other.

Similar to the first music videos you did with Devo.

Yeah, before they were called music videos, we were making short films, and having nowhere to show them. We would send them to the Ann Arbor Film Festival. And we won prizes at film festivals for them. That's how we actually became noticed. It wasn't through the music on its own. It was through our short films that ended up in short film compilations that toured.

It's kind of complicated in a way. Musically, I actually had some patrons at the same time I was going to college, and I was in the art department. And I got a partial scholarship in art, and so that's mainly why I went that direction. But musically, I was already experimenting with electronic instruments outside of school. So I was kind of thinking, "I don't like the tyranny of a keyboard," for instance. I didn't like what it made you do subconsciously — how you subconsciously made the same cliché choices, and it made it harder to break out into something else.

And so I was looking even then for ways to make music that didn't use keyboards, didn't accentuate the guitar like it did in Rock & Roll, or the drums like the kind of drum patterns you found in Rock & Roll. I was trying to do other things. And so I was looking to other places to be inspired and when I went to the music department at school, they're just learning like were doing scales, and we're learning theory and things like that.

And I thought that's exactly what I'm trying to be different from. The futurists, back in the 20s and 30s, were saying things like the orchestra of today is not sufficient — not the sufficient range of sounds to accurately portray an industrial culture. And I thought, "Yeah, that's how I feel about right now. I want to make mortar blasts and V-2 rocket sounds and ray guns and gamma rays and hydrogen bombs. And I want to do creepy sounds like in Pepto Bismol commercials of the little trail of liquid coming down into the stomach and coating the stomach and going into the intestines.

I liked elevator music. I was looking everywhere other than pop music for inspiration at the time. And I just felt like what they taught at school was all historical, and I wanted to go somewhere else.

Tell me about your first foray into film composing.

Because my schedule with Devo was so heavy, even doing the TV show, I was a little bit nervous about it at first. Because we were touring five or six months a year, and I was writing music for the band. And then Jerry and I would come up with our graphics ourselves, and we'd do our merchandise. And we designed it yourself way back when merchandise was — I remember getting chastised by Neil Young back in 1978, "Why are you guys selling merchandise in your album?" Why am I telling you that story? (Laughter.)

When Paul said, "Do you want to score this show," I was kind of like, "Do I have time?"

For episode one, he sent me a tape of the show on Monday, and I wrote all the music for the show on Tuesday. And then Wednesday recorded it, and Thursday I had to put it in the mail, because there was no Internet back then to send things on. So I'd put it in the mail. He'd get it in New York on Friday morning and they edited in the show and Saturday we'd watch it.

And it's like a whole album's worth of music, and then Monday it started over again. I went, "Sign me up for this job. I love this." Because being in the band, the part that drove me crazy was sitting in airports, waiting backstage after sound checks. What do you do for five hours, waiting for the show to start, you know?

It would take a whole year to write 12 songs. And the idea that you could write 12 songs worth of music in one week totally thrilled me and excited me, and made me go, "That's the job I want."

How much more control did you have being on your own, outside of a band?

I don't think you have more control, necessarily. Both of them, in my particular situation, because I wasn't a solo artist, it was with the band; it was collaborative. It was two sets of brothers, and no matter who it said on the album, a lot or most of them said I wrote them. But everybody in the band helped me, and if Alan had a great idea for something we incorporated, or my brother Bob — and Jerry, if he wrote something, then he probably started it, and then we all (finished).

I was used to collaborating, and when I got into TV and film I realized, "Oh, that's what a lot of it's about," because the director comes in, and he says, "OK, here is what I'm trying to do. I've been working on this movie for four years now. I finally got to shoot it. My lead actor had diarrhea during the big important week where we had love scenes to do, and he's just totally unbelievable, and I need you to help me." Or they come in, and they see it was raining all week. "We had to do something out in the sun. We had one hour where we could, but you still see glistening rain. I need you to make people know it's a bright, sunny day." And I kind of love that. I love those kind of abstract requirements and concerns and needs.

I found out early on that music is maybe the best part of working on films, because all the creepy stuff's been done before you're even brought into it. they have to fight for money, all the different people all scramble for their money, and who is going to make the most — the actors, the film company, the producers — everybody is going for their piece. And by the time it gets to you, they just need the film to be done. So you're kind of the last thing. You and the sound effects are the last things to be put on the film. And some directors come in, and they give their concerns, and some of them are really into it. They really love working and collaborating, and some of them just want to be done. They just, "Go ahead, do what you do."

It's always interesting to me, because you end up with a couple bad experiences, if you do close to 200 TV shows and films. You end up with some bad experiences in there somewhere, where you're like, "I'll be really glad when this is over." But it is always over. So that's the good thing, that it is eventually over, and it's not like your whole life forever. It's not like you're going to the same office where there's a jerk that you work for.

So then you start going, "These guys were really fun to work with. I'm going to keep an eye on what they're doing, and let them know I'm available whenever their films come up."

How do you establish a connection with a director?

You start creating a shorthand for communication. It's like, when you first start to work with somebody, and they say they want action music. What does that even mean? You don't even know exactly what that means. Or if they say they want something they never heard before. What does that mean? Or if they say something else — you're trying to figure out what it is that they're saying to you, and how much communication skills they have, and you take that and then you watch how they temp their film, (how) they put in (temp) music. And then you see how they react to their own temp. They go, "This is terrible. I hate this piece of music, but it was the closest we could find." Or you listen to something and go, "That doesn't fit, but I understand why they used that cadence," or, "I understand why they used those instrument choices." A lot of that stuff, after the first movie, you've already taken care of it. And it means you can get right to the fun part of working on a film sooner.

When you started composing for film, did your passion for making records change?

It became less interesting once I realized it was so easy, but there was a time when I was struggling between the idea of being a pure artist, and then even getting into the record business. And then realizing that the more success you had in the record industry, the more the record company tried to manipulate you.

The first two albums we put out, we were under the radar screen for Warner Bros. They weren't even paying attention to us. Even the third one, until "Whip It" was a hit, which was on the third album. Then after that, they started showing up at our recording sessions. The president of the company would come in, and he'd sit at the mixing console and say, "I used to mix. Let me see if I can fix this song." And you'd be like, "This is not where you're needed, you know?" They would put pressure on us, and say, "Hey, next album do whatever you want to do. Just do another 'Whip It.'" And it was kind of like, "Well, we don't even think that way." I remember reading an article where Sting said, "I wake up in the morning, and I can write a top-10 hit by noon." And I'm thinking, how do you even think like that? And at the time, to me, it was just really impressive that somebody could say that. Now I kind of understand how you could do that. You just grab enough clichés and put them all together, and make one little shift and there you go. Your brand new pop song.

To say, "difficult" is not really the way to think about it. But it is totally a different part of your brain. A pop song is a different part of your brain than a score. But a score for a movie, there's really a lot of directions you can go. One of the things that attracted me was that even on the Pee Wee show, I was working with jazz music and space-age bachelor-pad music and sci-fi outer space music, and over-the-top silent movie distraught music, and punk and hip-hop styles, and I got to bring all these — and Mr. Rogers. I got to bring all those styles and just smash them together, and then add electronics and Spike Jones elements to it. I just loved that it wasn't restricted. Because pop music — when was the last time you heard a pop song and you said, "That doesn't sound like anything I've ever heard before?" Never. They always sound like something that was out last month. They have like slight flavor changes, and that's about it. So, harder isn't really the thing (that's most exciting about film music). It's just what attracts you the most.

What are the limits of what film music can be?

I think it's a broader horizon. And just even in the time that I've been involved in scoring, scoring has really become much more diverse, and there's really a wide range of choices now that there weren't back in the early 80s. It's like electronics. All different kinds of electronics have gone through so many evolutions. Every five years, there's a different style. And you can blend in parts of that into something with an orchestra. It was an orchestral-electronic score for Lego (The Lego Movie). But it was kind of really modern electronics for Lego. I was using things that were more from the world of Deadmau5 and Diplo and that kind of sound, but I was using a very classical-sounding orchestra and a Greek choir of about 30 people that were just chanting things in the background.

I just love — that's what makes me want to keep coming back

to film scores. It's just a really satisfying mode to work in. And people can pick the area that they like.

Do you think you'll ever get tired of scoring films?

Well, if I thought I was going to live to be 150, maybe I would get tired of it. But I think, in a normal human lifespan, I'll probably find many things to keep me interested. I'm still curious. I see things now happening in electronics that, I just go, "How lucky to be a kid right now, and be interested in the arts!" Whether it's visual or sonic, but especially sonic. It's the kind of tools that I was looking for when I was a kid. I remember the first time I heard the first Roxy music album. There's a song on it that's not a very — it's kind of throwaway, it's a B-side — called "Editions of You." It's not one of their more popular songs. But I remember I was just listening to the album. Because, before that, I was trying to think, "How do I avoid keyboards, and just using the scale that we all know and are bored with?" So Devo had played a show with Sun Ra in 1974, 1975, and I saw them come out and play the keyboard, hitting it — kind of looked like a baby — but a mad man, because he was dressed in his African gear, and it was kind of intimidating but exciting to watch him just do this. And it sounded great. And the band was really good. And I remember thinking, "That's it. You just have no respect for that keyboard. That keyboard it's just meant to be punished."

I remember, even when we did "Whip It," I tried it at first on tour. I had set the whip crack sound up on my synthesizer, and I was trying to hit it with a whip and make it crack. But I was not a good enough whipologist or whipotronic or whatever the term is. I was not good enough at it. So it would hit exactly at the exact split second you needed the whip crack.

How has your record production background informed the way you produce a score, sonically?

I've run orchestras through ring modulators, which almost seems like, "Why would you even bother with an orchestra in the first place?" But we already had the orchestra recording, and it was able to dial it in, so that by the time you could really notice the ring modulator, it started going from being this organic human sound to turning into this kind of very digitalized electronica, noise. And it was really nice. It was a nice effect. We've worked with detuned pianos, where you just destroy the tuning, and then the studio then charges triple rental rate to try and get it back in proper tune again, and then they're angry with you. Gosh, I've used all kinds of toys. Because of Moonrise Kingdom, I just wrote some of the kind of more esoteric, conceptual pieces for the film.

So I did like field drums and marching snare drums that morphed into Indian tom toms, but like the kind you would think of from an old Hollywood movie. Not authentic. It would be more like rubber tom tom kind of sounds. And (Wes Anderson) sent me a piece of film, and it was these two kids running through the woods. And I remember looking at it going — and it didn't have sound with it — and I remember thinking how weird to look at these two kids running through the woods and you can't hear anything.

I thought it needs the wind, and it needs birds or something. And I have this collection of about 150 birdcalls. I just collect sound-making instruments and foghorns and all different kinds of things. But I started playing the bird calls just to kind of fill in, and I started playing a piano along with that, and then I lost interest in the film, creating something for the film, and I started making this bird call orchestra, and I started writing this music for a symphony of bird calls.

Then I realized it's impossible to play them right, because you need like 150 people to all be sitting there waiting for their turn to go. So I found this guy about five or six years ago that that built things for amusement parks, and he built stuff like, "Look at this, it can play a banjo." And it was this horrible, mechanical (thing), no, it was a great mechanical sound of like some machine playing a banjo, or a guitar, and you'd go, "Wow, it doesn't sound real, but it's kind of cool in a way. It's better in a way."

And I said, "Well, I'm trying to get all these bird calls to play," and he goes, "I never did that."

To make a short story long, we did like 60 or 70 of these birdcalls all on one machine, so I could play them on a keyboard through MIDI. And I started writing music for that. So it's because of that movie, I came up with an instrument that I'm writing music for now that I'm kind of super happy about.

SCORE

A FILM MUSIC DOCUMENTARY

SCORE-MOVIE.COM
FACEBOOK.COM/SCOREMOVIE

BOOKINGS

TO BOOK DIRECTOR MATT SCHRADER FOR A
SPEAKING ENGAGEMENT AT YOUR SCHOOL OR
ORGANIZATION OR FOR A SCREENING OF
SCORE: A FILM MUSIC DOCUMENTARY,
CONTACT INFO@EPICLEFF.COM.

25837321R00216

Made in the USA
Lexington, KY
29 December 2018